Henry Aaron Stern

The Captive Missionary

Being an Account of the Country and People of Abyssinia

Henry Aaron Stern

The Captive Missionary
Being an Account of the Country and People of Abyssinia

ISBN/EAN: 9783337134112

Printed in Europe, USA, Canada, Australia, Japan

Cover: Foto ©ninafisch / pixelio.de

More available books at **www.hansebooks.com**

THE CAPTIVES.

THE

CAPTIVE MISSIONARY:

BEING AN ACCOUNT OF THE

COUNTRY AND PEOPLE OF ABYSSINIA.

EMBRACING

A Narrative of King Theodore's Life,

AND

HIS TREATMENT OF POLITICAL AND RELIGIOUS MISSIONS.

BY

THE REV. HENRY A. STERN,

AUTHOR OF "WANDERINGS AMONG THE FALASHAS."

LONDON:
CASSELL, PETTER, AND GALPIN,
LUDGATE HILL, E.C.;
AND 596, BROADWAY, NEW YORK.

TO

LIEUT.-GENERAL THE RIGHT HONOURABLE

LORD NAPIER OF MAGDALA,

G.C.B., G.C.S.I.,

WHOSE WISDOM, ENERGY, AND VALOUR PLANNED, EXECUTED, AND, WITH
THE DIVINE BLESSING, SUCCESSFULLY ACHIEVED THE OBJECT
OF THE ABYSSINIAN EXPEDITION,

This Volume

IS, WITH PERMISSION, DEDICATED,

AS A

TOKEN OF PROFOUND REGARD AND ESTEEM,

BY ONE OF THE VICTIMS OF

KING THEODORE'S TYRANNY.

CONTENTS.

CHAPTER I.

Mutual Feuds and Hostilities in Abyssinia—Theodore—His Birth and Parentage—Leaves his Mother and flees to Tschangar—Atrocity of Dejatch Marou—Confou, Uncle of Theodore—His Death—Intestine Strife between his Sons—Theodore takes Refuge at Saragie—Turns Bandit—Schemes of Empire—Ancient Prophecies and Traditions—Theodore's Popularity and Growing Power—Woisero Menin attempts to crush him—Defeat by the Turks—Fever at Tschangar—Insulted by the Queen—Civil War—Defeat of the Queen—Ras Ali—Battle of Aishal—Victory of Theodore—Schemes for Subjugation of the Gallas—Shoa and Tigré—Battle of Semien—Capture of Amba Boahil—Coronation of Theodore—Treachery to the Princes—Victories over the Shoanes and Gallas—Quarrel with the Church 1

CHAPTER II.

Theodore Triumphant—His Conduct towards Egypt—France and England—Social Condition of the Empire—His Hatred of the Egyptians and Turks—He imprisons the Viceroy's Ambassador, and is unappeased by the arrival of another Minister from Egypt—Arrival of Consul Cameron and M. Lejean — Imprisonment of the French Representative — Consul Cameron's return — Theodore's Hostility to the English is excited—Success of the English Missionary . 27

CHAPTER III.

Return from Missionary Tour—Invitation from the King—Feast of St. John—Interview with Theodore—M. Bardel's Account of his Mission—Wounded Pride—Dismissal of M. Lejean—Gloomy Forebodings — Discordant Sounds—Departure for the Coast—Unfavourable Symptoms—Visit to the Royal Camp—Violence of the King—Execution of my Servants—Personal Maltreatment—Feeling of Desolation—Keen Sufferings—Abyssinian Surgery—Honest Tears—My Chains—My Consolation 38

CHAPTER IV.

Summons from the King—Painful Journey—Compassion of the Guards—Sagacious Servant—Note from the Aboona—Kind Assurances—Interview with the King—Camp Prison—Numerous Guards—Keen Sufferings—Stupor—Prison Diet—Appointment of my Judges—Arrival of the Missionary Agents—Postponement of Verdict—My Baggage ransacked—Vague Hopes—Suspended Negotiation—Generous Exertions of the Metropolitan—Redeeming Love an unfailing Comfort—Joseph's Forebodings—Fidelity of Servants—Thrilling News—Bright Anticipation—Misplaced Confidence—Vain Conjectures—Seizure of my Property—Photographic Lore—Brutality of my Gaolers—Crippling Fetters—An ever-present Saviour—Frugal Diet 63

CHAPTER V.

Conflicting Rumours—Vigilance of the Guards—Degenerate Taste—Midnight Discussion—Removal of my Foot-chains—Theodore's Court of Justice—Code of Laws—Forestalled Condemnation Charges against Myself, Mr. Rosenthal, and Mrs. Flad—Revolting Baseness—The Royal Pedigree—A Challenge—Sickening Existence—Dragged back to Prison—Visit of Executioners—A Dangerous Bill-hook—Fresh Maltreatment—Slow Progress of Time—The Tyrant's Speculations—Freedom at the Expense of Truth—Fluctuations of Hope and Fear—A Revolting Sight—The Prisoners Stripped—Terrible Night—Anticipated Execution—Mitigation of our Wretchedness—Valuation of Silks—Royal Messages—Strange Garments—Compelled to write Letters to Europe—Consul Cameron's unfortunate Request . . 89

CHAPTER VI.

Gethsemane a Captive's Comfort—January 3rd—Consul Cameron chained—Prison Discipline—Samuel's Smiles—Brave Conduct of Mrs. Flad and Rosenthal—Seizure of a Doll—Cross-fire of Questions—A Warning Text—Death deprived of its Terrors—Sham Reconciliation—An Accession of Prisoners—Fortunate Incident—Royal Inquisitiveness—French Consul's Protest—Release of Six Prisoners—Perplexing Stipulation—Extensive Conversions—Religion and Cannon—Confident Anticipations of Release—M. Bardel's Imprisonment—Charges against him—Sad Disappointment . 120

CHAPTER VII.

Prison Discussions—Release of Rosenthal—Dangerous Controversy—Isaiah's Censures—Dissatisfaction in the Army—Quarrel between the King and Aboona—Episcopal Visit—Trumpery Charges—Divine Support—The enraged Monarch—Rope Torture—Removal of the Cords—Fluctuating Emotions—Artfulness of Samuel—Renewed Tortures—Maddening Sensation—Royal Interrogations—Pandemonium—Thoughts of Suicide—Terrible Warning—False Alarm—Firmness of the Aboona—King's Confession—Reconciliation—A misunderstood Letter 143

CHAPTER VIII.

Winter—Unsheltered Prison—Foot Chains—Religion subdues the Temper—Prison Diet—Small-pox and Famine—Exchange of Fetters—An unhappy Couple—March of the Army—Revolting Sights—New Prison Ground—Deluging Torrents—Prison Rations—Cruelty to Prisoners—Gondar—Exorbitant Fines—Designs of the new Metropolis—A partial Amnesty—Festive Day—Exhausting March—A Wet Night—Advance to Ferga—Consul Cameron and M. Makerer—Remedy against Stoicism—Better Diet—Alcoholic Influence—Promised Release—Artful Rumour—Resignation—Departure to Magdala 169

CHAPTER IX.

Jan Meeda—Unappreciated Scenery—Strange Companions—Warning Beacons—Descent into the Beshilo—A Feast of Air—Makerer in Trouble—Ascent to Magdala—Forewarning Symptoms—Amba Home—Change of Manacles—Precautionary Measures—Prisoners' Wives—Prison Life—New Dormitory—Limited Space—Nocturnal Squabbles—Sunny Visions Eclipsed—Theodore's Perfidy—Destructive Foray 193

CHAPTER X.

Death of Ahmadee Busheer — Villany Triumphs — Revolt in Shoa—Guerilla War—Disastrous Campaign—Cruel Scene—Vain Negotiations—Prince Menilek—Want of Gallantry—Disagreeable News—Massacre of Gallas—Atrocious Orders—Good Advice—The Negoos and Metropolitan—Defiant Attitude of the Aboona—Unprovoked Resentment—Additional Fetters—Ingratitude—The Penitent Thief—Captured Galla Women—Royal Diversions—Fictitious Victory 213

CHAPTER XI.

Departure of the King—Seeking for Truth—Opposition of the Priests—Triumphs of Truth—Death in Prison—Smallpox—Sympathy Unappreciated—Chains Tightened—The Young Pilgrim—Brief Career—Mournful Funeral—Considerate Guards—Nightly Torments—Incipient Sickness—Colocynth Pills—Sickness Forestalled—Kerans a Dentist—Makerer an Oculist 230

CHAPTER XII.

Hope Deferred—Embarrassing Negotiations—Approach of Mr. Rassam — The Artisans' Disappointment — Delightful Message — Removal of Fetters — Strange Sensation — Departure from Magdala—Ominous Intelligence—Arrival at Gaffat—Camp of Mr. Rassam—Order of March—Samuel's Kiss—Theodore's Dissimulations—Malicious Charges—New Garments—Sham Trial—Alleged Offences—Forced Admission — Royal Satisfaction — Solomon's Seal — Suspicious Intimations 245

CHAPTER XIII.

Easter Day — An Ambiguous Compliment — Contemptible Trickery—The sullen Agha Farce—Delightful Ride—Unappreciated Attentions—Royal Missive—Confiscation of Valuables—Uncomfortable Position—Conflicting Rumours—Comfortless Lodging—Voyage across the Tzana—The Royal Robber—The Mission Arrested—Diplomacy Foiled—Grand Court—Meekness and Rage—Diplomatic Manœuvre—The Christian Diplomatist—Gymnastic Performances—Sworn Friendship 262

CONTENTS. xi

CHAPTER XIV.

Sensation Scenes—Brag and Bluster—Zeghee Pillaged—Cholera in the Camp—Abrupt Departure—The Penitent Tyrant—Death in Pursuit—Raw Recruits—Vice Dangerous—Prelude of Ruin—New Homes—Transient Honours—Royal Craft—Grateful Counsellors — Murder of a Beggar — Doubtful Parentage—Undisputed Claims—Dismal Dungeon—Royal Visit 284

CHAPTER XV.

Revolt of the Provinces—Sham Campaign—Churches Pillaged—Retributive Vengeance—Wanton Atrocities—New Prison—Foot Chains—Domiciliary Arrangements—Despatch of Letters — Abyssinian Honesty — Our Prison Library — Instruction of Inquirers—Prayerless Amar—Sundays in Prison—Stirring Incident—Diplomatic Correspondence—Butchery in the Camp—Desertions—Reign of Terror—A Midnight Massacre—A Wise Messenger—The Tyrant Defeated—Cannon Foundry—Unfortunate Fugitives .   . 297

CHAPTER XVI.

Hostile Movements—Sham Exploits—Valour at Zero—Plans of Escape—The lucky and unlucky Fugitives—Amba Desertions—Galla Hospitality—Midnight Assassins—Merited Penalty—Death of Aboona Salama—The Apostles of Abyssinia—Spread of Christianity—Truth and Error Blended—Abstruse Dogmas—Theological Squabbles—Indifference of the Laity—Advent of the Jesuits—Laxity of Morals—Protestant Missions—Unsatisfactory Converts—Enlightened Metropolitan—The successful Rebel—Artful Intimidation—Bishop Gobat's Efforts—Falasha Converts—Paradoxes Solved—Incipient Reforms 319

CHAPTER XVII.

Royal Messengers—Samuel's Terrors—Antidote to Fear—Letter from Menilek — His Approach—Sham Bravery — Jealousy among our Guards—Hostile Demonstrations—Perplexing Conjectures—Cowardice of Menilek—Schemes for Escape—Good News—Painful Suspense—Theodore's Mad Rage—Men Hunters — Royal Duplicity — Reward of Fidelity — Christmas Day—The King and the Peasant—Submission to the Tyrant—Flattery and Treachery—European Artisans in Disgrace 345

CHAPTER XVIII.

Theodore reaches Magdala—Change of Guards—Release of Dr. Blanc and Lieut. Prideaux—Royal Promises to the Envoy and his Companions — Change of Sentiment — Bardel's Warning—Mr. Rassam and Theodore—Prisoners Released —Faith and Trust — Summons to the Royal Camp — Gracious Reception — Harmless Brag — The Despised Letter — Seven Executions — Revolting Massacre — Providential Escape—Return to Prison—Battle of Arogie— Diplomacy in Requisition—Lord Napier's Firmness and Courtesy — Theodore's Confession — Suicide Prevented — Suspected Treachery—Sympathy of Natives—Audience Refused — Contradictory Commands — Royal Designs — Divine Interposition — Arrival in the British Camp— Delicious Sensation—Easter Sermons—Theodore's Despair —Visit to Magdala—The Dead King—Success of the Expedition—Thanksgiving Service 368

LIST OF ILLUSTRATIONS.

The Captives . *Frontispiece.*

Abyssinian Horseman . *To face Page* 48

A Priest and a Monk . ,, 128

King Theodore's House at Magdala . ,, 177

The Queen of the Galla Country, with her Youngest
    Son and a Mahometan Priest . ,, 218

Interior of Magdala, with Salasie in the Distance . ,, 296

Church at Magdala, showing Theodore's Grave . ,, 337

Magdala in Flames . , , ,, 385

PREFACE.

The strange and unparalleled captivity of a few missionaries and British officials on the rocky heights of Magdala, and their unscathed deliverance, have excited much public notoriety and interest. Circumstances which were beyond human control unfortunately made me the longest and the most tried of the sufferers. Providence ordered it so. I had neither committed a political nor a criminal offence worthy of the stick, fetters, the torturing rope, or fifty-two months' rigorous captivity. It is true King Theodore asserted that I had defied him—an assertion that was in perfect harmony with his conduct towards every one, whether ambassador, consul, or missionary, who could not minister to his wild ambition or swell the number of his white artisans. The following pages contain a succinct account of that eventful history, from my first beating on the plain of Woggera until that happy day when the flag of freedom and liberty, honour and power, fluttered to the breeze on the most impregnable fortress in Abyssinia.

To make my narrative complete, I was obliged

to devote some pages to King Theodore's rise and fall. This, I feel persuaded, will enhance and not detract from the interest of the work.

In retracing the events of that long imprisonment, I drew occasionally on some of my own letters and papers which have already appeared in public print. Willingly would I have avoided making use of these materials, had not truth and candour rendered it absolutely imperative.

Six of the sketches were taken by the Royal Engineers who accompanied the Abyssinian Expedition. The Secretary of State for the War Department kindly granted me permission to embody them in my narrative, and I gladly avail myself of the opportunity to tender him my most respectful acknowledgments for the favour. I had myself taken upwards of forty views of Abyssinian scenery and life, but—like all my other property—they were confiscated and destroyed by the king.

On casting a retrospective glance on that painful captivity, judgment and mercy, wrath and love, trial and succour, seem so wonderfully blended, that I cannot help believing that, for some still undefined reason, an invisible hand wove the Abyssinian difficulty, and, contrary to all human speculation, also brought it to a happy and successful termination.

London, October 26th, 1868.

THE CAPTIVE MISSIONARY.

CHAPTER I.

Mutual Feuds and Hostilities in Abyssinia—Theodore—His Birth and Parentage—Leaves his Mother and flees to Tschangar—Atrocity of Dejatch Marou—Confou, Uncle of Theodore—His Death — Intestine Strife between his Sons — Theodore takes Refuge at Saragie—Turns Bandit—Schemes of Empire—Ancient Prophecies and Traditions—Theodore's Popularity and Growing Power—Woisero Menin attempts to crush him—Defeat by the Turks—Fever at Tschangar—Insulted by the Queen—Civil War—Defeat of the Queen—Ras Ali—Battle of Aishal—Victory of Theodore—Schemes for Subjugation of the Gallas—Shoa and Tigré—Battle of Semien—Capture of Amba Boahil—Coronation of Theodore—Treachery to the Princes—Victories over the Shoanes and Gallas—Quarrel with the Church.

It is a complete anomaly that a people speaking one language, professing one belief, and united together by a common interest, should for ages be involved in mutual feuds and hostilities. Ties of blood, friendship, and affection have in all lands, and among all tribes, times without number, curbed the ambition of the proud, and restrained the greed of the avaricious. This salutary fear of severing sacred bonds and desolating happy homes has often served to keep the sword in its sheath and the arrow in its quiver. In Abyssinia, on the contrary, the loudest clamours for peace, and the most boisterous professions of a common Christian brotherhood, have only inflamed the passions and excited hostilities. Without unravelling the ponderous folios of monkish annals, which delight to depict royal exploits that were never achieved, and glorious battles that were never fought, we have in the authentic history of the last three centuries enough to demonstrate the cupidity and licentiousness of the Abyssinian people, and the rapacity and corruption of their rulers. Weary and tired of these perpetual conflicts between contending chiefs, whose road to power lay athwart the ruin and desolation they had created, the enslaved peasantry with delight hailed the advent of the great Theodore, who, according to ancient prophecy, was to introduce an era of unprecedented splendour and glory, peace and prosperity.

This wonderful personage, around whose infantine couch clustered the hopes and expectations of an enslaved race, was born in the year 1822, in the small province of Quara, close to the north-western frontier of Abyssinia. His father, Hailu Weleda Georgis, reputed to have been the scion of a noble house, died while the boy was still very young. The small property of the defunct noble was immediately seized and squandered by avaricious and extravagant relatives. The mother of Kasa—for that was the orphan's name—had no home to which she could repair, and no friends on whose liberality she could depend. Driven from the home that had so long sheltered her as a nominal wife, she repaired to Gondar, where, by the sale of kosso—a specific for the tapeworm—she eked out a miserable subsistence. The orphan boy betrayed in childhood those traits which distinguished him when he became a man. Impatient, passionate, and proud, he disdained the humble vocation of his mother, and in a fit of anger left her poor hut and took refuge in a convent at Tschangar, near the northern shores of Lake Tzana. In this asylum Kasa might have spent many years in dreamy indolence had not Dejatch Marou, a defeated rebel chief, invaded its sacred precincts, and in the mutilation of innocent boys resented the brave resistance of their victorious parents. Marou's wholesale butcheries did not remain unrequited. He had slaughtered the aged priest and his youthful pupil; but the boy who was destined to inflict a retributive vengeance on the murderer's race saved his life by a timely flight to an adjacent stronghold of his uncle, Confou.

In the home of this powerful noble, whose residence was the rendezvous of all the Amhara chiefs, the enthusiastic youth imbibed that ardent love for those brave and daring exploits which subsequently distinguished his military career. Dejatch Confou, the puissant ruler of the north-western provinces, frequently allowed his nephew to accompany him on those dangerous expeditions which still form the theme of the bard's fulsome effusions. Kasa on these occasions exhibited an undaunted valour and martial skill that elicited the admiration and applause of both friend and foe. Honours and favours were profusely lavished on the youthful hero, and he would probably have obtained a high appointment, had not death robbed him of his guardian and protector. The sons of Confou, animated by jealousy and lust of power, immediately after the death of their father, engaged in a fratricidal strife which weakened their forces and exposed them to the mercy of an encroaching foe. Woisero Menin, the mother of Ras Ali, and wife of Atze Yohannes, the shadow king, took advantage of the quarrel, and whilst her forces seized on the north-western portion of their patrimony, Dejatch Goshou, of Godjam, invaded the districts abutting on the Lake Dembea. Kasa, who had in this quarrel taken the side of the elder brother, fled before the ferocious legions of the south to a peasant's hut at Saragie, not far from his native province, where he met with a cordial and generous reception.

Panting for distinction and military fame, Kasa organised a band of freebooters, consisting of seventy men, and with these he infested the borders of the western lowland. Hated by his own gang, who wanted a chief to lead but not a master to rule, a conflict ensued, in which more than half the banditti lost their lives. It was at this period that Kasa, afraid of the vengeance of his former companions, fled to Matamma, the territory of the Tougrourees, where, as a grass-cutter, he found food and shelter in the stables of Sheikh Shuma. His new employment was evidently not suited to his taste, and ere a few months had elapsed the sickle was exchanged for the robber's sword, pistol, and lance. Prompted by a bitter hatred against the Tougrourees, which to some extent verifies the story of his degrading service, the bandit, with his newly-organised gang of desperadoes, for many months became the terror and scourge of every lowlander.

Disgusted with a freebooter's precarious vocation, he left the feverish wilds in the undisturbed possession of Shankgallas, Tougrourees, and other equally ferocious occupants, and reappeared on his own native soil. The squabbles and conflicts between the ruling chiefs inflamed the towering ambition of the retired robber, and he began in reality to cherish those schemes of aggrandisement which won him a kingdom and a crown. Such aspirations were not new to his heart. In the convent at Tschangar, where he was preparing for the niggardly preferments bestowed by the church, he became acquainted with many of the legends attributed to inspired and wonder-working saints. Among these was a prophecy of the advent of a great king called Theodorus. The story has not lost in romance by tradition. Born of humble parents, though of Solomon's royal line, the hero of many a romantic and eventful tale was for a limited period, like Moses in the solitudes of Midian, and David on the lonely green pastures, to be shrouded from the ken and observation of mankind. On his appearance on the wide stage of humanity, exploit after exploit was to crown his invincible arms. He was to exterminate the hated Turks, conquer the Holy Land, plant the cross on the site of the ancient temple, make Jerusalem the metropolis of the universe, and bring princes and rulers, nations and tribes in homage before the throne of Solomon's restored dynasty. This idea, which had evidently taken deep hold on the mind of Kasa and his adherents, paved the road for the success that attended his military expeditions. From all parts of the country the needy and ambitious, the disaffected and improvident flocked around the rebellious standard of the rising chief. Wherever he went, young and old welcomed him with bursts of delight. The proud and fair Amhara maiden, who a few years before would have disdained the attention of the kosso vendor's son, now rejoiced in his smiles and loving glances. Kasa was not insensible to the admiration he elicited, and the saint-like character after which he aspired was frequently tarnished by the gallantries in which he indulged. He had several sons and daughters, but, with the exception of Dejatch Meshasha and two daughters, they were, together with their mothers, discarded by the popular hero, who was as inconstant in love as in all other matters that did not suit his whims or capricious fancies.

Woisero Menin, the mother of Ras Ali, and nominally the queen of all the provinces west of the Tacazze, began to dread the growing power of the rebel, and, prompted by deep passionate animosity, which invariably characterised her proceedings towards those who defied her authority or did not minister to her corrupt taste, she dispatched a large force to crush the arrogant lowland robber. Informed of the expedition, Kasa, without delay, hastened to meet the enemy; but no sooner did the royal forces come in sight of their antagonists, than they took to their heels and fled. The treacherous woman, foiled in her expectations, had recourse to intrigue and fascinating blandishments, which experience had taught her were more formidable weapons than the lances of her legions. Kasa saw the snare and eluded it. Baffled and thwarted, the queen, with all the rancour of a passionate woman, was more than ever intent on entrapping the presumptuous rebel. To effect this she did not hesitate to sacrifice the honour of her own grandchild, the daughter of Ras Ali. The young wife, true to the generous instinct of her tender and guileless heart, instead of abetting her grandmother's infamous design, with a constancy and devotion seldom witnessed in that demoralised country, imperilled her own life to protect that of her ungrateful and faithless husband.

Unable to make the daughter forgetful of the duty of the wife, Woisero Menin hit upon a new scheme to compass her end. The Arabs on the north-western frontier, as in all undefined and wild border lands, had occasionally hostile encounters with their Abyssinian neighbours. Dejatch Confou, the uncle of Kasa, delighted in these forays, which afforded a wide field for his strategic skill, and considerably augmented the revenues of his overburdened exchequer. Menin was anxious to obtain this kind of tribute, but she had neither troops nor a chief capable to levy it. To get rid of a dreaded foe, or, if successful, to secure a rich booty, Kasa, under the specious pretext of avenging an affront, was ordered to proceed with a strong force against several Egyptian outposts. The bold soldier willingly obeyed a behest that promised to gratify his vanity and adventurous spirit. Sixteen thousand men, well equipped and full of ardour, started from the high land to rob and to destroy the detested Mahomedans, but scarcely 4,000, crestfallen and wounded, returned to their homes. The few Egyptian outposts had received intimation of the intended expedition, and with a rapidity that did credit to the few indolent and ease-loving officials, about 800 Bashe-Bouzouks—Turkish irregulars—were collected together and stationed behind a stockaded fence to watch the movements of the enemy. Kasa and his army, confiding in their prowess and valour, boldly advanced on the despised foe. Some pieces of brass and inflated skins, that were suspended in front of the slight defence of sticks and thorns, had a magic power in attracting the pillage-loving Amharas. In excited masses the impetuous host rolled on towards the fatal stockade till they were within easy reach of the defenders' muskets and artillery, when suddenly a destructive fire, that carried terror and death, came flashing into their serried ranks. Appalled and panic-struck, the discomfited assailants, in their savage bewilderment, instead of retreating, stood aghast and almost petrified on the fatal battle-field. Kasa, mounted on a gallant charger, with his sword flashing in the sun's fiery rays, and a countenance full of fury and wrath, like a demon of vengeance, sprang over heaps of dead and dying, shouting forth commands which in the confusion no one heeded. A well-aimed ball forced him from his saddle, and the pretended destroyer of Mahomedanism, with a mere remnant of his late numerous forces, had to flee from the pursuit of a contemptible handful of ill-disciplined Turkish troops. The disappointed queen, stung to the very quick by the failure of her design and the disasters of the expedition, did not conceal the deep repugnance she cherished towards the man who had brought troubles and misfortunes upon her. Basha Lamlam, a Magdala chief who was in the fight, frequently amused the captives with the account he gave of it.

Lamlam himself, one of the heroes of the day, as well as every one who had joined that ill-fated expedition, received several dangerous wounds. The majority who escaped were wounded in the back, which, whilst it did honour to their discretion, told a not very creditable tale of their valour. Poor Basha Lamlam fell on April 10th, 1868, in a fight with a nobler enemy than the Turks. He was a kind-hearted, good-natured man, and ought to have breathed his last on a bed surrounded by sympathising and affectionate friends, and not on a battle-field, and in the midst of hostile and unconcerned foreigners.

Stunned with the excess of his calamitous defeat, Kasa repaired to Tschangar, the home of his childhood, to tend his wounds, ere he again ventured on the stormy scene of war and bloodshed. The kind monks paid their distinguished guest and former pupil the most assiduous attention. Under their tender care his impaired health might speedily have been restored to its wonted vigour, had not a devouring impatience for action preyed on his mind and fed the fire of a delirious fever. The wiry frame, however, triumphed over the inroads of disease, and the patient was so far advanced in his recovery that the Hippocrates of Tschangar confidently undertook to extract the rankling ball which an infidel had lodged in his side, if a fat cow and a large jar of butter were given him. Kasa thought the doctor's prescription a good opportunity to remind the queen that he was still in the land of the living; but the proud though dissolute daughter of a noble line of Galla chiefs, who had been more than once defied and insulted by the Quara upstart, instead of complying with the request, sent him a joint of beef, with the bitter sarcastic taunt that men of low birth and rank were not entitled to a whole cow.

Frantic with rage, the indignant soldier bided the time required for his recovery, and then once more bestrode his war-steed, and hastened to Quara, where he collected his faithful followers, and then pressed forward to Dembea and Gondar, to extort by force, as he said, that deference and respect which his birth denied him. Convinced that no expression of regret and no assurance of royal favour could heal the breach or ward off the stormy contest, the Queen promptly despatched a strong body of troops to intercept the progress of the insurgents. The hostile forces met near Tshako, and, in a fierce encounter, the royalists sustained a most signal defeat. The loss of the Queen in arms, wounded, and prisoners was very great. Amongst the latter was Dejatch Wanderad, a noble chief who, in a council of war at Gondar, had loudly boasted that he would bring the kosso vendor's son, alive or dead, to the capital. Kasa, to whom this speech was reported, sent for Wanderad in the course of the evening, and, to the amazement of the assembled rebel chiefs, handed him a horn full of the obnoxious draught, with the biting sarcasm: "My mother did no business to-day; you will, therefore, accept this humble fare for your evening repast."

A war *à outrance* now began to rage all over Western Abyssinia. The Queen, anxious to redress past errors and failures, assumed the command of her army, and in a fierce conflict at Balaha, near the Tzana, displayed the daring and courage of a consummate general and dauntless warrior. The army, unfortunately, did not emulate the fearless bravery of their commandress, and the unsupported heroine lost the battle through her fiery impetuosity and mad valour.

Ras Ali, the son of Menin, and father-in-law of Kasa, now shook off that voluptuous sloth to which he had abandoned himself, and grasping the sword, which his hand knew well how to wield, he placed himself at the head of his followers, and marched against the presumptuous Quara rebel. The common people, who had hitherto continued indifferent to the struggle between the contending parties, were stirred to the very depth of their hearts by the exciting intelligence that a battle was about to be fought that would decide the fate of the realm and the destiny of the reigning family. At Aishal, in Dembea, towards the end of the year 1855, the hostile forces encountered each other in a most sanguinary conflict. The troops on both sides, stimulated by their leaders, fought with marvellous bravery. Kasa, repulsed in every direction by the Begemeder and Galla horse, had prepared an ambush, and artfully feigned a retreat. Flushed with success, the conquerors pursued the discomfited foe, spreading terror and death among the flying ranks. Unacquainted with the craft of their cunning opponent, they darted forward till they came close to some hedges and trees, when suddenly, from scores of small mirrors that hung suspended in the sun's rays, a dazzling light painfully glared on their swarthy countenances, whilst, in different directions, the undermined ground burst in deep furrows beneath their war-steeds' hoofs. The superstitious barbarians, imagining that evil spirits and demons were arrayed against them, stood nerveless and aghast on beholding these wonderful phenomena. Kasa immediately whirled round, and before the panic-stricken pursuers had recovered from their amazement, they were surrounded and butchered by the incensed foe. Ras Ali, as Mr. Bell, who was in the engagement, assured me, performed prodigies of valour; but despite the despairing effort of the doomed chief, the rule of the Galla usurpers had reached its end, and before night their last descendant was crownless and a fugitive.

The victor of Aishal, not much disposed to rest on his laurels, quickly marched to Quami Tsherk, in Godjam, to seize on the territory of the ruthless Birrou Goshou. In the evening preceding the conflict which freed Abyssinia from a moderate ruler, and gave it an insatiable, bloodthirsty tyrant, Kasa and his brother officers were discussing, over some reeking joints of broundo, the merits of their respective troops, when one of the great magnates, in the exuberance of his tedj-inspired loyalty, ejaculated, " What need we to fear? No one can resist us; how much less you, our gallant leader." The following morning, in a short skirmish, Birrou was unhorsed, and with a stone round his neck—the sign of humility and contrition—led as a prisoner into the presence of the man whom he had always treated with contempt and supercilious hauteur. The victor now asked his prostrate foe what fate he would have awarded him if their fortunes had been reversed. " You would have been executed," rejoined the unguarded Birrou. Instantly a score of swords gleamed over his head, and Birrou Goshou might never have uttered another syllable had not an authoritative voice ordered the murderous blades back to their scabbards. The prisoner's wife, a daughter of Queen Menin, unconscious of her husband's fate, with a strong force, had entrenched herself on Tshebella Amba, an impregnable fortress. Kasa, anxious to secure this strong position, sent an imposing deputation to persuade the lady to evacuate her stronghold. "And if I do," said the proud princess, "what will Kasa give me in exchange?" "Your husband," was the brief response. "He may take the Amba without restoring me my husband," was the quick reply of the fond wife. The request was granted, and Birrou Goshou to the end of his days will probably never again trust a female heart. He wore his shackles thirteen years; and probably only the grave would have unriveted them, had not the white man come and avenged Abyssinia's wrongs, and unbound her nobles' chains. Perhaps the school of adversity has taught him a salutary lesson, which he will apply to his own and his country's weal. He, with all the other great Magdala prisoners, was released on the memorable Easter Monday, the 18th of April, 1868, the last morning of Theodore's treacherous and cruel rule.

Godjam, Dembea, and all the western provinces had made their humble submission to the conqueror's sway. This did not satisfy the ambition of Kasa; he had still to subdue the Gallas, the hereditary enemies of his country, and to annex the independent governments of Shoa and Tigré to his dominions ere he sought new laurels beyond the legitimate boundaries of his own realms. Dejatch Oubie, the ruler of Tigré, a man of firm nerve and stout heart, was quite prepared for a passage of arms with his ambitious and unscrupulous opponent. Kasa, notwithstanding his late successes in Dembea and Godjam, hesitated to risk the hard-gained toils of years in the brief contest of an hour. Friends on both sides tried their utmost to prevent the unnecessary effusion of blood. Their humane exertions were not altogether unsuccessful. The hostile chiefs, by solemn oaths, agreed to submit their respective quarrels to the arbitration of nobles, whose decision was to settle every claim. Whether true or not, Kasa pretended that the nobles of Tigré intended to place Oubie on the throne, and that Aboona Salama had consented to crown him king. To intimidate the primate, the crafty intriguer put himself in communication with Mgr. Jakobi, the zealous, indefatigable, and unscrupulous chief of the Romish mission in Abyssinia. The political Jesuit grasped with delight what he imagined the opporunity which would annex the largest patrimony of St. Mark to the trembling domain of St. Peter.

Perfidy and perjury now joined hands for a mitre and a crown. Kasa, encouraged by his episcopal ally, cast his oath to the winds, and made secret preparation to attack his foe. The treacherous proceedings of the

Quara usurper reached the ears of the Aboona, and he threatened him with the severest excommunication of the Church if he did not desist from his wicked design. Kasa, with a nonchalance unknown in Abyssinian history, replied to the episcopal messenger: "Tell your master that if he bans me, my new Aboona Jakobi will absolve me and ban him."

Dejatch Oubie now foresaw the storm that was looming in the horizon. To prevent a sudden surprise, he instantly assembled a well-organised force, and amidst the alpine heights of Semien awaited the issue of coming events. On a cold, raw, and stormy day in February, 1856, the Amhara forces, after a long and fatiguing march, came in sight of the well-ranged lines of Oubie's extensive camp. With that activity and promptitude which has often done more for Kasa than his valour and prowess, he at once marshalled his forces into battle array, and commanded them to charge the enemy. On hearing this command, distinct murmurs of discontent, like the rush of the sea against distant rocks, broke from the agitated masses of warriors, and for some moments Kasa himself stood appalled in witnessing these symptoms of fear and insubordination. Fully convinced that in the fortune of that day the prospects of a crown, and perhaps of life, were involved, the resolute chief, in that clear and ringing voice which always electrified his followers, gave them a short and pithy address, in which he recapitulated in glowing terms their former achievements; and then, swinging his sword defiantly towards the enemy, he thundered forth, in soul-inspiring accents, "After all your numerous conquests, does yonder rheumatic dotard damp your courage? Do yonder guns, charged with powder and rags, cow your souls? Are yonder rocks and chasms a barrier to your bravery? Follow me, and to-morrow by this time my name will be Theodorus, and not Kasa, for God has given me the kingdom."

Roused by the stirring words of their chief, the countless host rushed on the expectant foe, who welcomed them with a shower of iron balls and well-aimed spears. The groans of the dying and the war-whoop of the living—the echoes of the cliffs and the reverberating thunder of the storm, all combined to mark that day as one of the most terrible in the annals of Abyssinian warfare.

Evening was fast approaching, and the shades of night were beginning to confound friend and foe; still the desperate struggle raged with unabated ardour, and the carnage continued with unmitigated fury. Oubie, who had on that day evinced a generalship and gallantry that recalled to many a scarred head the deeds of their former adored Sabogadis, was at last, unknown to his soldiers, forced by exhaustion and age to seek a brief rest in a deep dell at the outskirts of the battle-field. This almost unguarded retreat was discovered by a detachment of Kasa's troops, and before the old chief could recover from the sudden surprise, he was seized, and carried in triumph to the enemy's camp. The Tigréans, bewildered and panic-stricken at their leader's captivity, were immediately thrown into the utmost consternation, and before the different chiefs could summon courage to rally their disordered retainers, some had sought safety in flight, others in passive submission, and not a few in a soldier's honourable grave.

The following day Kasa besieged Amba Boahil, 13,500 feet above the level of the sea, the reduction of which rendered him master of that bleak and inaccessible mountain range. Treacherous himself, he did not admire treachery in others when it no longer served his designs, and as Mgr. Jakobi might have become a troublesome guest, he received a polite mandate to leave the country. Aboona Salama, though almost a prisoner, indignantly refused to comply with the request to crown Kasa. Urged by priests and laymen, soldiers and chiefs, he reluctantly assented to perform the odious task, and on the 5th, Kasa, the rebel, had the sacred meron poured on his head, and, amidst the prayers of the primate, the chants of priests, and the shouts of an enthusiastic army, was crowned in the Church of Mariam Deresgie by the pompous name of Theodorus, *negoos negest* of Ethiopia.

After the coronation the troops marched off to take possession of Amba Hai, on whose summit were the treasures and the two youthful sons of the fallen chief. The princes, who were respectively twelve and fourteen years old, refused to surrender unless commanded by their parent. Kasa knew that Oubie would be as reluctant to assent to this as he was to leave the rich booty. In this emergency, as on all perplexing occasions, he had recourse to stratagem. There resided in the neighbourhood of Hai an ascetic renowned for his wonderful sanctity. The king sent for this recluse, and, after kissing his hands and cross, told him, with many an oath, of the anxiety and solicitude he cherished for the princes and their attendants, who had scorned his most generous overtures. Amazed at such obstinacy, the holy man volunteered his good offices to induce them to exchange their cold eyrie for the more genial atmosphere of the royal court. The words of the santon were received like the oracles of inspiration, and the whole party, in obedience to a decree it was sin to resist, left their lofty rampart, and, in the company of the saint, repaired to the royal tent. A present of a handful of dollars rewarded the envoy, who, unaccustomed to the din and tumult of a camp, gladly accepted his *congé*, and, with his dollars and sanctity intact, retired to the quiet solitude of his untainted hermitage. "So you trust a monk, and not a king," were the cutting words addressed to the amazed princes on the departure of the recluse, by the man who had sworn to shelter and protect them. "Well, you were right, and if the chains in which you will be fettered are ever taken off, you will afterwards be more cautious and prudent."* In fetters they remained until the day when the British flag of liberty fluttered to the breeze on the ramparts of Magdala; but it may be doubted whether these two princes, during the many years of their hard captivity, acquired much wisdom from their sad experience.

The treasures on the Amba exceeded the anticipations of the king. There were heaped up on that high rock seven thousand muskets, two cannons, a great quantity of gold and silver, and above forty thousand Maria Theresa dollars, besides a vast number of copper utensils, and gorgeously-coloured berilles, which the Abyssinians use instead of wine-glasses in drinking their hydromel. Thus did the base treachery of that ruthless man triumph over every obstacle that opposed his schemes of aggrandisement, or ensured safety to a doubtful friend or open foe.

Tigré was subdued; the Aboona apparently reconciled; Oubie and his sons in chains. Prophetic utterances were about to become historical facts. It

---

* The two princes, Kasai and Quanquoul, who were my companions in chains for sixteen months, gave me this account of their capture.

is true the Wollo Gallas, those hereditary enemies of the Amharas, were still unsubdued, and Shoa, a fief of the Gondar crown, was governed by an independent prince. These were, however, trifling achievements after what had already been accomplished. The march southward to subjugate the two countries that had not yet volunteered submission, was, after the conquest of Tigré, prosecuted without delay. On the plain of Bola Worka, not far from Ankobar, the southern capital, the Shoa and Amhara forces measured their strength. The Shoanes, anxious to maintain their old renown, rushed to the charge with a courage that defied every resistance, and overcame all opposition. Theodore's quick eye at once perceived that the very violence of the assault would exhaust the vigour of the assailants. "Stand firm, and do not divide," was the command. The royalists murmuringly obeyed. Mad with rage, the Shoanes, in scattered groups, attacked the enemy's compact hosts. This immobility, so new to Amhara warfare, they foolishly attributed to the cowardice of the enemy. They did not know that Theodore had received some lessons in the art of war from Baron Heuchlin, and other Europeans, who taught him that unity of action ensures victory, or renders a retreat comparatively safe. Recklessly they poured in detached columns on the concentrated masses of the impassive foe. Quick as lightning the serried lines opened out, and ere the chiefs could reassemble their dispersed hosts, they were encompassed by the Amharas, and compelled to surrender. Fresh from the victorious battle-field of Bola Worka, the impetuous conqueror, with his countless multitude of Shoa, Tigré, and Amhara forces, torrent-like, rushed on the unprepared Wollo Gallas, drenching field and meadow with the blood of the young and the old, the weak and the strong. The campaign was most successful, and King Theodore, the ruler of all Abyssinia, laden with spoils, and accompanied by weeping and disconsolate multitudes of captive boys and girls, retraced his steps towards Gondar, the metropolis of his realm. To protect his newly-acquired provinces, he fortified, according to Abyssinian fashion, the rocky heights of Magdala, which he garrisoned with faithful troops, under the command of Af Negus Work and Dejatch Alamee, two tried and trusty chiefs. On Amba Geshen, about thirty miles east of Magdala, to intimidate his turbulent newly-acquired Yedshoo subjects, he also placed a large troop under the command of a Bengal Christian Jew, a man most faithfully devoted to his interests. These two positions, garrisoned by men in whom he could place implicit confidence, were quite sufficient to defend the country against any foreign invader; but Theodore, bent on chastising the Turks and on conquering Jerusalem, wanted to make his own dominion impregnable, and so another small Amba, called Quoied, near the Beshilo, had also to receive its quota of lancers. To occupy these strongholds was easy enough, but not so the means of provisioning them. His chiefs reminded him of that difficulty. " Ah! you donkeys," was the curt reply, " haven't I got peasants enough? and if these do not suffice, we shall soon get Turkish slaves to do the work."

Winter, that season of inactivity, wet, and cold, had now fairly set in. Theodore, inured to bustle and the tumult of the camp, could ill brook the quiet and confinement of the Gondar Castle. To while away his time, he was obliged to find some objects worthy of the royal diversion, and as he could not make any distant forays with his tired and weary troops, nor plunder loyal and devoted provinces, he selected the Church for this special service.

Ever since the reign of Yasou, A.D. 1680, the Abyssinian Church, partly by intrigue and partly by voluntary bequests, had acquired vast landed property. Free from all imposts and taxation, the ecclesiastical domains, which amounted to a third of all the landed property, was a great eyesore to King Theodore. Anxious to appropriate these extensive possessions for his own use, he artfully promised to provide for the wants of the clergy, whilst at the same time he proposed to release them of all secular concerns so incompatible with their holy vocation. The hierarchy, with the bishop at their head, were not so easily gulled. They understood Theodore better than the peasantry, and contrary to his expectation, all unanimously declared that they would not be slaves dependent on the royal bounty. The tyrant, at whose bidding legion after legion of his armed countrymen had laid down their weapons and sworn fealty and allegiance, was little prepared for this outburst of priestly opposition. In his wrathful ebullition, he would probably have evoked the sword to decide the quarrel, but his faithful advisers reminded him that the sympathies of the troops and the nation were with the priests, and that serious consequences might ensue if he provoked their superstition and bigotry. The furious despot, unaccustomed to be baulked in his schemes, like a lion at bay, in his rage rushed on Wagshum Tafaree, the mouthpiece of the counsellors, and probably would have transfixed him with his lance, had not his better genius, and perhaps an opportune recollection of ten thousand Lasta and Yedshoo horse under his command, curbed his fiery passion.* Mr. Bell was not such high game, and the lance intended for the Wagshum sped its flight over the Englishman's bending form, and fell blunted against an opposite wall. The storm soon abated,

* This chief, the best informed and most gentlemanly of all the Abyssinian nobles, and who may yet play a significant part in his country's history, related the whole occurrence to the Aboona, to whom he was devoutly and sincerely attached.

and the tyrant, convinced of the unreasonableness of a conflict that might, at the very outset of his reign, convulse the whole realm to its very centre, yielded to the dissuasions of his friends, and the Church spoliation plan was suspended till 1860, when it was carried into effect.

CHAPTER II.

Theodore Triumphant—His Conduct towards Egypt—France and England—Social Condition of the Empire—His Hatred of the Egyptians and Turks—He imprisons the Viceroy's Ambassador, and is unappeased by the arrival of another Minister from Egypt—Arrival of Consul Cameron and M. Lejean—Imprisonment of the French Representative—Consul Cameron's return—Theodore's Hostility to the English is excited—Success of the English Missionary.

THEODORE had gained his object, and was now sole ruler of Abyssinia. His army, which exceeded 150,000 fighting men, was devoted to his interests, and implicitly obedient to his will. "I am the *barea* (slave) of the king" rang through the air from morning till evening, and from evening till morning, and often enough interspersed with adulations so extravagant, that they degenerated into horrid blasphemies.

The incense of adulation so profusely offered before the shrine of the sable Moloch, inflated his pride and fed the devouring flame of ambition that was burning and flickering in his insatiable heart. Egypt he grossly insulted, and perhaps the Viceroy would never have condescended to notice his coarse effusions, much less have honoured him with an embassy, had not consular pressure made itself felt in the councils of that most conciliatory power. England he treated with a little more deference on account of the projected embassy which, under the guardianship of Consul Plowden, then a hostage in his power, was to visit the Court of St. James's. Towards France he openly avowed an intense hatred, and if he could have caught his former friend, Monsignor de Jacobi, he would have resented on him and his companions the sins they and the government whose protection they claimed had committed in his eyes. His foreign policy was not more crooked and perverse than his internal civil rule. Under the pretext of love to his people and solicitude for their welfare, he perpetrated with impunity the most atrocious deeds.

Nobles of renowned pedigree, and hereditary chiefs of powerful clans, for real or imaginary crimes, were, without trial or investigation of the charges alleged against them, put to death, their property confiscated, and their families distributed as slaves amongst favourites or a new-created aristocracy. The terrors pervading the upper classes found no responsive chord in the heart of the lower orders. The peasantry were weary of the incessant conflicts between rival chieftains, and the fate of those who had again and again disappointed their expectations did not concern them, so long as their harvest was unmolested, their homes secure, and their persons protected. Taxes, grievous and most exorbitant, which were imposed upon them, they willingly paid, as experience—bitter experience—had taught them that it was more advantageous to be subjected to the spoliation of one than of scores of oppressors. Here and there a district sought to assert its claims to a just and legal taxation. An appeal to law they knew was useless, since the king was above all law; and to submit to a perpetual grinding taxation, they felt was ruinous. In this emergency, they had recourse to the chiefs of their clans, or, rather, the lords of the land, and these were only too glad to encourage a rising against one far beneath them in origin or possessions, but who, by tact, energy, and daring, had swung himself into the seat of their ancient kings. Theodore, by the rapidity of his movements, and the slow proceedings of the insurgent leaders, generally nipped these outbursts of dissatisfaction before they could take deep root and effloresce. This was the case with Gerad, the murderer of Consul Plowden, who, together with sixteen hundred followers, was nominally immolated to the manes of his victim, Consul Plowden, and the outraged dignity of Britain, but, in reality, to the vengeance of the king, and the mortification of the many disaffected proud nobles. A rebellion in Tigré, under Agow Negusee, could not be so easily quelled; but duplicity and craft, blended with artful promises and bombastic proclamations, combined to secure the tyrant's triumph.

The punishments inflicted on the rebels and their abettors were unparalleled for their atrocity and brutality in the annals of Abyssinian history. Godjam, which had partially raised the standard of rebellion, was cowed by the feeble resistance of the rebels in the north-eastern provinces, and, in their dread of the royal vengeance, many deserted their chief, Tadlo Qualou, whilst those who adhered to him sought refuge on the inaccessible Amba Tshebella.

Having thus by his own indomitable energy reduced the jarring elements of disorder, and diffused the blessings of peace and unity over a realm hitherto torn and distracted, he ought to have forestalled, had he possessed the requisite prudence, all future troubles that cast their ominous shadows over the present calm aspect of the discontented provinces. This he could have accomplished without weakening his power or creating any formidable foes. The peasantry, ground down by crushing taxation, without venturing openly to express it, longed for a relief from their heavy burdens. To modify the imposts without diminishing the rabble hosts that swelled, but did not strengthen, the ranks of the army, would have been an impossibility. "Let the people perish; if I have troops, I can gain new countries and fresh subjects," was his response, whenever any one ventured to broach such a delicate topic. Besides his ambition for territorial aggrandisement, there rankled in his heart a deep burning hate against the Egyptians, and that merely because, half a score years before, they had inflicted so terrible a lesson on the impotent reasserter of Abyssinia's ancient domain. For the disastrous defeat of the 16,000 Ethiopians by 800 Bashe-Bezouks, the Egyptian government was not responsible, since Kasa himself, and not the governor of the Soudan, was the aggressor. This, however, the arrogant monarch would not admit, and day after day, and week after week, his rankling hostility against the Turks assumed more and more the form of a passion that seemed to absorb all his thoughts and feelings. The Viceroy did all that was consistent with his dignity to pacify a savage, unscrupulous neighbour. He dispatched to his court a most flattering embassy, represented by no less a personage than the Copt Patriarch, the acknowledged successor of St. Mark, and the Supreme Pontiff of the Abyssinian Church. Unfortunately, the successor of the apostle loved the aromatic weed of Latakia; animadverted a little freely on raw, reeking collops; censured, perhaps, in too severe terms the mode of life adopted by his spiritual children; and in many other matters gave offence, and brought upon himself the wrath and indignation of the monarch whose favour he was sent to conciliate. These assumptions the proud Theodore could not allow to pass unpunished, and the unguarded Patriarch, together with his subordinate, the Aboona Salama, had both to do penance for their common indiscretion by five days' durance vile in an Abyssinian camp prison. Of course, his Majesty found numbers of apologisers for his harshness towards the representative of a friendly foreign power, and among these the few Europeans in the country were not the last to raise their voice. A Turkish ruler to send a Christian ambassador? What indignity! What insult! What contempt! Unfortunately, weak Egypt listened to the bawling of interested sycophants and selfish courtiers, and Abdul Rachman Bey, an orthodox Mahomedan, was dispatched with presents worth more than £10,000 to retrieve the errors of his impolitic apostolic predecessor. Alas! alas! for political acumen. This genuine, true, and faithful follower of the Prophet was addicted to what all good Moslems are addicted, and this the immaculate Theodorus deemed an offence worthy of the most condign severity. Poor Abdul Rachman Bey pleaded, and pleaded justly, that the morals of Egypt were superior to those of Abyssinia, and yet the "Effendina" did not subject a man to a prison, or mulct him in a fine if he indulged in greater excesses than his neighbours; and that, in particular, foreign diplomatists enjoyed in this respect the greatest immunity and the greatest privileges an exalted personage could possibly desire. The king's ear was deaf to all arguments, and the representative of Egypt had to repair to the well-known "Hotel des Ambassadeurs," at Magdala. The English Consul, who had in the interval fallen a victim to a rebel's lance, escaped certain impending troubles, whilst the tyrant, robbed of his victim, adroitly applied the disappointment to his advantage in his direct and indirect intercourse with the British Government. France—glory-loving, progress-loving, idea-loving France—stimulated by a desire to emulate British influence in north-eastern Africa, immediately dispatched a consul with presents and a most courteous bland letter to the sensitive Negoos, who cherished an old grudge against "la grande nation" on account of the support extended to the late Tigré rebel. M. Lejean, the representative of the Emperor, who reached the Abyssinian coast a few months' later than Consul Cameron, his English confrère, met with the wonted courteous reception. The proud barbarian, admired by England, courted by France, wooed by Egypt, sought by Austria, and honoured and complimented by Prussia, began to believe that if he could not claim to be the real Prester John, or Solomon, he was certainly a being equal, if not superior, to these historic personages. Confident in his exalted position and fancied invincible power, he boldly burst the barriers which had hitherto restrained his impetuous temper, and threw aside the garb of sanctity which had disguised his true character. The veil of decency once cast aside, the hero, whose praise had so long been the theme and glory of an enslaved people, daringly defied the opinion of men and the laws of God. Vice was henceforth rewarded, and virtue, such as Abyssinians can exhibit, punished. Deeds the most revolting were no longer subject to legal investigation, nor crimes the most heinous censured by royal lips. Every passion found an apology, and every atrocity a plea. The camp, heretofore, comparatively speaking, the purest spot in the land, was deluged with a polluting stream dark as night and black as hell. Provinces were pillaged, villages burnt, and thousands of defenceless people indiscriminately butchered. M. Lejean, to his horror, discovered that the atmosphere of the court of Theodorus was too hot for his French constitution, and, confiding in the wide-spread fame of his imperial master, he humbly craved permission to seek a more genial clime. The request was peremptorily denied, and its reiteration visited with strong and massive manacles. The missionaries of the London Jews' Society and the Scottish Church, during the whole of this stormy period, continued unmolested at their post in Genda. Schools were established, Scripture-readers engaged, itinerating tours initiated, tracts written, books translated, catechumens instructed, and other efforts for the enlightenment of the people, and the regeneration of their benighted land, were carried on without interruption or impediment.

An ominous dread—the prelude of coming troubles

—now and then clouded our visions, and imparted a pall-like tinge to our sunny views. During an interview with his Majesty in Dembea—when he had just chopped off the hands of two loitering soldiers, and inflicted the giraff on his faithful Asash Gabrio, the governor of the province—he was serious, but not sullen; taciturn, but not morose; nay, on inquiring whether I could visit the lowland province of Armatgioho, he politely rejoined: "You can go where you like, and if you want grain, money, or anything else, let me know, and you shall be supplied."

The impending catastrophe, though postponed, was, however, sure to come at last. In June, 1863, Consul Cameron came back to Abyssinia. His Majesty, on being informed that he had returned without a reply to the letter he had entrusted to him for her Majesty the Queen, was indignant, though he tried to conceal the wound which his pride had sustained. In his interviews with Consul Cameron—at which some, if not all, of the missionaries were generally present—his conversation, bland as it was, betrayed that, beneath the soft words that fell so smoothly from his thin lips, there lurked a tone of asperity which all his craft could not effectually conceal. There was a calm, but the heaving of the under-current prognosticated to the experienced eye the approach of a storm. The mission-premises, on which Consul Cameron resided, quite unnoticed hitherto, now became the subject of severe animadversion. The houses—though merely thatched conical huts—were too large, and their number—though limited to only seven, inclusive of a chapel and a school-house, too great. In fact, it was obvious that we had incurred his Majesty's displeasure, without being conscious of the cause. The spot we occupied, the houses we inhabited, the converts we made, the people we employed, and the schools we founded—all, all, as I heard from the Aboona, who had his spies around the king, were regarded with suspicion, and denounced as unlawful. Take care! take care! was the primate's admonition on July 3rd, 1863, that your people do not divulge to the Negoos the number of the proselytes or catechumens that you have gathered from among the Falashas! This intimation—kind, generous, and affectionate as it was—fell on my ear as the death-knell of our mission, and the funeral-note of our buried hopes. My only object now was to improve the brief period that we were still tolerated in disseminating over the troubled land those heaven-born truths which, even in the absence of the living teacher, if blessed from on High, could make those mountains and valleys redolent with a fragrance far more sweet than that of its scented shrubs and aromatic herbs. That such a period was approaching, unmistakable signs palpably indicated. A power invisible had touched the hearts of many, and awakened a responsive chord. There was now seen what was never witnessed before, a thirst for the Divine Word, a yearning for Christian instruction, and an honest, confiding trust in the foreign teacher. I had wandered over many a tract, district, and province where the voice of the messenger of glad tidings had never fallen on fond, listening ears; but wherever I roamed and wherever I strayed—on the verdant plain, and on the picturesque mountain slope; in the sequestered wood, and beneath the isolated shady tree —every spot became a centre of attraction, and every retreat a temple for converse and communion with troubled, agitated, and alarmed truth-seeking fellow-men. The day of salvation had indeed dawned, the shadows of unregeneracy had indeed fled, and the morning of joy and praise was about to break over this region of sin and this home of spiritual night, when events fraught with anguish, affliction, and despair, marred our hopes, and disappointed our most hallowed anticipations.

CHAPTER III.

Return from Missionary Tour—Invitation from the King—Feast of St. John—Interview with Theodore—M. Bardel's Account of his Mission—Wounded Pride—Dismissal of M. Lejean—Gloomy Forebodings—Discordant Sounds—Departure from the Capital — Unfavourable Symptoms — Visit to the Royal Camp — Violence of the King—Execution of my Servants—Personal Maltreatment—Feeling of Desolation—Keen Sufferings—Abyssinian Surgery—Honest Tears—My Chains—My Consolation.

IT was towards the end of September, 1863, that I returned to our station at Genda from a missionary tour through the north-western lowland provinces, delighted with all that I had witnessed and experienced. On my arrival, Mrs. Flad told me that she was glad that I had come back in the very nick of time, as on that very day she had received a letter from her husband at Gondar, requesting me in the name of the king to repair thither, as his Majesty wanted to communicate to all the Europeans the answer M. Bardel had brought to the letter he had dispatched by him to the Emperor Napoleon. Captain Cameron received a summons of similar import from the king himself. We immediately made our few necessary preparations, and the following day set out for the capital. The feast of St. John, which was then solemnised, imparted a festive aspect to the camp and city. Eating and drinking, singing and dancing, resounded from hut and tent, palace and church. All were plunged in merriment and gaiety. The myriads and myriads of beeves plundered from the Zeelans, and liberally distributed among the hungry broundo-loving gourmands, amazingly enhanced the savage carnival. We had now approached within a respectful distance of the imperial palace, where etiquette warned us to leave our saddles. Hosts of greasy terpsi-chorean performers met us at every nook and corner of the labyrinthine Etcheque Beit, where the royal domicile stands out in bold and picturesque relief from the midst of a mass of indescribable rickety tenements. Careless of the sweltering fetid throng, we steered, like a ship with sails all spread, through the stormy and boisterous living ocean, up to the precincts of the royal court, in the hopes of meeting a sober courtier who would inform his Majesty of our advent. The bacchanalian votaries were all, however, too much absorbed in their peculiar merriments to pay any attention to two white strangers; and, as we were too fond of pure air, we tacked our course out of the stifling atmosphere towards the dwelling of a debterah, where we knew a friendly welcome awaited us. On our way we encountered M. Bardel. He did not see me, and this perhaps removed all restraint from his tongue. During the short converse with

Consul Cameron, the words, "I shall crush them all"—which might have had reference to the missionaries, workmen, or French Consul—fell with appalling import on my startled ear.

Sunday was undisturbed, but early on Monday morning we were ordered to repair to the royal residence. Of course we instantly obeyed the summons, and hurried to the palace. Two gorgeous tents, which stood conspicuously on the grassy lawn fronting the royal saloon, indicated that some business of import was about to be transacted. In one of these gaudy pavilions was M. Lejean, the French Consul, and in the second, to which we were directed, were already assembled in barbarous state uniform his Majesty's white workmen. A few minutes had only elapsed when half-a-dozen officers of the palace made their appearance, and requested us to follow. An ascent of about fifty broad steps landed us on the vestibule. Here another cluster of officials conducted us into the audience hall, which was still redolent with the odours of the previous day's raw beef banquet. His Majesty was seated in the deep recess of a glassless window, surrounded by books and papers, which merged the savage African into the polite and polished Ethiopian. He was more than usually dignified and polite in his deportment, though it was evident that beneath that assumed blandness and forced condescension there lay an under-current of anger and asperity which his best acting—and he was a consummate actor—could with difficulty conceal. All being seated on the carpets which, in a crescent form, were spread a few yards from the Negoos, M. Bardel, the royal envoy, received an intimation to rise. The favoured courtier in a trice was on his legs, and like a man who knew what was expected from him, stood with an air of confidence awaiting his master's commands. "Aito Bardel," in subdued accents, the king then said; "how were you received by the Emperor?" "Your Majesty," the crafty envoy rejoined, "I met with a most uncourteous reception at the court of France." "Did they provide you," returned the king, "with a house, food, and all that you required?" "No, Janehoi," was the response; "I got neither a house to dwell in, nor food nor money to supply my daily wants." "What did the Emperor tell you," continued the king, in the same smooth tone, "when you presented him my letter?" "His Imperial Majesty asked me a variety of questions about Abyssynia," quoth the envoy, "and he seemed favourably disposed to my proposals, when he turned to his adviser, M. d'Abbadie, who was in the reception hall, and consulted him about the matter embodied in your Majesty's despatch. M. d'Abbadie's observations immediately produced a change in the Emperor's conduct towards me, and he dismissed me with the sarcastic sentence, 'I will have no direct intercourse with a sovereign who cuts off the hands and feet of his subjects.'" That this whole interview was a fiction of M. Bardel's own inventive genius was palpable, but I could not venture to express such a conjecture, without endangering my life, to any one except Consul Cameron. The Emperor, though unwilling to have any direct intercourse with the court of Abyssinia, the envoy further stated, was not desirous to terminate all future relation with Ethiopia, and this induced him to order his minister to write an answer to the document he had conveyed to France. This letter, which was most courteous, and replete with wise and sensible suggestions, was now handed for perusal to the assembled conclave. Consul Cameron was ordered to read it aloud for the edification of all. When this was done, his Majesty seized the document, and dashing it on the ground, remarked in accents of bitter irony blended with wounded pride, "Is this an answer to my letter? Napoleon may think himself great, but I am greater still; his genealogy is only of yesterday; mine, on the contrary, I trace back to David and Solomon. True he is rich, and I am poor; he is powerful, and I am weak; he has fine palaces, and I only ruins; but"—and he paused a few seconds, whilst his hypocritical eyes were devoutly upturned—"glory, wealth, and renown will yet be my portion!" A few unimportant questions were now interchanged between the Negoos and the disgraced French representative. M. Lejean tried and tried hard to convince his Majesty through the delegates (for a personal interview, though urgently solicited, was not granted) that he laboured under an erroneous impression, and misunderstood the sentiments of his master the Emperor, who cherished the highest regard and esteem for the king. To corroborate his statement, he most assiduously craved permission to present to the Negoos the despatches he had received from his government, which positively stated that the Abyssinian embassy would be accepted so soon as the arrangements for their passage through Egypt had been satisfactorily settled. Neither diplomacy nor persuasion could, however, appease the incensed monarch, and M. Lejean and his companion, Dr. Legard, instead of chains, with which they were to have been favoured, had not the Aboona interfered, received peremptory orders to quit the country. The departure of the French Consul; the doubts and suspicions about an answer to his letter from the British Government; the report that a strong Turkish force had taken their position at Matamma, on the northwestern border; the consciousness that he could not cope with a foe whom he had insolently challenged to a combat; together with the fading vision of ever obtaining by diplomacy the coveted possession of Senaar to the north-west, and the isle of Massowah to the north-east, soured his temper, and stimulated him to perpetrate deeds which led to the ruin of his country and the loss of his crown and life. Ominous indications of coming events henceforth cast their dismal shadows athwart our serene and hitherto unclouded horizon. No one, of course, had the remotest idea in what shape or form the impending crisis would develop itself. I believed the royal indignation would burst on the missionaries in an order for their immediate expulsion, and on the British Consul in a mandate for a forcible unfettered detention. I communicated the fears I felt to Captain Cameron, but he did not share the dismal forebodings in which I indulged.

The object of my mission was by this time completely attained, and, to avoid all unnecessary delays which might perhaps have retarded my return, I mounted my mule, and bade farewell to scenes and associations that, I still faintly trusted, would prove centres of light and truth to irradiate far and wide the thick darkness of Abyssinia's superstitious gloom.

It was on the memorable October 13, 1863, that I entered on my disastrous and fatal journey. The sun on that ill-omened day rose in its wonted tropical splendour; hills and valleys, fields and meadows, all sparkled and glittered in the lovely splendour of a tropical morn. To the north rose, in bold relief against the azure sky, massive rocks, which, for many hours per day, cast a deep shadow over the sacred quarter of Kudus Gabriel. Opposite, on a verdant sloping ground, lay in peaceful repose the large division of the town called Etcheque Beit, intersected by churches embosomed in the shady foliage of the juniper. Beyond these, in a south-west direction, extended, as far as the eye could reach, the tents of the king's army; whilst due south and west, at the extremity of the lovely plain, lay, like a sheet of burnished gold, the isle-dotted lake of Dembea. The silence of death, broken only by the chants of the officiating priests, which, till now, fell in melancholy cadences on the ear, was gradually superseded by less harmonious strains. Bleating flocks, accompanied by the jarring notes of the shepherd's shrill reed-pipe, here scaled a steep ascent towards an upland plateau; there a peasant, cracking his terrible giraff, lazily followed his beeves to an upland field. From one house resounded the harsh voice of a virago, who poured forth volumes of unmentionable epithets on a truant daughter or indolent husband; from another were heard the oaths of a drunken soldier who refused to pay for his libations, intermingled with the shouts and imprecations of a merchant who would not yield his property to the spoiler. This din and confusion, as if not enough to stun the ear, was now and then heightened by the sharp rattle of a rusty musket, which, as it floated across the plain, gathered strength in the distant rocks, where it reverberated for miles with a deep crawling echo, or by a savage war-whoop, that reminded one forcibly of a large travelling menagerie. In my own domicile all was in harmony with its dignified occupant. Servants and slaves noiselessly performed their various duties; even the beggars, who beleaguered the doorway, in subdued accents solicited their alms, quite contrary to their wonted boisterous clamour. My mind, excited by the anticipation of the journey, the fears and doubts of its successful termination, and a variety of distracting reveries—the prelude of coming troubles—forbade repose, and I rose exhausted and feverish. The bustle of packing, the hurrying to and fro of domestics, and the excitement of leave-taking, relieved my spirit, and banished those dismal visions which, in defiance of all resistance, presented themselves to my imagination. My host, the bishop, in the retirement and sanctity of an inner court, which it was sacrilegious to cross without previous sanction, promised me, the preceding evening, an early interview; but, forgetful of his engagement, and wrapt in sweet daylight slumber, he tested my patience not a little by his unreasonable hours. Unwilling to delay longer, I had the temerity to penetrate his sanctum. On seeing me he stretched out his hand, and observed, "I am later than usual; but this," he added, smilingly, "must be attributed to the holy Georgis, who, like myself, does not want you to desecrate the day devoted to him by travelling." I expressed a different opinion, but he ridiculed my secret surmises. I then discussed again various unimportant matters, partook of a substantial breakfast, arranged some business affairs, and then, followed by his own and Father Joseph's (his confessor's) best wishes, took my departure out of the hospitable episcopal residence. My animals being loaded and already on the march, I at once mounted my mule, and, accompanied by my Armenian servant and some natives, rode up to the Etcheque Beit, to bid farewell to Consul Cameron. He had already anticipated this parting visit, for his mule stood saddled in the court. To avoid the noonday's sun, we bestrode our animals, and trotting through rugged narrow lanes and over hills impregnated with all sorts of unmentionable odours, hurried on towards the foaming and dashing Gaha. Bardel joined us near the river, and he and the consul, with their numerous followers, formed quite a respectable cavalcade. As the king was on the march, masses of soldiers, with their ragged followers, were in a confused motley, forcing their course in the same direction, in order to join their respective chiefs. The panting and gasping, hungry and tattered multitude, formed a host whose very appearance augured desolation and misery to any province they might have to traverse. To us they were tolerably civil, though, as I afterwards recollected, there was not that deference which had hitherto been evinced towards the white man. Had I been less engaged with my own thoughts and more with the rabble host, I might have divined, from the coarse jests and gibes, the rude gaze, and impertinent throng of the semi-savages between whom we defiled, that the white man had sunk in position, and that there were already indistinct murmurs which prognosticated his impending doom.

Some servants of Consul Cameron and Messrs. Staiger and Brandeis, who, with despatches and letters for the coast, had on the previous day, by order of the king, been plundered and maltreated, confirmed my suspicions. Al Tassab, one of the party, and who was delighted to find a refuge among my people, lost twelve dollars, all his earthly possessions. The packets were conveyed to Gondar, and there Samuel, as I heard from his own lips, concealed, but did not destroy them. His object was to keep on good terms with the favourite Chrishona artisans and their missionary brethren, Staiger and Brandeis, till he had wreaked his vengeance on Consul Cameron* and those whom, like myself, he considered more directly connected with England.

---

* Samuel had a most inveterate hatred against Consul Cameron. In his capacity as "baldaraba"—viz., spy—he watched all his movements, which he reported to the king. The letters he sent from

ABYSSINIAN HORSEMAN.

Two hours' ride was beguiled by pleasant converse about the future destiny of the country, of whose beauties and capabilities we could judge by the surrounding scenery, and then we bade each other a cordial farewell. Followed by my Egyptian servant, I sped my way through the ever-increasing crowd up a regular succession of steeps, and about mid-day landed on the verdant plateau of Woggera. Here, to my disagreeable surprise, I saw, about ten minutes' ride to the left, the camp of the king. Immediately I consulted with my people, who had been waiting for me, whether we should encamp. They unanimously declared that it was my duty to halt till I had paid my respects to the king. I did not particularly admire this advice, but as a deviation from the established etiquette might have been misinterpreted into rudeness or contempt, I accepted with the best grace a not very pleasant suggestion.

A fair, green spot, abounding with fragrant shrubs and shady trees, invited us to alight. The royal camp, though near, was not near enough to attract the inquisitive and curious, the lazy beggar and the proud military chief, to our halting-place. My tent was soon erected, and on a bed of sweet herbs I

Boghos when he accompanied him down the coasts with the royal despatches were dipped in venom, and contributed materially to our misfortunes. He admitted that he wrote letters, but denied that they exaggerated or misrepresented any fact.

enjoyed a happy and calm repose after the fatigue and toils of the journey.

The idea of visiting the white tent of royalty, which shone brightly in the clear atmosphere on a hill about half an hour's distance, depressed my spirits with a melancholy I could not explain. I tried to dispel this ceaseless gloom by writing and jotting down notes, but, notwithstanding my utmost effort, I found it impossible to banish the presentiment of an impending disaster. Conscious that, neither by word nor deed, I had merited the king's ill will, I strove against the warning of the internal monitor, and, throwing my shama around me, like a man anxious to get over an unpleasant task, I went, accompanied by two of my people, towards the hill, on whose summit stood conspicuously the imperial pavilion. As I approached, all previous surmises and misgivings vanished, and, confiding in the consciousness of my integrity, which I thought would be a shield strong enough to guard me against the machinations and malice of insidious foes, if I had any, I boldly advanced till I stood within a respectful and becoming distance of the never-to-be-forgotten spot.

Whilst waiting for the approach of an officer or domestic of the royal household who would announce my visit, groups of drunken military chiefs and district governors came staggering, in most unseemly attitudes, out of the royal banqueting tent. Many gazed at me in stupid bewilderment; others, with heavy tongues, bawled forth a compliment or abuse on the white men, who had brought into disrepute the faithful lance and trusty sword by the introduction of heavy muskets and unwieldy cannons. I felt disposed to retreat, but to this, for sapient reasons, my companions justly objected. I then suggested that we should seek the shelter of a shady tree or bush till the banquet was over and his Majesty visible. This proposal was equally rejected as incompatible with Abyssinian rule. The last jar of hydromel had at last, as a royal page, *en passant*, assured me, been quaffed, the last reeking joint had been devoured, the last batch of rioters had at last vanished, when the folds of the tent were thrown aside, and his Majesty, surrounded by half-a-dozen officers and several pages, strutted out into the open air. My companions quickly prostrated themselves into the dust; whilst I, without imitating their servile obeisance, made a humble and deferential bow. "Come nearer," shouted the attendants. I obeyed, and advanced a few steps. "Still nearer," reiterated several stentorian voices. I complied, and made another forward movement. "What do you want?" sharply demanded the flushed and drink-excited Negoos. "I saw your Majesty's tent," was the response, "and came hither to offer my humble salutations and respects to your Majesty." "Where are you going?" "I am, with your Majesty's sanction, about to proceed to Massorah." "And why did you come to Abyssinia?" "A desire to circulate the Word of God among your Majesty's subjects prompted the enterprise," I rejoined. "Can you make cannons?" "No," was the reply. "You lie," was the laconic retort; and then, turning with a withering glance towards Negusee, one of my companions, and a servant of Consul Cameron, he imperatively demanded to know the name of his province. "I am from Tigré," tremulously responded the poor man. "And you are the servant or interpreter of this white man?" "No, your Majesty; I am in the employ of Consul Cameron, and only accompany him down to Adowa, whither I am bound to see my family." "You vile carcass! you base dog! you rotten donkey! you dare to bandy words with your king. Down with the villain, and *bemouti* (by my death), beat him till there is not a breath in his worthless carcass." The order was promptly obeyed, and the poor, inoffensive man, without a struggle, ejaculation, or groan, was dashed on the ground, where, amidst the shouts of the savage monarch, that the executioners should vigorously ply their sticks, the animated and robust frame was, in less than a minute, a torn and mangled corpse. "There's another man yonder," vociferated the savage king; "kill him also." The poor fellow, who stood at a considerable distance, was immediately dragged to the side of his motionless companion, and, without having breathed a word or syllable that could possibly have irritated the sanguinary tyrant, doomed to share the same unhappy fate. I was amazed, bewildered, and surprised. In my agitation I might, unconsciously, have put my hand or finger to my lips. This the cruel tyrant construed into an act of defiance, and, without one warning or reproof, he rushed upon me with a drawn pistol, like a lion balked of his prey. For an instant I saw the glittering weapon sparkling in the rays of the sinking sun, and then, as if checked in his fell design by an invisible power, it disappeared again in the case suspended round his waist. "Knock him down! brain him! kill him!" were the words which rung appallingly on my ear. In the twinkle of an eye I was stripped, on the ground, and insensible. Stunned, unconscious, and almost lifeless, with the blood oozing out of scores of gashes, I was dragged into the camp, not, as my guards were commanded, to bind me in fetters, but, as they thought—and I heard it from their own lips—to bury me.*

---

* The six chiefs who administered the sticks subsequently became my best friends.

A stifling sensation, I well remember, roused me to something approaching consciousness. I tried to speak, but my throat and mouth, full of clotted blood, forbade the attempt. I sought to look around me, but my eyes were glued, and I did not dare to open them. I endeavoured to recollect the events of the last few hours, but my swimming and giddy head rendered the effort abortive. Rousing myself from this state of painful lassitude and stupefaction, my mind, though sadly confused, retained some faint recollection of the last hour's terrible scene. The soldier to whom I was fastened, and whose shama my bleeding wounds had thoroughly saturated, noticed that I was in great agony and distress. The gentle touch with which he lifted the chain convinced me that he was not one of Theodore's hardened ruffians. "What do you want?" he kindly inquired. I pointed to my parched and feverish lips. "Woha" (water). "Tenisu" (get up), "and you shall have some." With difficulty I raised my cold, shivering, and stiff limbs, and, together with my kind guardian, crept to a watchfire, where there was a party who had a skin full of water. "Hit (go), Turk," they shouted, "for our Christian cups shall not touch a Moslem's lips." "I am not a Mahomedan," I mournfully sighed, "but a Christian, and a believer in a blessed Trinity." These faintly-breathed words acted like a galvanic battery on their insensible hearts. Promptly the water cup was raised to my quivering lips, and a place vacated for me near the fire. A good, cold draught roused me to a knowledge of my misery and wretchedness, loneliness and desolation. I was alone; a stranger in a strange country. No bosom was open to my sorrow; no heart shared my grief. The world around me was dead to a white man's anguish, and indifferent to his woes: but though far removed from the sight of those whose words might have soothed the aching, lacerated, and bleeding missionary; whose hands might have bathed his throbbing temples, stanched his bleeding wounds, and protected him from the chill morning blast, there was One present who, in the utter despondency and despair of the storm-tossed heart, could point to His own solemn and touching words: "Fear not, for I am with thee; be not dismayed, for I am thy God. I will strengthen thee; yea, I will help thee; yea, I will uphold thee with the right hand of My righteousness."

The long, interminable night of suffering and trial, with its dew and cold and darkness, at length drew to a close, and the dawn revealed, in its dim, pale light, the mountain-tops that guarded, like impregnable ramparts, the south-eastern confines of the wide-spreading Woggera plain. Twilight in those latitudes speedily yields to the full blaze of sunlight, and cold night to the warmth, if not heat, of day. The camp was now full of life, activity, and bustle. Tents were struck, mules loaded, and horses saddled. Women and men, chiefs in silken shirts, and common soldiers in greasy shamas, vied with each other in clearing the camp and road before the approach of the royal cavalcade. In the midst of that hum and din I alone was most indifferent and unconcerned. Many of my wounds had, indeed, ceased to bleed, but that did not mitigate my excruciating suffering. During the cold and damp of night the inflammation, if not subdued, was at least checked, but the wind and sun, acting on the unswathed and exposed gashes, produced the most exquisite and indescribable torture. Death, the dreaded intruder on many a happy home, would then to me have been an angel of mercy; but though I yearned most impatiently for his visit, he would not come. The fetters fastened around my native companion's wrist were unriveted, and my swollen, palsied arms, instead of being held in irons, were pitilessly grasped by two savage ruffians in the service of a notorious villain, Ali Woobeshat,* the governor of

---

* This man, like many others who had a share in my sufferings, perished under most excruciating tortures.

Woggera. Excited to a pitch almost verging on frenzy, I tried to shake off the dastardly poltroons, but the exertion exceeded my energy, and I sank prostrate at their feet. Forced to get up, I was partly carried and partly dragged out of the detested camp. The physical effort was too much for my failing strength, so that, despite the goading of the zealous myrmidons of Ali Woobeshat, I had to rest again and again. Water! water! was my entreaty. This mournful cry several parties of soldiers who passed by heard; but although they cast many a pitiful glance on the disfigured and woe-begone stranger, not one had compassion enough to allay the maddening thirst of my burning tongue. At last I saw a chief, a native of Genda, strutting along, who had formerly been in Egypt on an errand of his royal master, where, as I heard from his own lips, he had been most hospitably entertained. That man, I felt persuaded, would act the part of the good Samaritan, and relieve my distress. He halted, looked at me, listened to my pathetic appeal, and, with the withering scowl of a demon on his lean, ugly face, rode quietly away. Ah! tell me not that there is a hidden fount of kindness in every heart, which needs only to be touched, and it will gush forth in streams of love, tenderness, and mercy! This may be the case—nay, I believe it is the case, in countries where, as in this happy isle, the Gospel has refined the asperities of a selfish nature; but such was not my experience in Abyssinia, and in the camp of the crime-stained Theodore. Pushed on by the cowardly savages, who imagined that a man who could not stand might yet be able to run, I crawled forward, and at length, to the satisfaction of the custodians, was safely housed in a peasant's reed-built cabin. Two chiefs, Hassan Ali, the nominal governor of Yedshou, and Basha Medeka, a noble of Woggera, who had the previous evening broken their sticks on my head, received me. Whether my wretched and almost dying condition moved their pity, or whether they thought that my decease might draw upon them the wrath of their master, I cannot positively assert. I know that they were attentive to my wants, and, together with the villagers, did everything in their power to mitigate my sufferings. Hassan Ali, an amateur dabbler in the chirurgical art, kindly examined the depth of my wounds. The operation, though well intended, was very painful, for the instrument—a hard stalk of straw—was not the best probe for a white man's skull. The swarthy amateur doctor was evidently displeased with his patient's condition, and, to convince himself thoroughly of the state of my cranium, he ordered me to press firmly a piece of cane which he put between my teeth. I tried to obey, but the swollen and aching gums refused to perform the imposed task. By dint of perseverance I at last succeeded. The kind physician watched the operation with intense interest, and then, like a wise man, without expressing his opinion, probably not to compromise his reputation, he gave a sapient shake to his butter-besmeared wig, and squatted down.

It was now about eight o'clock, and as I had not yet heard or seen anything of my servants, I began to be suspicious about their safety. My guards kindly assured me that nothing had happened to them, and that in a short time they would be conducted to my abode. This, for the nonce, proved true, for before noon they all made their appearance. The sight of their disfigured, prostrated, and wounded master, who only a short day before had left them cheerful, strong, and happy, arrested their breath, and, in rapt speechlessness, they stood gazing at me. Their pent-up grief gathered strength during this brief silent interval, and then gushed forth a flood of tears and convulsive sighs so genuine, honest, and touching as to awaken a responsive sympathetic chord in the bosom of the groups of villagers who had collected around my desolate couch.

Past noon there arrived from the infamous

governor, Ali Woobeshat, a pair of hand and foot chains, which, at the command of royalty, were to be fastened around my swollen limbs. The guards, hardened as they were to every better sentiment, I could perceive from their looks, did not quite approve this fresh infliction of suffering on a dying man. There were many whispers, consultations, and animated debates; but, as I anticipated, it all ended in a unanimous decision that the royal mandate must be obeyed. My poor servant Joseph, a native of Aleppo, on perceiving that his master's lacerated, torn, and bleeding limbs were to be manacled, threw himself before the guards, and, in melting accents, implored that they should not perpetrate such a ruthless deed on a stranger and a Christian. I believe they would gladly have acceded to his prayer, had not the image of their terrible master floated, like a dreaded phantom, before their frightened imagination, and steeled them against another's woes. They still hesitated a little, and not till I told them to do whatever they felt disposed, did they proceed to perform the disagreeable operation. The ring round the wrists was expeditiously hammered on; not so around the ankles. The inflammation, which had continued to increase and increase till the leg had assumed a most formidable size, rendered it impossible to fasten the hoop so that the foot could not slip through. Baffled and perplexed, they at last resolved to rivet the right hand to the left ankle, the least injured—an operation which, I must confess, they performed with a care and tenderness that did honour to their humane feelings.

Utterly unconscious that I had perpetrated any offence or crime to merit this harsh treatment, I consoled myself in my terrible position with the illusive hope, that after a day or two the tyrant would regret, or at least relax in, his unprovoked severity, and permit me to crawl on as well as I could to Massowah. I had not yet penetrated the depth of Theodore's malice, nor experimentally learnt that man in barbarous, and sometimes also in civilised countries, is most vindictive towards those on whom he has inflicted the deepest wrongs.

The sunny visions in which my enfeebled imagination loved to indulge alleviated my oppressive solitude; and I sank for several hours into what I so much needed—a kind of stupid reverie. Dawn—cold and dismal dawn—had already lit up the rickety stockade walls of my prison, when, chilled by the damp winds that poured in gusts through every hole and crevice, I awoke to the fearful reality of my sad position. A few verses out of the sacred volume, adapted to my circumstances, imparted a peaceful serenity to my chafed and harassed mind. "Neither shall there be any more pain." I had read these words, pondered over them, and preached about them, but not till that moment did I feel the energy they infuse, the consolation they afford, and the sweet resignation they communicate. Delightful thought!— no more torture to rack the frame—no more fetters to cripple the limbs—no more buffetings to mark with blood the Christian preacher's entangled path —no more oppression and tyranny, scorn and derision such as fell to my lot the day before—but rest, peace, and joy in the home of our God, in the mansions of glory near the centre of creation, where tyranny cannot enter, nor cruel despotism have the sway; where no chastening stroke is felt, and no bitter cup is swallowed; where is the tree of life, beneath whose shadow we shall repose, and the fountain of life, whose water we shall drink.

Such were the thoughts which beguiled my mind, and dissipated the maddening gloom.

CHAPTER IV.

Summons from the King—Painful Journey—Compassion of the Guards—Sagacious Servant—Note from the Aboon—Kind Assurances—Interview with the King—Camp Prison—Numerous Guards—Keen Sufferings—Stupor—Prison Diet—Appointment of my Judges—Arrival of the Missionary Agents—Postponement of Verdict—My Baggage ransacked—Vague Hopes—Suspended Negotiation—Generous Exertions of the Metropolitan—Redeeming Love an unfailing Comfort—Joseph's Forebodings—Fidelity of Servants—Thrilling News—Bright Anticipation—Misplaced Confidence—Vain Conjectures—Seizure of my Property—Photographic Lore—Brutality of my Gaolers—Crippling Fetters—An ever-present Saviour—Frugal Diet.

AT sunrise there was a clatter of hoofs, and then there appeared a number of horsemen at my prison-hut. They came from the camp of his Majesty with a message that I should accompany them. This behest descended like a blasting storm on my devoted head. I was, however, resigned to my unhappy fate. The servants did not share my feelings; on the contrary, they saw an uncomfortable indication of coming evil; and afraid to betray their latent surmises, they rushed out of the hut, and sought a lonely spot where to weep. I wanted a change of garments, as those around my shivering frame were saturated with blood, but this the guards would not sanction. "Your property belongs to the king, and is no more your own; and nothing must be touched." To this unreasonable order I bowed in silent submission. All being ready, I was lifted on to the vacant saddle, and the sad cavalcade turned its back on a scene that will, so long as life lasts, form the darkest episode in my chequered career. It was a most painful trip, that short ride to Gondar. Every step, every move, every twist and shake of the mule caused a convulsive shiver to my bruised and bleeding frame. The guards, inured as they were to such exhibitions—perhaps because I was a stranger and friendless in a foreign land—manifested more sympathy towards me than I had reason to anticipate. "Fear not," they whispered in my ears; "the king will have mercy on you. It is your intimacy with the Aboon that brought you into trouble; but he is powerful, and will satisfactorily arrange the unfortunate misunderstanding." Upon inquiring whether I did wrong in calling on Janehoi late at noon, they smiled at the very suggestion. "Wrong!" Hassan Ali, in perfect amazement, rejoined; "why, if you had not called, we had orders to arrest you, and who knows whether the stick alone would have been the penalty you would have incurred!"* Balambras Tesamma, subsequently one

---

* I mention this, because so many misrepresentations on the subject have appeared in public print.

of my friends—a man well known to Mr. Rassam and his companions—quite unsolicited, assured me that my visit would have averted from me all harsh treatment had his Majesty not been in a bad humour about the failure of his expedition against the rebel Taousie Gobazie. Even the wife of one of my escort, an Abyssinian lady of rank, displayed an interest in the unfortunate white man that did credit to her untutored female heart. Repeatedly she gave me birs (a mixture of honey and water something like sherbet), and whenever any of the common soldiers rudely approached me, her soft voice kindly interposed to spare the wounded man the gratuitous insult. Late at noon we neared Gondar, where my conductors ordered a brief halt whilst they tied a strong belt around my waist and arm—a precaution which they considerately omitted on the road, but did not dare to neglect on entering the camp. Silently and in measured steps we marched on, when one of the party noticed that a servant had absconded. Quick as lightning two of the chiefs galloped away towards Kudus Gabriel, where, as by instinct, they guessed I had dispatched him on an errand to the Aboon. They were not deceived in their conjecture, for the fugitive, as they told me themselves, was in earnest converse with the primate as they deferentially, and with many gesticulations, crossed his threshold. Not wishing to offend the puissant church dignitary, they made no inquiry, but merely requested the honest fellow to accompany them. Quite delighted with his feat, the poor man approached my mule, which, like myself, was held by a soldier, and with a knowing twinkle in his eye, pressed into my hand a small paper. Shading my head with the shama, I glanced at the paper, and found that it contained two notes, one from Consul Cameron, and the other from the Aboon. Both expressed their deepest sympathy with my sufferings, and the Aboon added the solemn and emphatic assurance that no effort should be spared to effect my liberation. In passing through the wide-spreading camp, my wretched appearance elicited many ambiguous comments. To all such remarks, whether kind or unkind, rude or gentle, I had in a few days become wonderfully impervious, so that they produced no more impression on me than the breeze which played among the trees, or the declining sun that tinted the evening clouds. On, on we proceeded, till our steps were almost arrested by the royal fence. Here I was lifted out of my saddle, and placed in the centre of a circle of vigilant guards. The precaution was certainly a display of over-zeal, as I could not move a step unaided; but a cringing subserviency rendered such an exhibition indispensable. After sunset it was announced that the Negoos had returned to his tent. All immediately girded themselves, that is, they folded their capacious overgarment around the waist, and in this court attitude awaited the summons. With my aching head resting on a stone, I became oblivious of the terrific past, the gloomy present, and the portentous future. "Tenisu" (get up), and almost simultaneously with that imperative shout, I was raised up and hurried before the dreaded tyrant.

"Why did you come before me on the road?" demanded his Majesty in a stern tone. "I came," was the rejoinder, "to offer my salutations and respects to your Majesty." "Who gave you permission," continued my interrogator, evidently at a loss to palliate his cruelty, "to take my people to your country?" "Your Majesty is misinformed," I replied, "for I never intended to take a single Abyssinian to Europe. This my servants, who are all standing here (they had all been arrested), can testify." "Why did you insult me when I punished two of my subjects who did not conduct themselves with becoming propriety in my presence?" "Your Majesty," I solemnly replied, "there is a God above, and He knows that courtesy prompted me to approach your Majesty's tent." After a pause, during which he evidently tried to work himself into a rage, he abruptly and angrily said: "You white men hate me, and I hate you. I allow you to come and stay in my country merely because I want to get some of your *belhad* (arts). England and France boast of power and riches; I defy them both." Then turning to the servants, he inquired why they accompanied me. The response, as might have been expected, was, "Because he pays us." "And where are you going?" Several at once replied, "To our home at Adowa." "And cannot I pay you more, vile peasants' sons, than that white slave?" grunted forth the artificially excited monarch. "Guards, seize them!" Instantly they were seized, stripped and buffeted; then turning in the direction where the chiefs of my escort stood, he said: "Watch him well, and do not allow any one without my sanction to approach him." I was immediately in the grasp of half-a-dozen officers, who led me to the tent which had been erected for my camp prison. The small canvas shelter was already crowded by a whole host of volunteers who, under the pretext of wishing to see their friends, had really come to have a good view of the unfortunate Cocab. Sick, feverish, and exhausted, I was not allowed to stretch my weary limbs in peace and quiet on the hard uneven ground. I was a prisoner, but without fetters, and until these were riveted around my swollen ankles and wrists the gaolers could not partake of the repast provided by the royal purveyor. Manacles, with which each chief must be provided, whether on a march or in the camp, at home or abroad, were quickly enough brought into the prison. There was, as ever, some altercation about the weight of one and the length of the other. These preliminaries were, however, amicably arranged, and the passive victim of wanton cruelty had patiently to yield his aching limbs to the merciless infliction of a malefactor's manacles. Bread, broundo, and tedj were now in due proportion served to the faithful lieges of the great king. The smell of the reeking collops and fetid assembly did not improve my position. My eyes were swollen, my nerves unstrung, and my head was throbbing as if every pulsation would be the last, and yet the agony did not cease, nor my wretched existence terminate for ever. I moved from side to side; now my shama covered my quivering frame, then again I had madly thrust it over the soldier to whom I was tied; one moment I bit it in agony with my chattering teeth, the next I almost unconsciously applied it to a bleeding sore. I do not know how long this struggle between pain and restlessness, wakefulness and somnolency continued. A stupor akin to insensibility overwhelmed me, from which I could not rouse myself till daybreak next morning.

Soon after sunrise the number of my guards was diminished by the dismissal of Ali Woobeshat's myrmidons, and I had the melancholy satisfaction of a foot or two more space. Trifling as this may appear, it was an advantage and boon I highly appreciated. I could now, at least, by stretching out my fettered right hand, turn from side to side without coming in unpleasant contact with my new unwashed, uncombed, and unclean companion, to whom I was tied by a heavy massive chain. Food I neither got nor wanted. I had flour and smoked meat in abundance, but a biscuit dipped in water was all I could or cared to swallow. There was a report that the king had ordered liberal rations for his prisoner. Whether the rumour was well founded or not was, and will remain, a matter of insignificance to me. From well-ascertained facts I know that some persons, for the sake of the dollars they got, tried most strenuously to palliate the king's conduct towards me. "He had a kind heart, deep religious impressions, and was sadly misunderstood!" This, however, was to be expected. Base flatterers abound in Europe as in Africa, and the most revolting deeds, if perpetrated in high circles, find hosts of unprincipled apologists.

I was conducted to Gondar on Thursday. On the following Saturday, I believe at the request of Consul Cameron, Mr. Flad came to Gondar. He and M. Bardel immediately sought an interview with the king. His Majesty was in church. On coming out it was evident that his devotions had not improved his temper. He was angry and out of humour. On seeing the two white men, he halted, and in conformity with his habit when in a passion, he launched forth in a tone of keen severity against all Franks. Having exhausted his own peculiar vituperative vocabulary, he sharply adverted to me, and the sins I had committed, and then concluded with the challenge, " You, the Genda and Darna Frendjoj, shall judge who is the transgressor, I or Cocab."

A messenger was promptly dispatched to the two missionary stations, and on Monday the missionary agents, four in number, exclusive of Mr. Flad, who was at Gondar, reached the capital. In conformity with the summons, they expected an immediate audience; but after waiting for some time near the royal fence, they were informed through Samuel that his Majesty was engaged and could not see them that day. On Tuesday the anticipated interview, under various pretexts, was again postponed. He was evidently embarrassed. This the guards themselves noticed, for they repeatedly told me, and that without any reserve, that the king was conscious he had done me wrong, and that probably he would condone the injury by a large sum of money, and dispatch me to my country. I cherished similar hopes, and in my illusion I not unfrequently worried my mind with all sorts of conjectures about the application of the money the tyrant might give me, of which, as it was extorted from his subjects by the torturing rope and mutilating knife, I would not retain a farthing in my possession. I played with shadows, and was beguiled by idle fancies. It was about noon on that very day which I thought would bring me freedom and liberty, that Messrs. Flad and Bardel, Aboona Matti (a Copt), the king's Arabic clerk, Aliga Engeda, the royal scribe, and Aito Samuel, were dispatched to examine my luggage and to seize any letters that I might have in my possession from Consul Cameron or the Metropolitan, Aboona Salama. The three natives ransacked and threw everything into confusion, not with the object of finding dangerous documents, but merely to satisfy their own curiosity. My photographic sketches, and a well-assorted collection of insects, particularly attracted their attention, and in their admiration of some beetle or butterfly, a mountain scene or a village group, they entirely forgot their commission, and reduced the search to a perfect farce. Feverish, excited, and almost demented, my mind was perpetually dilating on the king and the guards; the tented prison and cruel fetters. Every coloured man who wore a sword or carried a lance I dreaded as an enemy, and every white man I loved as a friend. I had still to learn, that a kind, sympathetic look does not always indicate a generous and true heart.

Wearily the days of misery passed away in the canvas tent of the isolated captive. I expected every morning a visit from Aito Samuel and the Genda Frendjoj, whose united efforts I vainly imagined would, perhaps, appease the pretended royal anger, and restore me again to liberty. Wednesday and Thursday came and went without bringing me either joy or grief, gladness or sorrow. I was in the power of a lawless tyrant, and had to submit to his capricious whims. On Friday, the long-expected Genda Frendjoj received an order to visit me. The instructions communicated to them were very brief: "Go and ask Aito Cocab why he insulted me." My friends faithfully delivered their message, and then took back the apology, in which I reiterated the assurance that I had always felt regard and esteem for his Majesty, and if, by an unconscious movement of my hand or any other outward expression, I had unwittingly offended him, I would, with a stone on my neck, crave his forgiveness. The delegates immediately took back my apology to the king; but, as he pretended to be busy, they were ordered to come again the next morning, and to bring with them at the same time a letter from Consul Cameron, embodying the views and feelings entertained by the British Government towards Abyssinia and its monarch. The consul was immediately informed of the request of the king, with which, I believe, he promptly complied. The following morning the small band of intercessors repaired again to the royal camp, where they expected to meet, according to previous arrangement, a messenger with Consul Cameron's despatch. Aito Samuel, in his blandest tones, welcomed the deputies; and if gracious smiles and low bows conveyed any meaning, I was a free and happy man. The affable courtier hastened to present to his Majesty the salutations of his visitors, to whom, after a brief pause, he returned with a most condescending response. "Have you brought Consul Cameron's letter, as his Majesty requested?" now inquired the worthy mouthpiece of royalty. Almost spontaneously, every one turned round to see whether the expected messenger, with that important document, had arrived; but, alas! though they shouted, inquired, and searched, he could not be found. Angry, black, scowling, the excited courtier disappeared within the folds of the royal pavilion. Tremulously the little group awaited the issue of this exciting and shifting scene. Their patience was not long tried, for the folds of the tent were once more lifted, and Samuel, not radiant with benignity, but frowning like a fiend, stood before them, and, in an assumed tone of offended dignity, blended with the coarse bombast of low vulgarity, ordered them, in the name of the king, to return to their homes. My expected liberation was thus postponed from day to day and week to week. There were many natives, and some Europeans, who were anxious to have the manacles knocked off my limbs; but they had no influence, or were too timid to put it to the test. Aboona Salama, the Metropolitan, alone, was most indefatigable in his exertions. He threatened and implored, gave rich presents, and made glowing promises; spared neither time, letters, or money; in fact, he did everything in his power, and beyond his power, to move the pity of the tyrant towards the victim of his ferocity. At one time he seemed inclined to relent, and the next I was again more closely watched. Perhaps, I thought, the malicious monarch finds a satisfaction in the agonising suspense of his captive; or he seeks some plea to gloss over the infamy of his base conduct; or, what appeared not improbable, he intends in the dying throes of the white man to demonstrate before obsequious serfs the greatness of his power. Such were the dismal phantoms with which my diseased imagination beguiled the present, and sought to foreshadow the future.

A fortnight thus elapsed, a fortnight that appeared a century, for who can compute the length of those weary hours that hang immovable on the dial-plate of

Time, offering neither hope to despair, rest to trouble, or comfort to misery. At such a period—I say it solemnly—the punctured head, the riven side, the pierced feet, and the heavy cross of redeeming love, is a sight that nerves and supports the drooping and desponding spirit. In my distress and sorrow, I threw myself on the bosom of a sympathising Saviour, and if I was not happy I was at least resigned.

The king, whether impelled by a whimsical fit of charity or a secret intelligence that the long-expected letter from the British Government had reached Massowah, relented in his severity. My sequestrated keys were given back, my confiscated luggage was restored, and I was treated with indifference, if not consideration. All, indeed, seemed to augur well for the captive exile. There were secret inquiries from his Majesty after his prisoner's health, the progress of his wounds, the food he ate, the water he drank, the words he uttered, the sentiments he cherished, nay, even the prospects he entertained. I tried to interpret this sudden transition from anger to pity, but the task exceeded my impaired faculties. Joseph, my nurse and companion in affliction, and who had imbibed an intense hatred to the king and his rabble hosts, tried to solve the enigma, but even to him the mystery was shrouded in impenetrable darkness. "I have got it, I have got it," he shouted, after a night's profound reflection. "And what is it, Joseph?" curiosity made me inquire. "Ah, master, don't ask me. A Habashee (Abyssinian) is what the Arabs call a *hanash* (serpent), and you will discover when I am buried"—he added, in a melancholy, funereal tone, as if he already felt the approach of the shades of death, which a month later were glazing and fixing his vision—"that you have fallen, like the man who went to Jericho, into the hands of a cruel, treacherous, heartless ruffian." "Suppose, Joseph, this is true—and I believe it is—cannot God save us, as He saved the ill-fated pilgrim?" "Yes, He can, if He had a Samaritan to send you." And then, after a pause, he added, "You have faith, I only malice, rancour, and gnawing animosity against our oppressor and his crew." "I see, Joseph, that you are sad, and, to dissipate the vapours of a restless night, I advise you to go up to Gondar, and get from Mackerer, or the consul, some tidings that will cheer us both." The permission of the head gaoler, who knew he would get a bottle of arackee, was immediately obtained, and gladly enough he hurried out of the detested camp. He might now have decamped, and, being of a dark complexion, the chances of his escape were almost beyond doubt. Such a thought, however, never entered his mind. Once, on the way from Woggera to Gondar, I suggested it to him and my native followers; but, notwithstanding the dreadful fate of their two companions, they all said, in their own metaphorical style, "We have been with you in sunshine, we will not desert you in the storm." This faithful attachment to an unfortunate master was, perhaps, as regarded poor Joseph, the natural result of his lonely position, in a foreign land, and among a strange people; but this was not the case with the rest. They were in their native land, and within easy reach of friends and kindred, so that their continuance in my employ could only be attributed to an affection, most creditable to their kind and tender hearts. In about two hours Joseph returned. His red face and flashing eye indicated something significant. I waited patiently for the intelligence he had to communicate. "Master," he at length commenced, "don't mind this black (*hada el aswad*) to whom you are shackled, for the days of our captivity are numbered." After this epigrammatic sentence he became more calm, and, without indulging in his usual rhetorical flourishes about *abeed* (slaves) and their bad hearts, he told me that he had heard news in Consul Cameron's house that made his heart and soul thrill with joy. On perceiving my curiosity, he remembered that, in the excess of his delight, he had forgotten to communicate to me the intelligence that I was most anxious to know. This checked the wild raptures of his exuberant nature, and, in a voice almost stifled with emotion, he told me that he had heard in the consul's house, that a steamer had reached Massowah with letters and presents for the king, and that, on their arrival in the camp, we should, together with an embassy to the English court, start for the coast. The heated fancy of the Oriental had evidently exaggerated the report, till it tallied with his own wishes; still, after every proper deduction being made, it conveyed facts that operated like an opiate on my chafed and perturbed spirit.

Meekly I now wore my galling chains, submissively I bowed to my adverse fate, and cheerfully I sustained the most glaring wrong which unprovoked malice and conscious guilt could inflict. I had a support in the brightening future, and a solace in the prospect of a speedy release from that wasting confinement which rendered the present so sickening. My frame, inured to fatigue, and steeled against hardships, unimpaired by potent hydromel, and still more potent arackee (alcohol), which only on special occasions, and in the presence of royalty, polluted my lips, began to recover from the shock it had experienced. The wounds and scars which only a week before, even under the most favourable changes, threatened to cost me my right hand, and perhaps arm, began to heal, the swelling subsided, and I could, without great effort or support, stand erect. All looked serene and cheerful. That my papers and diaries, in a foreign language, containing facts, incidents, and observations on the occurrences of each passing day, which no traveller or missionary could, or ought to, entrust to memory, should ever offer a pretext for renewed severity, never for a moment presented itself to my mind. Besides this, who would suggest to the king the perusal of a stranger's letters and notes? M. Bardel, who hated missionaries, might do so, but he pretended to cherish a special regard for me; and then his apparent efforts to effect my release, strengthened the confidence I reposed in him. Aito Samuel, the ex-baldaraba of Consul Cameron, I knew, was capable of any vile action, if it tended to injure the white man, whom he hated, or enhanced the royal favour which he laboured to secure. He had, however, been most injudiciously bribed* to conceal what he ought never to have known. Had I possessed less candour and some duplicity, not a written line in my possession would ever have gratified the sight of the king or his unscrupulous minions. It is true I ought to have remembered Richelieu's aphorism: "Give me two lines from any man, and his head shall roll on the

---

* Flad gave him, on account of the Jews' Society, a hundred dollars, and the other four missionaries, from their private resources, ten, and Bardel cancelled a claim on him of a hundred dollars. This sum I repaid to Bardel at Zeghee, through his countryman and friend, Bourgeaud, although Samuel protested that Bardel owed him money, and not he Bardel.

scaffold." I was deceived. Several times I intended to give a few dollars to my native companion, and, in the absence of the guard, try to destroy every scrap of paper in my possession; but then, again, it appeared to me quite a superfluous precaution to remove notes and memoranda that were useful and intelligible to me, but almost valueless and incoherent to a stranger. My book, of which I had a copy—the only one in Abyssinia—I would never have concealed, for the history of the king's life which it embodied I imagined could not fail to be flattering and grateful to the despot's pride. The well-founded statement that his mother sold kosso, I felt sure the most cursory reader of the volume could perceive, was not written to depreciate, but to do justice to the humble chieftain who, by his own skill, dexterity, and valour, had, through the lines of hostile nobles and cringing serfs, made his way to a sceptre and throne. Such were the conjectures that sometimes flashed across my mind, without leaving a real or abiding impression. The possibility of an interview with the king, the probability of a reconciliation, the removal from prison, the mode of travelling, and the joyous restoration to friends and home; these, and not the dismal anticipation of a protracted captivity, and more rigorous treatment, were the pictures that danced before my eyes and exhilarated my spirits.

It was exactly twenty-eight days after my fatal encounter with the king on the Woggera highlands, that, about noon, friend Samuel, with a flushed countenance and averted look, strutted into the prison-tent. The guards, of whom a good number were accidentally with me, as well as myself, received his most courteous salutation. I requested him to sit down, but, without heeding my invitation, he entreated, in the sweetest tone that he could adopt, that I should resign to him the keys of my luggage. "Samuel," I said, in a voice which neither betrayed anger nor grief—"Samuel, I know what this request signifies, only take care that you do not bring new troubles on an innocent man; for if you do I may die, and if your own acts, and those of your abettors, escape with impunity here, they will not remain unvisited hereafter." "Don't think ill of me, I am your friend," and then, turning to the guards, he shouted, "Seize this luggage, and carry it up to his Majesty." Joseph, who sat petrified and stunned, the courtier now touched by the arm, and, in a cajoling strain, said, "Joseph, ibn Arab, you must come with me." The bewildered man gave him a glance that would have pierced his very soul, had it not been encased in a triple brass covering, and then, without uttering a word, obeyed mechanically the injunction, and marched off.

Adversity had again blighted my prospects, and

marred my best hopes. I was not sad. I was not in despair. I was callous, reckless, and indifferent. My senses were blunted, and my mind unhinged. Robbed of liberty, and chained like a wild beast, I did not, at that moment, dread the knife, nor fear the gallows. The cup of misery was full, and I was sick—sick to loathing of that wretched existence. My agitation keenly affected my nervous system, and I sank, worn out with all kinds of horrible ideas, on the hard pallet. Samuel, who, with the lens of my photographic camera, came back to the tent, was, as he subsequently told me, quite frightened to gaze at me. My whole appearance had undergone a change. My face was red, my eyes fiery, my lips compressed, and I stood before him — to use his own words—more like an enraged Bedlamite than a humble manacled captive. I adjusted the glass, gave the requisite explanation, and then stretched myself again on the comfortless couch. An hour, at least, had elapsed ere I became fully aware of my position, and the dangers by which I was encompassed. I roused myself from this painful lethargy, and, entering into conversation with my inseparable companion, whiled away another hour. About sundown Joseph, pale and haggard, followed by the bearers of the luggage, returned to his master's prison. Sobs and sighs for some minutes sealed his lips. "Oh, master!" he at length ejaculated, "you are in the clutches of wicked men, and they will kill you," he added, with sad solemn emphasis. My books, papers, manuscripts, and a good number of valuable presents, in the shape of skins and silver ornaments, which I had received from the Aboona, were all sequestrated. Mr. Samuel, and his coadjutor, M. Bardel, according to Joseph, manifested the most eager desire to find obnoxious and compromising papers. The king several times got tired of the business, and ordered the various articles to be put back into their places, but the zealous examiners were so intent on their agreeable task that they scarcely heeded the royal command. The sketches in my book, and my brush and comb, particularly elicited his Majesty's admiration. He made a variety of inquiries about me, the illustrations in the book, and the mode and method of taking photographs; Joseph, who was supposed to be initiated in all the mysteries of his master's lens and collodion, gave the most elaborate, and, no doubt, most lucid explanation of the process. Samuel tried to assist him; but it was quite evident, from his own words, that he did not feel disposed to share the honours of his profound photographic lore with an ignorant, self-conceited African. "I allowed him," he said, contemptuously, "to make his own comments on the comb, which his savage master, the king, stuck in his mop, for I would not argue with him on such a topic. Photography is, however, quite a different thing, and I was determined to oppose, if I could not humble, his arrogant pretensions." This conversation cheered us up a little, and we were both thinking of composing ourselves to rest, when a whole troop of ruffians, headed by Jaque Obey, a notorious, merciless poltroon, rushed into the tent, and ordered me to follow him. "Short shrift," I ejaculated. The soldier to whom I was linked guessed my surmises, and, drawing the fetters by which we were fastened to each other a little tighter, he said, in bated breath, "The king is angry, and has given you in charge of more rigorous guards." "Mashanyies" (leather thongs), bawled out the head gaoler, as we approached the lines under his control. "Are these ruffians going to tie me with ropes?" I remarked to my servant. The good man, in the bitterness of his heart, curtly rejoined, "Master, these blacks are fiends." In the twinkle of an eye the ropes were brought, not, as I suspected, to inflict on me the torture of the *quad*, but to wrench off the old easy chain around the wrist, which allowed me to stand upright, and to give me in its stead a double chain, to bend and cripple the whole frame. The operation of fastening on these cruel fetters confirmed my previous bad opinion of that atrocious villain, Jaque Obey, and his bullies. Held by about a dozen of these wretches, which rendered me quite helpless and passive, my right leg was violently seized, and an iron bar put on the ankle. To tighten this long, broad, and lockless piece of iron, so that the foot might not slip through, and afford the prisoners facilities to escape, a heavy hammer, or large stone, is plied till the oblong bar forms a hoop around the leg, which no giant arm, unaided, can burst. In the present instance, probably to augment the agony of the captive, many a stroke, as it descended, fell, not on the insensible iron, but on the white man's unresisting limb. One or two of the executioner's satellites manifested some compunction, and addressed a few words of encouragement to me. "Beat on," vociferated the infamous leader of the band,* "and, if he moves, let his white skin feel a black hand's strength." Several volunteers, among whom were some servants of the Negad Ras, a protégé of Consul Plowden, and formerly in his employ, perhaps to resent an old grudge against their master, took a particular delight in battering the shrinking limbs of the defenceless Frendjoj. The operation on the right leg being completed, the left, and then

---

* The dastardly ruffian, unable to return to his own country, where the enraged peasants would have torn him to pieces, remained with the king to the last. He assisted in digging his late master's grave. Mr. Kerans, who superintended the ceremony, told me that he felt his hand itch to imprint on the murderer's face the stamp of a strong Irish fist. The moment was, however, as he justly observed, inopportune.

the right arm, had to submit to the same merciless treatment. No criminal of the deepest dye, no outlaw with the brand of infamy on his brow, no fugitive from the just sentence of the law, could possibly have met with a harsher treatment than was accorded to me on that dreadful night by Jaque Obey and his crime-stained crew. I was indeed sick—oh! sick to loathing—of a life fraught with ever-increasing troubles and trials. The warbling and bleeding words of Job found an echo in my bosom, and, like him, I also wished to be "where the wicked cease from troubling, and where the weary are at rest." Alone, and in an African prison, amidst beings who, though they had a human form, were dead to every human sentiment, I sought then, as ever afterwards, refuge and protection beneath the shadow and shelter of the cross. The Saviour was indeed with me, and His presence diffused peace and comfort around the captive home of the crushed missionary. Another week had been added to the never-ending period of affliction and sorrow, without bringing me release or lighter fetters. Food I had none, nor did I much care for it. A flat teff cake, baked by a servant of the gaoler, and a little pepper flour mixed with water, constituted my breakfast and dinner. Consul Cameron sent me every day a most liberal repast, but the soldier, who charitably proffered to convey it from his house to my canvas gaol, unscrupulously appropriated all to his own and his brother's table. Unhappy man! little did he dream that in a few months more that very brother whom he fed with provisions robbed from a white captive's scanty supplies—that the same brother would arrest his step, and with his own hand and spear transfix the deserter's faithless heart.

CHAPTER V.

Conflicting Rumours—Vigilance of the Guards—Degenerate Taste—
Midnight Discussion—Removal of my Foot-chains—Theodore's
Court of Justice—Code of Laws—Forestalled Condemnation
—Charges against Myself, Mr. Rosenthal, and Mrs. Flad—
Revolting Baseness—The Royal Pedigree—A Challenge—
Sickening Existence—Dragged back to Prison—Visit of Executioners—A Dangerous Bill-hook—Fresh Maltreatment—Slow
Progress of Time—The Tyrant's Speculations—Freedom at the
Expense of Truth—Fluctuations of Hope and Fear—A Revolting
Sight—The Prisoners Stripped—Terrible Night—Anticipated
Execution—Mitigation of our Wretchedness—Valuation of Silks
—Royal Messages—Strange Garments—Compelled to write
Letters to Europe—Consul Cameron's unfortunate Request.

A VARIETY of conflicting rumours, some favourable and some unfavourable, enlisted my attention, and counteracted that dull feeling of apathy to which I was disposed to yield. There were reports that a treasonable correspondence between the bishop, Consul Cameron, and myself, about certain church property, had been discovered; next, that a Frendjoj was making every effort to compass my death; and last, that I had indulged in reflections on the king, that would, even without the white man's aid, cost me my life. These stories were rapidly succeeded by others of a more encouraging character, viz., that the long-expected letter and presents from

England were positively on the road; that his Majesty was about to be reconciled to the Aboona; that all the Europeans, non-artisans, were to be expelled; that, to compensate me for my past sufferings, I was to receive a thousand dollars; and many other statements, that exaggerated or misrepresented, reached my ears in rapid succession, and acted like an artificial tonic on an exhausted and worn-out frame. My guards, as ever, notwithstanding the good or evil tidings which, according to their tenor, appalled or delighted me, were unwearied in their vigilance over the prisoner. Twenty-five soldiers and five chiefs had the charge to watch me in turns day and night, and I must praise the fidelity with which they discharged their onerous duty. Not a movement I could make, not a step I could walk, and not a jerk I could give to the detested fetters, without having half a dozen eyes glaring upon me. Even during the silent watches of midnight, when sleep lulled me into forgetfulness, a couple of legs were stretched across my cramped limbs, to prevent what they must have imagined a miraculous escape. No stranger was allowed to approach my tent. A slave of the principal gaoler, with whom I shared my frugal meals, brought me, according to his whims, daily, or, if he was annoyed at something, every alternate day, a leather bottle of drinkable water. In the luxury of a wash, I never did and could not indulge; even my hair, which was long and matted, had to dispense with comb and brush, as I possessed neither of these useful articles. I had unwillingly degenerated into the savage, and, incredible as it may appear, found amusement in the very garments which, under more prosperous circumstances, would have caused me a shudder. On November 10th, I was bound hand and foot, and on the Monday following I heard that all the missionary agents from Genda and Darna had been brought in fetters to the camp. On the evening of the same day I was informed that they had all been released; then again that one was still in irons; and, lastly, as if to add to my perplexity and bewilderment, M. Mackerer (formerly a French soldier), in the service of Consul Cameron, sent me word that the longed-for letter from the British Government would arrive in two days, and that on Friday I was to be liberated. The arrival of the European workmen from Gaffat, to whom the king wrote a fortnight before, "If you think that I have tortured Cocab (the name by which I was known in Abyssinia) long enough, and if you approve of it, come and reconcile me with him," imparted an air of plausibility to the last part of M. Mackerer's message. The subject of my release also formed, during the long night, the staple of conversation among my talkative guards. "What is Janchoi to do with him?" quoth Jaque Obey.

"Is he not a priest? and have we not already more than we want? He might kill him; but then what white men will come to our country and teach us their *belhad* (mechanical skill)?" "And is it true," inquired several well-greased pates, simultaneously, "that Janchoi is angry with the queen of their sunless country?"* "He is," rejoined the sapient chief, "and if she is not quick in transmitting the tribute, by St. George (a favourite adjuration), her realm will soon be devastated by our brave hosts." I had enough of this intellectual conversation, and would have gladly closed my ears and eyes in sleep, had not a suffocating, rancid odour, rendered the effort useless. Daylight did not dissipate the vision of impending deliverance; nay, the removal of my foot-chains, and the more friendly deportment of the gaoler, invested the story with a palpable reality.

After sunrise, the usual numerous guards were reduced to two. One of these, suspicious of the nimbleness of his charge, held firm the chain around my wrist, just as shepherds in the East hold a savage dog when a friendly stranger passes along the road. Perfectly ignorant of the ordeal that awaited me, I beguiled the slow progress of time in converse with a lively Galla lad, the slave of a

---

* Many Abyssinians believe that beyond Jerusalem, the limits of their geographical knowledge, the sun never shines.

guard. Jaque Obey, contrary to his custom, came nearly every hour, and put his shining, buttery wig into the tent, to see that all was safe. I could not bear the glitter of that basilisk glance; and whenever it accidentally lighted on me, without disguising my sentiments I turned away from it in inexpressible disgust. The tramp of feet, the hum of voices, and the rattle of shields and spears, rang ominously and solemnly on my ears. About noon my fierce chief guardian, accompanied by half-a-dozen satellites, marched into the tent, and commanded me to accompany him to his Majesty. "Hold him firm," shouted the leader of the ruffianly gang; an order which, in less time than I can write it, stamped on my sides and arms the shape and size of several tawny hands. Not knowing, and not even caring to know, whether I was about to be led to execution or freedom, I unresistingly allowed the dastardly cowards to drag me to the spot from whence proceeded the muffled noise that had puzzled me the whole morning. Here, to my surprise, I found the *élite* of the whole army drawn up in a square, with the furthest line occupied by a throne, on which, in proud dignity, sat the savage king, shaded by two gigantic silken umbrellas. "Bring the Falasha forward," said, in a sharp and shrill voice, the recumbent figure on the throne. Quick as lightning, the heaving mass formed a passage in the centre of the line, and there the pompous despot had the satisfaction to behold his victim, manacled, haggard, and exposed to the rude gaze of a despicable, servile mob. Averting my eyes from the execrable tyrant who had brought on me all that misery, I leisurely and fearlessly surveyed the throng that stared on me in wild, stupid wonderment. Many a face in that gorgeous royal judgment court was familiar to me, though not one had the heart or the courage to extend to the culprit even a sign of recognition. Messrs. Bardel and Zander, the imperial counsellors, were to the left, and the dignitaries of the church to the right of the dais. Fronting this most uninteresting assemblage, there was a vacant space, covered with new and old, bright and faded carpets, from Turkey, Europe, India, and Persia. From this sacred spot, where none dared to venture unsummoned, extended another line of carpets, on which sat, facing each other, the king's European workmen, her Britannic Majesty's Consul, and the missionaries. The consul was in his uniform; Messrs. Josephson, Staiger, and Brandeis in their European garb, over which hung, in approved Court fashion, the white shama; and all the rest, who were knights of the shirt,* shone

---

* The investiture of the silk shirt admits the recipient into the ranks of the nobility. King Theodore conferred this dignity on the lowest villains and ruffians.

and sparkled in the dazzling glitter of tawdry harlequins.

Undaunted by a subservient multitude, and confident in the purity and integrity of my actions, I calmly awaited the issue of that day's pomp and ceremony. The sight of Mr. Rosenthal, in fetters, and guarded, gave me quite a shock, and my Christian fortitude (I do not say it in a boastful strain), which always rose higher as the danger became more imminent, almost faltered and flagged. Perfectly ignorant of the offences laid to his charge, I forgot my own misery by reflecting on that of my companion. The distress, agony, and grief of his desolate and friendless young wife, roused every dormant passion of my heart, and impotent as I was, had it been prudent or practicable, I would that moment have rushed on the craven savage, and defied him in the very midst of his rabble hosts. In my excitement I unconsciously shook the abominable fetters by which I was tightly held. A pull from the gaoler that made my arm ache reminded me that patience and submission, and not boldness and candour, were the virtues I had to practise. Aliga Fanda, the expounder of the Fetha Negest, a code of cruel laws, erroneously supposed to be based on that of Justinian, was then read. The servile scribe, who cared for his master's favour, and not for the maintenance of justice, in a hurried tone, as if ashamed of his own baseness, declared the prisoners worthy of death. Poor man! he has expiated his cringing, criminal subserviency to an unscrupulous despot by the same terrible death of mutilation which he often pronounced on others. His innocent wife and her five children experienced a more lenient treatment, for the tyrant spared them the maddening pain of the knife, and graciously dispatched them in the flames of their blazing homestead. An indictment without a proof, and a verdict without a trial appeared inconsistent, even to the ruthless savage; and to invest his proceedings with an air of plausibility, the charges against the prisoners were read. Ten articles, I believe, were preferred against me. They were nearly all garbled, perverted, and disconnected extracts from notes and diaries, which the base minions of the tyrant, in the hope of favour and reward, had dexterously disposed to suit their own and their employer's murderous design. The most formidable crimes alleged against me were, that I had stated his Majesty had no good counsellors; that he had plundered various districts, and among these the episcopal domain of Genda; that he was no friend of our mission; that he was provoking the hostility of France, and the aggression of Egypt; that the Abyssinians had no legal marriages; that I had charged Mrs. Flad with dishonesty;* that I had said that at Dubark, on the Woggera plateau, the king had murdered in cold blood between 700 and 800 people; and, finally, that I was in correspondence with the Metropolitan, and had a few harmless letters from him in my possession. The only offensive statement in my book, of which I had one solitary copy, that was sent to me by post, consisted in the correct and well-ascertained pedigree of his Majesty.

Rosenthal's sins, which were shifted on my shoulders, though I knew not a word of what he had written till that moment, consisted in some reflections on the king's domestic life in a private letter to his brother-in-law in London, and in a remark that Abyssinia would probably enjoy greater security under the sway of Egypt than under the sceptre of its native sovereigns. Mrs. Flad had also fearfully compromised herself in a note addressed to me, and which contained the treasonable observation, that his Majesty still bragged that he would invade England and conquer Jerusalem. Her Darwinian theory of development at an inverted ratio—

* This false charge was quite irrelevant to the accusation; but the manufacturers of the indictment had their own special reason for fabricating it. Samuel on the preceding evening had urged Consul Cameron and others to pronounce on me the verdict of death. This, he assured him, would so please the king, that vindicated justice would instantly be followed by Christian mercy, and the culprit, instead of death, would receive a magnanimous pardon. The scoundrel knew that if his master once imbrued his hands in the blood of a white man, he would not soon stop.

viz., that the Abyssinian lion had degenerated into a tiger—the considerate translators had omitted, probably to avert a little longer the hostility of the favoured artisans. She was, of course, arraigned before the august tribunal, but luckily her historical knowledge of the cruelties perpetrated by the Turks in Europe, and which she dreaded to see, during the king's absence on his distant expedition, re-enacted in Abyssinia, together with her husband's doubtful position at court, to my delight, gained her the royal clemency and pardon. Such was not the merciful verdict accorded to the other culprits. They were the victims of malicious intrigue and revolting selfishness. They were encompassed by foes who, whilst they professed friendship and devotion, sought revenge and honours by circumventing their destruction and that of other Europeans with whom, at the very moment, they were eating, drinking, and interchanging courtesies. Oh! it chills the blood, arrests the pulsations of the heart, and makes one blush to think that beings endued with a soul and conscience could remorselessly seek to gain their own nefarious ends by compassing the ruin and death of innocent fellow-creatures! Let philosophers praise, poets admire, and moralists speculate on the innate human virtues: daily experience verifies the old and much-abused truth, "that the heart is deceitful and desperately wicked."

The mock trial, which lasted about three hours, was diversified by a few most ludicrous episodes. Thus, at one period, the tyrant was quite enraged with his temporal and spiritual chiefs, because they blundered most egregiously in tracing the royal descent. From Adam to Solomon all went on smoothly, and every one appeared satisfied that Isaac was the father of Abraham, and Jacob the progenitor of both. Such immaterial deviations from the sacred text did not affect the purity of the royal line, and name after name was bawled forth by the leader of the scribes, with a fluency that did credit to his patient toil. Down to Fasilidas, who reigned three hundred years ago, there was no fatal hiatus in the nomenclature; but suddenly the scribe became confused, wavered, and paused. The mantling visage and flashing eye of the monarch brought a score of squatting ecclesiastics on their legs, and these all, in the most boisterous confusion, repeated a genealogical register that must have convinced the most incredulous that the ash-coloured Theodore was the son of a very doubtful father, and that doubtful father a son of Adam, if not of Solomon. The important question of the paternity of Menilek's successor being settled, the learned and noble assembly proceeded to examine the family of the mother. The debterahs, as ever, were infallible, and their glib tongues ran on smoothly over the list of rugged names. Suddenly the tide of ugly hissing words was arrested in its flow, and Iteghie Mantoub, the pious friend of Bruce, opposed all onward progress. Once more the scribes rake their dull memories, the priests (their coadjutors) nervously count their ivory beads, and the monks—poor imbecile fanatics—mutter paternosters; but the effort is of no avail, and the glory of the royal Theodore's maternal ancestry is extinguished in a harsh antique name. The Tigréan nobles, the proud pretenders to an aristocracy more ancient than the days of our grey world, now jumped up, and in the bold assurance which stupidity often assumes, they adverted to such a multitude of ancient families, and branches of ancient families, that in their confusion they demolished the very fact their master was so intent upon confirming. "Rogues, villains, knaves!" shouted the enraged king; "I shall teach you to remember who I am, and from whence I come;" and then turning to the trembling hierarchical party, he poured forth a volley of abuse that established beyond all doubt his true origin. To appease his devouring rage he turned his tiger gaze on me, and in a blustering jumble of impassioned phrases challenged me to single combat. I did not reply. This increased his fury, and forgetful of the dignity which he generally tried to maintain, he almost sprang from his lofty seat, shouting, "Well, if you are not a woman, will you take the choice of the weapon, sword, spear, pistol, or even cannon, and fight me?" Calmly, and without manifesting either fear or contempt, I rejoined: "I am a priest, and do not fight." Whilst this colloquy was going on, two of the chief guards, who were stationed close to Mr. Rosenthal, suddenly, as if struck by an invisible arm, dropped down, and were carried insensible out of the heaving and surging lines. This incident one might suppose would have made some impression on the superstitious mind of the tyrant and his hordes, and move them to compassionate the strangers whom he had so outrageously wronged; but no, nothing could move a heart that was dead to every better feeling, and steeled against every foreign woe.

Arrested in the midst of life, activity, usefulness, and enterprise—far, far from friends, kindred, and home—my thoughts on that dark and desolate day did not wander to other scenes, but were concentrated on the unsympathising crowd that stared and gaped on the ill-fated objects of their cruel sovereign's rage. Among the white advisers, jury or audience—for they were invested with that triple character—two only looked pale and agitated; but the rest grinned and chuckled in unison with the dark visage that rolled from side to side on the soft silken pillows and coverlets the good and generous Aboon had, unsolicited, presented, with other valuable gifts, to effect my release. It was my Gethsemane, and I had alone, unaided and unpitied, to sustain the conflict, and to fight the battle in which I was involved. The charge of pride, to which, in the absence of a better plea, despicable pusillanimity sought a refuge from censure for a guilty indifference to the sufferer's woes, was unsparingly alleged against me. I had unhesitatingly rebutted the accusations of the tyrant, accused of malice the translators of my papers, and, undaunted by multitudes, asserted that the very book from which my enemies had extracted mutilated passages to effect my condemnation, unequivocally demonstrated my regard and esteem for his Majesty. But if every one shrank from defending my cause or interceding in my behalf during that terrible afternoon, I was not forsaken or abandoned; there was One with me, and His presence supported me in my trouble, strengthened me in my weakness, and conducted me safely through all my exhausting conflicts.

The taunts, insults, and indignities to which I had been exposed for several hours, keenly jarred on nerves that had already been fearfully shattered. Till that very day I cherished a faint hope that the tyrant would relent in his wanton barbarity towards me; but the treatment to which I was exposed, the injustice I had experienced, and the verdict which was pronounced by the court, and imprudently confirmed by the Europeans, dispelled the illusion, and I longed—longed most ardently—that no new incident would protract the final crisis.

"Sabinyee (guards), lead away your prisoners!" now shouted the king. Instantly we were in the clutches of a crowd of ruffians who, instead of dragging, in the excess of their zeal, roughly lifted us above the moving masses that were hurrying to their different camps. The petty tyranny of the servile wretches awakened in me a feeling more akin to pity than anger. Crouching slaves, they fawned, grinned, and bowed before the very man who had ruined their country, murdered numbers of their relations, and, in many instances, desolated their own houses and homes. Depressed and faint, I would gladly have slumbered away the recollection of the last few hours, had not the terrible Jaque Obey torn me from my hard couch, and in his merciless method hammered again the galling fetters around my aching and tired legs.

Saturday and Sunday passed away without any other infliction of sufferings beyond those to which I, and, to some extent, my companion, had already become inured. This was not the case on Monday. With sunrise on that morning we were most disagreeably surprised to see a whole division of Agha Faree Meshesha's notorious bands of executioners come into our tents. The blood-stained gang, with a consideration we had no right to expect, at once informed us that their errand was not to beat, whip, or scourge the prisoners, but to confiscate the property I had still in my possession. This intelligence caused me no regret; nay, I felt a kind of melancholy satisfaction to see the tent disencumbered of articles I could no longer claim as my own. To a revengeful spirit, a straw in the path, or a feather tossed about in the air, will afford a pretext to veil past injustice, and an incentive for fresh and greater atrocities. Thus, among my re-rummaged bags and boxes a bill-book was found with the seal and motto of the London Jews' Society on the margin. One of the king's wellknown European advisers was immediately consulted; and, according to the report of the guards, he assured his Majesty that the book, as the episcopal insignia proved, was a gift from the Aboon, and empowered me, when I came to Egypt, to draw money on his account. "I always suspected," rejoined the king, "that Cocab, for other reasons than the black cowl, respected that Copt; I'll take care that the treacherous monk shall not remit my subjects' money to the Turks, nor his friends have an opportunity to spend it. Jaque Obey, strictly guard Cocab."

It was already late when our chief tormentor returned from his duties as Agha Farce (gate-keeper)* to the charge of the two miserable captives. I at once perceived that he was irritated, drunk, and in bad humour. For two or three minutes he sulkily squatted down, and conversed with another chief, Basha Hailu, on the discovery made among my baggage. Abruptly, as if impelled by a demon-spirit, he broke off the colloquy, and, fixing his ferret eyes on me, in accents that made me start, hissed out: "If I had my sword I would cut off that white dog's head. Never mind. Get up, you slave, and let me see your fetters!" He did not permit me to obey the injunction, but, suiting the action to the words, he pulled me forward, and began mercilessly to batter the iron hoops around my legs. Wounds, bruises, gashes, all were unheeded by the besotted savage. His friends begged, his subordinates entreated, even his own servants—wretches who envied the morsel of bread we ate—implored him to desist, and not to break my bones, and still the ruffian persevered in his barbarous work. I quailed and shivered beneath every stroke, but the ferocious Agow would not desist, till he actually saw me drop, faint and almost insensible, on the knee of

* The Agha Farees perform the functions of royal gate-keepers, executioners, and military commanders.

my poor Joseph. Mr. Rosenthal's chains he also inspected, but as they could not be made tighter, he merely gave him a kick, that sent him rolling into his lair. The horrors of that evening and some similar scenes are so vividly impressed on my mind, that I shall remember the spot and the persons to my last hour.

Slowly passed the days and nights of anguish and pain. The former we spent in converse and prayer, the latter in struggles with tormenting guards and other tantalising visitors. Bibles—the solace of the Christian sufferer in sad, painful days—we were not allowed. The petulant despot, in his rankling animosity against the victims whom his dastardly resentment had wronged without just reason or honest motive, would not extend to them any indulgence that might indicate a regret for his unjustifiable severity, or an overt intimation that he had gratified his vile passion at the expense of all equity. No, he has done wrong, and arrogant pride must not avow it; he has been guilty of gross injustice, and his sham rage must not disclose it. "Let the white men perish, and their death will enhance my reputation, strengthen my power, and lead my people to believe that I am what I claim to be—the scourge of the Turk, and the destined occupant of Solomon's throne." Such, no doubt, were the arguments which swayed his decision, and prompted his atrocious proceedings towards us. Had this not been the case, he would never have wasted a moment on two insignificant and obscure individuals, whose detention, he had heard, involved no inquiry, and whose death, he was assured, entailed no risk. To adopt the latter alternative was his intention, as I heard from his own lips; but then, why should he sacrifice two insignificant missionaries, and leave untouched a big Consul? would not this half measure be construed into pusillanimity, and this moderation into cowardice? Besides that, was it not a palpable fact that his proceedings against the priests was dictated by other reasons than those he alleged, and more artful designs than he pretended? "Away with this wavering and vacillating policy, and let extreme measures supersede temporising expedients, and bold defiance artful compromise. If England wants her Consul, he is in my camp, and shall soon writhe in my chains; and if she demands satisfaction, I have soldiers, and will fight. The conflict may be severe, but in the end I shall be the winner; and if nothing else is obtained, Massowah and Sennaar will be annexed to the land over which I rule." Thus did that unscrupulous and intriguing despot persuade himself that the incarceration of a few helpless strangers, and, if needful, their execution, would increase his reputation, secure him the applause of his people, and give a sea-port and an Egyptian province to his prostrate and distracted empire.

One morning, soon after the seizure of my property, Basha Olash, a Yedsho chief,* and the worthy Samuel, came to my prison, and, in the name of his Majesty, promised me a free pardon and numerous favours if I confessed that through the family of Ras Oubie's wife, the commander-in-chief of the royal forces, I had obtained the information about the royal descent. To the surprise of the delegates, I deprecated all acquaintance, direct or indirect, with a family I only knew by reputation. They imagined that my answer was a mere artifice to extort a positive concession; but on reiterating that I could not purchase freedom at the expense of truth and honour, they ceased their importunities, and marched off.

A spasmodic calm, like the lull of the elements before the outburst of the storm, now crept into our tent. We attributed this to the arrival of the impatiently-expected letter from the British Government—an intelligence which, without any foundation, was industriously circulated.

---

* Wretched man! his faithful services were rewarded with imprisonment and a year's torture in fetters, ere he perished under the mutilator's knife at Debra Tabor.

Every day some new incident came to our ears that roused our hopes or intensified our despair. Now our dimmed eyes imagined that they saw the glimmer of a better day; then again some fresh incident occurred which cast a shade over our prospects, and once more held us in suspense between the agonising extremes of a happy freedom and the dread of a cruel and violent death. Depressed or elated, the days of misery slowly glided away, bringing us neither the longed-for liberty nor a more rigorous confinement. On December 4th, without any previous intimation, the manacles were removed from our legs, and, escorted by a detachment of soldiers, we were led before the king. On our arrival near the fence which separated the royal domicile from the enclosure in which all public business was transacted, we found his Majesty occupied in some legal proceedings. Not to irritate the chafed lion, we bowed most deferentially in the direction where he was seated. He took no notice of our salutation, but continued to investigate a quarrel between half a score of peasants and their despoilers—a number of pillage-loving soldiers. The decision was, as might have been anticipated, designedly adverse to the peasants, and, to impress the white culprits with the severity of Abyssinian justice, they were indiscriminately condemned to the revolting penalty of the giraff.

The verdict had hardly dropped from the judge's lips, when a band of hangmen, under Agha Faree Meshasha, pounced on the offenders, and whilst two held tight their hands and two their feet, two more alternately wielded the formidable whip, that furrowed their backs with every descending stroke. It was a painfully revolting sight to see these muscular, stalwart peasants knocked down robust, hale, and full of life, and then, after a few minutes, to behold them rise lacerated, faint, and dying. A young woman who had been condemned to the same punishment the tyrant pardoned, and that simply, as he himself stated, because he did not wish that the Frendjoj should say, "King Theodorus gives women the giraff." His apparent mercy was cruel in the extreme; for the poor creature, ere she reached the fence which conducted into the open camp, was bereaved of a husband, brother, and two neighbours. One more, it was reported, expired at the outskirts of the camp.

This giraffing process lasted at least two hours. During the whole of that time we were obliged to stand close to the executioners, without being permitted to betray, either by word or signs, sympathy or compassion for the suffering and dying men. The malicious grins of the fell executioners as they wiped the blood from their whips, or, by a dexterous whirl, spirted it on our faces, led us to anticipate a similar treatment. I felt no fear; I dreaded no death. All that harassed my mind was the number of strokes I might be able to stand, and the length of time their infliction would occupy. A hundred, I was quite certain, my frame, shattered as it was, would be able to sustain, and these, administered by the vigorous arms of two expert Shankgalla giants, I computed, would not occupy more than nine minutes. These reflections engaged my attention, till Samuel, who had been standing at some distance, approached, and authoritatively ordered the guards to advance with the malefactors into the inner fence.

"Are you afraid now?" interrogated the tyrant, in a tone of revengeful irony. This remark had evidently reference to some words that accidentally dropt from my lips one evening, when a set of vicious guards almost worried me to madness with a revolting description of the various methods by which criminals were dispatched in Abyssinia. Unable to retain my burning indignation, I told the scoundrels: "You may sport with human life if it delights you, but if you believe that your flippant prattle frightens me you are mistaken: I fear God, and not man." "Are you afraid now?" once more reiterated the dark, squatting figure before the royal pavilion. There was again no reply. "Why did you insult me?" peremptorily demanded that same clear and distinct voice. Silence being dangerous, I fearlessly but respectfully rejoined: "We had no design to insult your Majesty, nor have we written a single word in the language of this country; but if we have done wrong, we humbly crave your Majesty's clemency." Samuel, who acted as interpreter, had not quite finished the translation of the whole sentence, when the irritated despot ordered our shamas and shirts to be torn off. Quick as lightning was the behest executed; and the denuded captives, amidst crowds of gaping legions, were led back to their prison lair.

Our brave watch, terrified lest the fear of a speedy execution might induce us to make a desperate attempt to effect our escape, or that a miracle might happen, and wrest us out of their clutches, had a long consultation about the manner of guarding us. Some said that it would be best to watch us outside the tent, as the cold would benumb us, and render flight impossible; others maintained that we should occupy a vacant space in the circle they would form. Jaque Obey did not approve of either proposition. "To leave them in the open air," he wisely observed, "is dangerous, for these white men have *toungle* (tricks) which we don't understand; and to place them in the midst of a circle of guards affords them the comforts of a warmth they don't deserve. No, let them remain in the open tent, with two soldiers, and all the rest must encamp around it." Stretched on the hard, bare ground, and exposed to the sharp, keen blasts, we passed our last night, as we anticipated, in fervent prayer and devout meditation.

Cold and chilly was that night; dreary and dismal appeared that morning. Sick of captivity and weary of life, death had lost its terror, and the grave its gloom. The vision of a desolate home and sorrowing friends, of hearts that refused comfort, and of tears that will not cease to flow, caused many a pang, and embittered many solemn moments; but we had to seek composure and peace for our drooping spirits in the contemplation of scenes where separation cannot sadden or death create an aching void.

Our chief gaoler, who had gone to the king, we fully expected, would, on his return, announce the approach of our last moments. It must have been nine o'clock when he reappeared, accompanied by a royal slave, who carried a bundle of soiled, discoloured, and blood-stained rags. Jaque Obey, hardened in crime and insensible to human misery, in looking at the shivering forms of the two strangers that stood before him, must have experienced something of compassion, for, in the gentlest tones he could assume, he told us that the king had relented in his anger towards us, and that probably we should, ere long, receive a complete pardon, but in the meantime, to mitigate our wretchedness, we were to put on the garments with which he had been charged to supply us. This very act of mercy partook so much of the character of a malicious taunt, that for some moments neither Rosenthal nor myself made the customary bow of acknowledgment. The gaoler generously attributed our indifference to the royal favour to surprise, and, without any acerbity, he said: "Down on your knees, and thank the king that he has had compassion on you." Mechanically we performed this act of homage; and then the messengers, perfectly satisfied with our gratitude, went to carry the report of what had taken place to their master.

Respite, and not release, did not ease our anxieties or alleviate our cares. Arragow, a native lad* in the service of Mr. Flad, accompanied by a friendly soldier, occasionally crept to the door of our tent, and, by signs, kept us informed of what was going on in the world out of which we were banished. On his last visit he intimated, by pointing to his legs and spreading out his arms, that

* Mr. Flad, when dispatched to England in 1866, took him to the Chrishona, near Basle, where he is receiving an education.

our chains were to be unriveted. The civil and less obtrusive conduct of our guards indirectly confirmed this report; they manifested little or no restraint in their intercourse with us. It is true they would not, and perhaps could not, tell us the design of their master in the detention of a number of Europeans; but if they were uninformed about the future, they were well acquainted with the past, and, without the least reserve, they told us that our lives had been in most imminent danger, and that on the day the king took away our clothing our hands and feet would probably have shared a similar fate, had not the energetic remonstrances of the Etcheque (Prior) averted the catastrophe.

A deliverance so signal, and that, too, at the intercession of a stranger, *acted like a tonic* on our spirits, and roused us from a depression that verged on idiotcy.

Fifteen days more of anxious solicitude and corroding care rolled away. Our couch was still the bare ground, and our only covering the tattered filthy shamas given by the king. We tried to communicate with Consul Cameron, Flad, and Mrs. Rosenthal, but the soldier who acted as our messenger invariably gave us some agreeable intelligence of his own fabrication, and not the message entrusted him by our friends. One morning in December we were, however, surprised by a visit from Flad, Samuel, and several of the bishop's and king's personal servants. My body being bent and crippled by the chains, I was requested not to rise, as the visit was merely to ascertain the price of certain silks which the Aboon had presented to the king.* The valuation of the various stuffs which I had myself purchased for the Aboon did not take many minutes; but my visitors, instead of retiring, said that I must try to get up and hear the royal message. Samuel, the royal mouthpiece, after clearing his throat, which he always did when he spoke to me, as if his guilty conscience stifled his utterance, calmly informed me that it had been the design of his Majesty to kill me, and probably he would also have done it had God permitted it. "His Majesty," continued the courtier, "is now desirous to afford you an opportunity to regain his forfeited favour, if you comply with his condition, and assist him to obtain, through Mr. Flad, who is going to Europe, one or two powder makers, and the requisite machinery. If Mr. Flad is successful," he proceeded, in a calm, deliberate tone, "his Majesty will, on his return, overwhelm you with presents and honours that will make your name famous in Africa and Europe. During the

---

* The Metropolitan, as already stated, presented the king with most valuable presents, in the hope of effecting my release.

interval, you will have to accompany his Majesty on his campaigns, and take photographic sketches of the sceneries he may visit." I was disposed to object to all these propositions, but I was advised not to contradict the despot, as it might involve me afresh in serious troubles. The following day his Majesty ordered our hand-chains to be unriveted; but, on Mr. Flad's representation that my legs were swollen and inflamed, the order was reversed, and the foot, instead of the hand fetters, taken off.

Our affairs, though still undecided, began at last to assume a more favourable aspect. We were again allowed to have a servant, and more decent clothing. Unfortunately, such a thing as a wardrobe was a luxury that belonged to the past, and the male Frendjoj in the camp we knew would have nothing to spare in the shape of undergarments. In this emergency we had recourse to Mrs. Flad and Mrs. Rosenthal, and ludicrous as it may seem, the white shifts of these ladies, our tabagies—excellent judges—assured us were most becoming substitutes for gentlemen's shirts. What we, however, most prized were two Bibles—a comfort and solace we had not possessed for six long and trying weeks. Poor Joseph, whose constitution suffering, hardships, and privations had entirely sapped, received the royal sanction to leave the camp for the greater quiet of a house at Gondar.

Here the poor fellow lingered on a week longer, and then breathed his last. He had been faithful to me in all my trials, and his death caused a most sensible gap in the limited circle of my sympathising friends.

Two or three days after the above interview, Messrs. Flad and Samuel visited me again, and requested that I would write the letters I intended to send to Europe, to ensure the success of the proposed mission. I put the best looks on an ugly business. The crafty Samuel noticed it, and, when out of my hearing, he said to Flad something to the effect that the indignant dashes of my pen in the shackled hand betrayed the disgust with which I performed the requested task. The king himself communicated his arrangements with me to the European employés at Gaffat. Through pity for the sufferer, and perhaps a secret surmise that one or two good artisans from Europe might divert to some extent the favour and dollars of the king into another channel, they wrote a petition to the despot, in which (so it was reported) they remonstrated against my further detention and captivity, and promised to provide the required machinery and gunpowder. The king admitted the plausibility of their argument, and, to effect a complete reconciliation, they were ordered to come to the camp at Gondar. Samuel himself, who came to my prison on some business of his master, told me to "be of good cheer, for your liberation is not far distant." Consul Cameron, perhaps unacquainted with the court intrigues, or perhaps anxious to quit a country in which he was an unfettered prisoner, just at that critical moment, in compliance with the instructions received from his government, solicited the royal sanction for his departure to the coast at the expiration of the ensuing three days. This demand exasperated the tyrant, and marred my own and Mr. Rosenthal's prospects of release.

CHAPTER VI.

Gethsemane a Captive's Comfort—January 3rd—Consul Cameron chained—Prison Discipline—Samuel's Smiles—Brave Conduct of Mrs. Flad and Rosenthal—Seizure of a Doll—Cross-fire of Questions—A Warning Text—Death deprived of its Terrors—Sham Reconciliation—An Accession of Prisoners—Fortunate Incident—Royal Inquisitiveness—French Consul's Protest—Release of Six Prisoners—Perplexing Stipulation—Extensive Conversions—Religion and Cannon—Confident Anticipations of Release—M. Bardel's Imprisonment—Charges against him—Sad Disappointment.

OPPRESSION and tyranny, hardships and sufferings, had already tested the powers of endurance to the utmost, and the mind almost involuntarily began to shrink from the idea of entering on a new, indefinite period of heart-rending and heart-wasting martyrdom. In this hapless situation the troubled soul would have sunk into utter despair, had not a still small voice whispered, "Think on Gethsemane and the cross, and you have an antidote against the bitter cup which it is your Heavenly Father's pleasure you should drink." Such thoughts—and they were not the suggestions of a morbid sentimentality—continually occupied my mind, and nerved me for every species of cruelty and death savage ferocity might inflict. Nearly three months of unmitigated terror had already passed over me, and about seven weeks over my companion, Mr. Rosenthal. During this long and dismal Lent, the few faint and dim glimpses of a better time coming cheered and sustained us amidst the troubles and trials of a stormy existence. Thus day after day wore away in unvarying wretchedness and misery. Christmas had passed over us; the new year had been ushered in; yet the chains hung inexorably on our fettered wrists. On Sunday morning, January 3rd, 1864, some of our guards informed us that the Negoos was sending and receiving messages from the "Frendjoj," and that we should probably be liberated. Tossed about on a sea of trouble and care, any intelligence of this kind—even from the lips of an Abyssinian—did not fail to excite our depressed spirits to renewed courage and confidence. About mid-day, our truculent gaoler rushed in breathless hurry into our tent, and, after convincing himself that all was right, ordered, in the name of his Majesty, a detachment of troops to proceed on an important errand. I did not at the moment pay much attention to the command, though the promptitude with which all sallied forth convinced me that they were either charged to arrest a prisoner or to seize some property.* Late

---

* Subsequently, we heard that they had been dispatched to Gondar, to arrest the consul's people, and to seize his property.

at noon our redoubtable Jaque Obey again made his appearance, and in an imperative tone commanded us to accompany him to the king. On leaving, Rosenthal said to me, "What do you think this summons signifies?" "On a Sunday," I rejoined, "both whip and stick are in abeyance: we have no cause to apprehend anything inauspicious." A group of curious idlers followed us within the fence that divided the royal camp from that of the troops. A second central enclosure, on the top of a small eminence, occupied by white and black tents, revealed the abode of his Majesty and the royal household. We thought that we were to be conducted up to that busy acclivity, where, a few weeks before, we had such a mournful interview; but, instead of this, our guards escorted us to a white tent on the left, that ominously faced an elevated bank, on which two four-pounders, mounted on rickety ship-carriages, ostentatiously displayed their unpolished brazen fronts. A profusion of ragged carpets covered the entire space between these pieces of ordnance and the pavilion —a parade of regal pomp quite unusual, except on grand gala days. Our excited imagination immediately ran riot with all sorts of pleasing conjectures, which even now, after the lapse of so many trying months, I recall with satisfaction, as they afforded me a passing relief from perpetual trouble and care. The happy illusion in which I indulged was dispelled on a nearer approach. His Abyssinian Majesty had for some months felt disposed to quarrel, or, as he emphatically styled it, "to humble the pride of Europe;"* but the lingering expectation of a favourable reply to his letter to the British Government imposed a kind of temporary restraint on his towering pride. The consul's request to start for the coast confirmed his conviction that all friendly intercourse between Abyssinia and England was at an end; and to resent this insult, which, as he himself often enough confessed, deeply touched his honour and dignity, Consul Cameron, the missionaries, and every other European not in the royal service, was unceremoniously arrested. Ignorant of all that had occurred, and seeing every one sad and desponding, diffidently, as if I dreaded the inquiry, I said, "What is the meaning of all this?" With forced calmness they responded, "We are all prisoners, and about to be chained." The manacles were, indeed, soon brought, and, under the auspices of Basha Olash, hammered around the wrists of the culprits. The custom of attaching a soldier to each prisoner was, in the present instance, not strictly followed; one black to two white men the chief considered quite sufficient guarantee to ensure the safety of the culprits,

* By Europe he meant England and France.

a precaution which was not even enforced in the case of the old malefactors, who were deemed harmless and inoffensive beings. The relaxation of the strict prison discipline during the day was, however, not sanctioned during the night. No sooner did the shades of night thicken around us than there appeared a numerous and well-armed guard, who took their stations in and around the tent. No movement was now unheeded, and no incident, however trifling, unobserved. We were watched like criminals, and that, too, like criminals who were suspected of a skill that could burst impassable barricades, and elude the vigilance of the most watchful guards.

It was late, and most of the prisoners had already composed themselves to rest, when Samuel entered the prison tent, and in kind accents, which were contradicted by the smiles of satisfaction that lit up his sharp features, inquired whether Consul Cameron had his bed and wonted comforts. He also benignantly favoured me with an oblique glance, and, *en passant*, remarked, " I hope you are happier now, in the company of friends, than in your former isolated position." He relieved us of some of the guards, who most inconveniently thronged the tent, and then, bidding us an "egziabeher asfatachou" (may God deliver you), slunk quietly away. The next day the servants of our fellow-prisoners, who at the first alarm had sought the bush, on obtaining better tidings, came again straggling into Gondar, from whence some found their way to their incarcerated masters.

Chains and imprisonment one might have thought were penalty severe enough to atone for the real or imaginary grievances of the sensitive successor of Solomon; but no, he had been insulted by France and slighted by England, and for these offences a few defenceless strangers must, in addition to durance vile, part also with their little property. The order was promptly given, and the greedy royal banditti hurried away to enrich themselves with the spoils of the Frendjoj. In the tents of the consul and the missionaries they seized unopposed every article that was of value or use—an exploit they could not so easily achieve in the house of Mrs. Rosenthal and Mrs. Flad at Gondar. These ladies, roused to a pitch of frenzy, defied heroically the cowardly attempts of the ruffians to rob them and their helpless babes of their necessary food and clothing. Mrs. Flad particularly distinguished herself in the encounter with the undisciplined savages. "Go, tell your king," she said, energetically, to the leader of the band, "that we are weak, oppressed women; yet, if he wishes to kill us, we, together with our infants, shall deem it a mercy to be dispatched at once, rather than be subject to a slow and lingering torture.

This message was delivered verbatim to his Majesty, and he swallowed the smarting rebuke, by merely observing, "these white women compared to ours are perfect d—s." Even Mrs. Rosenthal, with her limited knowledge of the language, boldly faced some of the depredators; and one bravo, who had forcibly wrested from her a few pieces of sugar she had carefully husbanded for her sick babe, she pursued courageously through the compound, and would not give up the chase till the fellow restored the stolen and valued article. Another ruffian, amidst coarse ribaldry, wanted to test the comfort of an iron-folding chair, which his huge frame would have smashed at the very first touch. Mrs. Rosenthal immediately hastened to close it, but Mrs. Flad had already laid hold of the leg, and the ponderous savage, before he had tasted the luxury of a civilised seat, to the amusement of his companions, tumbled heavily on the stony ground. Poor little Anne, Flad's eldest girl, about four years old, had her temper also ruffled during the pillage. Her rag doll, which she had carefully concealed in a particular nook, was accidentally discovered, and confiscated by the unfeeling robbers. With tears, and "by the King's death," she protested against this illegal seizure; but the ruthless heroes were deaf to her entreaties, and for more than half an hour capered madly around it, ere they yielded it up to the sobbing child.

While such and similar scenes were enacted at Goudar, a cross-fire of questions and answers was lustily kept up between his Majesty and the Frendjoj. The vexatious topic of the unfortunate letter, and certain personal favours bestowed on England's representative, formed the staple of the queries put to Consul Cameron. From the tenor of the questions, one could perceive that his Majesty began to be conscious that, in his conduct towards all, he had exceeded the bounds of a ruler and a professing Christian; but, strange as it may seem, the very knowledge that he had done wrong inflamed his vindictive rage, and, in the haughty language of an irresponsible tyrant, he informed Consul Cameron that he knew her Britannic Majesty would send some great man to inquire into his proceedings towards her representative and the other Frendjoj, and that his answer would be: "I can do in my country what I please." Consul Cameron's business being dismissed, Samuel, the royal delegate, turned his vulture eyes upon me, and demanded to know what I meant by the statements contained in my papers, that, "if the Negoos provoked the hostility of the French, or the aggression of the Turks, the conflict would probably break the enthralling bonds of intolerance, and confer the boon of religious liberty on Abyssinia." "His Majesty," I responded, "is already acquainted with the views of the Emperor Napoleon on this subject, as they were embodied in the letter conveyed to the king through Monsieur Bardel, and it would, consequently, be a superfluous task for me to give a comment on language that was plain enough." "And what will England do if such a contingency should arise?" rejoined my interlocutor. "The British Government," I returned, "has always cherished the most friendly feelings towards Abyssinia, and it might be, if they thought religious toleration would enhance the moral and material welfare of the country, that they would support, without insisting on, such a concession." Samuel carried these answers back to the king, and then returned again, and, in a stern tone, said, "The Negoos has heard your replies, and, did he deem it expedient, *he could tell you a secret about England; but what does it matter, time will reveal it.*" I was anxious to discover the meaning of this mystery, which evidently was some mischievous intelligence communicated by the lying tongue of an unprincipled royal parasite. Samuel saw the drift, and as he had perhaps ample reason to evade an explanation, he promptly slided the interrogations into a new groove, and, in the name of his Majesty, proudly insisted that I should mention the name or names of the parties who had furnished me the particulars about the royal ancestry. Here a war of words ensued. Samuel dexterously tried to extort the names, and I adroitly eluded his request.

A PRIEST AND A MONK.

Baffled and thwarted, the indignant courtier arrogantly demanded that I should tell him the title I had bestowed in my book* on the parent of the Negoos. Too much candour here betrayed me into a serious mistake, for, instead of saying that I had stated his Majesty's father was the Duke of Quara (sic), I lowered him to the grade of a mere "bellada" nobleman, a dignity arrogated by many a despised peasant.

This day of intense misery tardily at length drew to a close, and, freed from our tormentor, each one, according to his inclination, was once more allowed to chew the bitter cud of his own ill-boding imagination. In the evening, our tyrannical gaoler, Jaque Obey, on resuming his night-watch, brought the Amharic New Testament, and, pointing to the last verse of the first chapter in the Epistle to the Romans, which stands on the top of the page, commanded me and Rosenthal to give the Negoos an explanation of the passage the next day. The awful import of the text, and the frightful verdict it denounces on the guilty, made me at first doubt whether I was among sane or mad savages; but when I recollected the dire emphasis Samuel had laid on the words which, in the course of the interrogations, had escaped my lips, "If it please God to bring me back to England, I shall know how to

* "Wanderings among the Falashas."

correct the pedigree of his Majesty," all misgivings vanished, and I anticipated without dread or terror my approaching doom. For weeks and weeks I had, indeed, been weary of this lingering torture and incessant misery; and now, when the ominous warning came, the knell of parting life was to me merely an emancipation from the cruel and bitter tyranny of earth to the glory, peace, and rest of heaven. Our heartless gaoler, who, I believe, never felt any other emotion in his petrified bosom than that caused by the love of rapine and plunder, on hearing from Mr. Flad the contents of the verse—for he was quite guiltless of the knowledge of letters—compassionately remarked: "They are not bad men, but this is a bad business."

Gradually the night rolled away, and daylight, with its cheering sun and bustling hum, broke upon the sad and lonely prisoners.* There was no conversation, and no interchange of thought; every one had sorrow engraven on his brow, and gloomy misgivings concealed in his heart. Anticipating every moment the fatal summons, faith, invigorated by Divine grace, triumphed over the throes of impending death; and, without one of those ever-

---

* Subsequently, Consul Cameron, Flad, and Cornelius told me that during those anxious hours they had frequently cast secret glances on the vacant paddock near our tent, to see if the gallows, on which the victims of tyranny were to suffer, was in course of erection.

shifting fluctuations of hope and fear which, under such circumstances, naturally agitate the human breast, I watched calmly and composedly the flying hours of time. Mid-day passed, noon declined, evening approached, and still no royal messenger made his appearance. Another night of earthly cares slowly waned away, and a new day of troubles stole quietly in upon us. At length, about noon, Samuel, that messenger of evil, appeared in our prison. After a condescending salutation, which, even in the moment of the basest intrigue, he never omitted, M. Rosenthal and myself were requested to rise, and, in the best Arabic of his rejected Koran, he ordered me, at the behest of his royal master, to expound the pointed-out passage of Sacred Writ. Instantly I seized the New Testament, and, commenting on the whole chapter, told the messenger that the terrible indictment of the Apostle against an unbelieving world had not the remotest connection with the offences charged against us; but, if his Majesty thought the reverse, we both deplored to have incurred his displeasure, and craved his clemency. Samuel now read the chapter himself, and, as he came to the revolting catalogue of crimes alleged against the fallen posterity of Adam, he unwittingly vented his astonishment at the unhappy selection in the ejaculation, "O Janchoi! Janchoi!" "Oh, King!

King!" His Majesty himself, rather ashamed of his quotation, or satisfied that he had inflicted sufficient sufferings, on the return of the messenger, informed us that the unlettered Jaque Obey had stupidly placed his fingers on the last verse of the first chapter, instead of the beginning of the second. The reproof he now designed to administer was obvious, and so, without expatiating on the propounded passage, I sought to mollify the hard heart of our oppressor, by soliciting Samuel to inform him that both Rosenthal and myself lamented to have involuntarily offended him, and, in imitation of the compassionate Saviour to repentant sinners, recorded in the first Epistle of St. John, chapter i., verses 8 and 9, we implored him to accept our apology. Samuel soon returned with the message that his Majesty had read the passage, and, as he hoped to obtain forgiveness of his sin, he also extended pardon and entire oblivion of the past to us, "and henceforth," added the servile courtier, "you will pray for the Negoos, as the Negoos charges me to tell you he will pray for you." The shadows of death, in which we had been enshrouded for twice twenty-four hours, were now dispelled, and, relieved from the spectral vision of a cruel, torturing martyrdom, we once more speculated on liberty and freedom. Pardoned, but in chains, restored to royal favour, but in prison, may appear puzzling paradoxes; but it must be remembered that the great Negoos was still smarting beneath the insult he imagined he had received from the British Government, and, in the swing of his towering ambition, he revenged on those near the mistakes of those far away.

On the same day that the Negoos manifested a faint inclination to generosity and mercy, the rest of the white prisoners, consisting of Mrs. Flad, Mrs. Rosenthal, Joseph and Schiller, two German ornithologists, Kerans, McKelvy, and Makerer, two Englishmen and one Frenchman in the service of the consul, were conducted from Gondar down into the camp. The two ladies, who were not treated like regular prisoners, were taken by Samuel to that part of the camp occupied by his establishment; and the rest, after receiving their chains, were located in a tent opposite to our own.

Moved by caprice, or, perhaps, satisfied revenge, the king ordered a few of the most worthless articles among the pillage to be restored to the prisoners. Here an incident occurred which strikingly illustrated the guardian care of our Heavenly Father, and inspired the depressed soul with unwavering faith and trust. About the middle of November, 1863, Mr. Kerans arrived at Gondar with a packet for the consul. Amongst the letters there were several for me; but, as I was a closely-guarded malefactor, and unapproachable, Mrs. Rosenthal took charge of them. On the day that her property was a second time entirely confiscated, these longed-for epistles from distant friends were safely concealed in a secret drawer in her work-box. Anxious to destroy everything that might compromise me afresh, she tried hard to abstract them, but the keen eye of the guard rendered the attempt abortive. In the evening, to her delight, the box was restored; and, though forced open, the clumsy depredators did not discover the hidden recess. Mrs. Rosenthal immediately communicated to me this fortunate recovery, and, at my request, she and Mrs. Flad perused the letters, ere they were consigned to the flames. I was afterwards informed that they had all been harmless, except one, which contained questions about the Negoos that might have roused his suspicion and ire.

Settled down into regular prison habits, our days were wiled away in listless inactivity or anxious care; our evenings were generally a little varied by a quarrel with the guards, who, reckless about space, thronged in groups into our tents, and filled the already stifling atmosphere with the putrescent odours of their fetid garments and buttered heads. The Negoos, too, occasionally relieved the dulness of our existence by an ambiguous message, the gift of a cow, or a few sheep. Sometimes, also, he sent and requested to know the meaning of a pirated sketch of the *Illustrated London News*, sometimes of a Bible picture, sometimes of an illustrated advertisement torn out of an unfortunate monthly; but most of all was the inquisitive descendant of Solomon interested in the caricatures of *Punch* which lay scattered among the plundered archives of the British Consulate. These friendly communications rendered the dreaded presence of Samuel quite amusing, and his visits, which were neither few nor far between, became quite diverting and agreeable. One day he walked into our tent scowling like a fiend, and handed to the consul a large, full-written sheet of paper. As I was standing close to him, curiosity made me look on the formidable document that had ruffled Samuel's temper. It was a protest of M. Lejean, the French Consul, on the subject of the treatment he had experienced during his stay at the court of Abyssinia. The articles, I believe eighteen in number, were couched in energetic and peppery language. Consul Cameron, after glancing over the foolscap, exclaimed, "Samuel, Samuel! this is a sad business!" but the stern delegate, without attending to his words, urged him to read it. Having complied with the request, he handed the precious document to me, and commanded that I should give him the contents of it in Arabic. Uncharitable as it may seem, I confess it afforded me some satisfaction to obey the order, and heedless about the wrinkles which each fresh sentence wreathed on his frowning brow, I translated every word, not omitting even the brutal conduct of his Majesty in chaining the representative of a potent foreign sovereign in full uniform. The outraged envoy restrained his boiling passion till I had concluded, and then he gave vent to his impotent rage in a profusion of ridiculous epithets: "Dog, liar, donkey! why did you not tell all this when you were in the king's country?" The diplomatic note, which mercilessly exposed the vanity, weakness, and barbarism of the monarch, in perusing it, rankled like a barbed arrow in his ambitious breast. In the absence of any other white men on whom to retaliate, we expected that our treatment would be more ruthless and severe; but whether guided by gentler emotions, or actuated by a presentiment that the day of retribution was approaching, matters continued in *statu quo*, and *Punch, Illustrated London News*, advertisements of razor and chandelier makers, and even an occasional full-dressed, rosy-coloured beauty in *Le Follet*, though no one pretended to know how she had crossed the African Alps, continued to pour into our prison tent. About the end of January reports reached us that M. Bardel, who had gone on the service of the Negoos to Cassala, the capital of Soudan, to espy what the Egyptians intended to do, was on his way back, and that on his arrival the European workmen at Gaffat would also come to the camp, whither they had been summoned to attend a special council. The rumour proved true, for on the 3rd of February M. Bardel returned from his secret mission, and on the 5th the Europeans arrived from Debra-Tabor. Immediately on their advent they repaired to the royal tent, from whence, after a lengthened conference, they were dispatched to our prison.

Messrs. Flad, Steiger, Brandeis, Josephson (since gone to his rest), Joseph, and Schiller, were instantly liberated—a clemency not extended to the rest, who were considered more exalted, or more dangerous characters.

The delegates, it is true, did not deprive us of all hope of release; on the contrary, they assured the consul that if he pledged himself that the British Government would not insist on satisfaction for all that had passed, they could, without endangering their own lives, effect our liberty, and perhaps gain permission to quit the country; if, however, this stipulation exceeded his authority, they promised to use their influence to secure us an unchained asylum, either at Gaffat or some village in the neighbourhood.

They had certainly many interviews with his Majesty, and that, too, sometimes of long duration. The questions discussed were, however, entirely confined to their private affairs and the casting of cannon.

His Majesty, to compound for his numerous sins, in a fit of remorse unexpectedly assumed the character of a missionary. The forcible conversion of the Falashas, which he had attempted in the beginning of October, and intended to carry into effect a month later, at my urgent representation to the Aboon, who was then on tolerable terms with the despot, was suspended for three years. That of the Mahomedan Gallas, who had no powerful intercessor, met with less opposition, and on October 15th, after a public discussion, the sword and spears of Theodore, and not the inspired writings of the prophets and apostles, induced them to throw off the leathern cord around the neck—the badge of Islamism—and to suspend in its stead one of silk, the mark of Christianity. The laurels he had already gained on the difficult field of missionary enterprise might, perhaps, have led him to seek still greater fame and renown on more distant scenes, had not the factious and insurrectionary disposition of his insubordinate subjects, who most unreasonably refused to be despoiled and then butchered, forced him to throw off the garb of the evangelist for the sterner garb of the warrior.

A ravaging disease and numerous executions quelled the threatening tempest of rebellion, and once more revived the dormant zeal of the royal apostle. The Gallas were converted; the Falashas wavering, but inquiring. Where now was the enthusiastic preacher to find objects on which to display the exuberance of his flaming zeal? In this perplexity his ever wakeful eyes lighted on Bishop Gobat's missionaries and their white companions in the cannon foundry. Zander, a native of Anhalt-Dessau, and Protestant by name, had already transferred his allegiance to the Abyssinian Church. Mr. Schimper, the next in rank, and a very old sinner, was well worthy of every attention, but as he had unfortunately already changed more than half a dozen times from Protestantism to Romanism, and from Romanism to Abyssinianism, his faith was rather suspected of being too marketable and cheap an article for a great king. M. and Madame Bourgeaud and family, devout Catholics, at the suggestion of their great teacher, found no difficulty in acknowledging the successor of St. Mark at Alexandria as good and holy as the successor of St. Peter at Rome. This was not the case with the avowed adherents to the Helvetian confession. St. George and Tecla Hamanot, Abo, Claudius, and a host more, might be very good men, but then it would not do to allow them to supplant Zwingle or Calvin without certain inconveniences and troubles.

But to oppose a liberal king and forfeit bags

of Maria Theresa dollars is imprudent. Well, they have made cannon, cast mortars, and manufactured gunpowder, and if this wisdom and skill does not smack of inspiration and proclaim the veracity of their creed, there is no true religion in the world. The devout king heard these arguments, and whether more anxious for the cannon his workmen produced than the weal of the souls they possessed, remained an open question. Probably he thought them impenitent and hardened sinners, and as he wanted mortars and powder, he abandoned their conversion, and stimulated their diligence by presents that were intended for the Queen of England.* The general opinion in the camp confirmed the expectation of our release. On the very day that the manacles were struck off the wrists of our companions, several chiefs who had some business near our prison, in reply to our interrogations, averred most solemnly that the king had sworn by "Confou yemout" (by the death of Confou), his most solemn oath, that we should not many days more sigh in captivity. Zodee, the chief spy and purveyor of the Europeans at Gaffat, and who was continually near the king, gave us the same hopeful intelligence. Even the

---

* The king was so sure of a favourable reply from England that he had already prepared the presents that were to be conveyed to her Majesty by the ambassador.

Etcheque, the father confessor of his Majesty, sent us tidings of a similar import, accompanied by a significant hint that we should not forget him in more prosperous circumstances. These reports kept us in a state of eager expectation and feverish excitement.

Early on the morning of February 4th, intelligence reached us that the king was angry with M. Bardel, and that he accused him of being the author of our misfortunes and sufferings. The young lad in the service of Mr. Flad, to whom I have already adverted, confirmed the intelligence, with the addition, that our freedom would lead to the imprisonment of M. Bardel. About noon the report received its verification, and M. Bardel, conducted by a detachment of troops, was actually led into our tent, there to await his royal master's pleasure. Discussion and inquiries were at their height, when a most formidable and imposing deputation from the king made their appearance. On former occasions, Jaque Obey, Samuel, or an officer of the household formed the medium of communication between the king and his white prisoners; but in the present instance, to give *éclat* to the message, greater etiquette was observed. Among the crowd which constituted the delegates, was our old acquaintance Zodee, Jaque Obey, Madrigal (formerly a pupil in the Malta Protestant

College), and a host of high functionaries and attendants. Jaque Obey, after making a scrutinising survey to see that all the prisoners, in deference to royalty, had girded their shamas round their waists, in a calm and deliberate tone said: "M. Bardel, Janchoi is angry with you, because you have misrepresented the prisoners and caused him to chain them. You have also spoken ill of the Negoos himself, and you have further, by unfounded assertions, tried to sow distrust and suspicion in his heart against your countrymen at Gaffat." Madrigal, for the benefit of all, translated every word into English, and the accused, without denying or admitting the charges, simply replied, "How! how!" This indirect apology for unmerited sufferings gave birth to fresh hopes of home and dear friends. Every hour now sped on heavily, and every messenger from the Europeans created a thrill of excitement. Day after day, however, was swallowed up in the relentless womb of time, and still the chains hung degradingly on our wrists. At last—I believe it was the 14th of February—Flad sent us word that all the king's European workmen, and the liberated prisoners, were to set out for Gaffat. This was a severe blow to our expectations, though the excess of the disappointment only stimulated the moral and physical energies of the soul to renewed courage and patience.

CHAPTER VII.

Prison Discussions—Release of Rosenthal—Dangerous Controversy—Isaiah's Censures—Dissatisfaction in the Army—Quarrel between the King and Aboon—Episcopal Visit—Trumpery Charges — Divine Support — The enraged Monarch — Rope Torture — Removal of the Cords — Fluctuating Emotions — Artfulness of Samuel—Renewed Tortures—Maddening Sensation — Royal Interrogations — Pandemonium — Thoughts of Suicide—Terrible Warning—False Alarm—Firmness of the Aboon—King's Confession—Reconciliation—A misunderstood Letter.

CONSIGNED once more for an uncertain period to fetters and a prison, each one, according to his peculiar taste, sought some occupation to beguile the long hours of the almost never-ending days. The accession to our numbers introduced also new topics of conversation. Popery, scepticism, and infidelity formed the staple of our discussion during part of the day; whilst our evenings were not unfrequently occupied in explaining the tenets of our faith to the loquacious guards. On the 29th of February the king asked me, through Samuel, something about a certain passage of Scripture, which Mr. Rosenthal, who stood near me, happened to answer. Samuel was exceedingly affable—a symptom by which we obtained a cue to the royal sentiments towards us. Our speculations that matters were again more promising were not unfounded, for in the afternoon the royal favourite came back, and released Rosenthal from his shackles, who now, together with his wife and babe, was permitted to enjoy the luxury of an unguarded tent; whilst to us he held out the prospect of a speedy happy change from prison to liberty. I had lost all confidence in his assertions —nay, invariably understood when he promised us freedom (a fact now incontestably ascertained) that he was toiling to effect our destruction and death.

A few weeks before Easter his Majesty one noon requested that I would prove to him from the Bible that fasting was not a Divine injunction, nor necessary to salvation. I readily obeyed the mandate, and message after message was carried in rapid succession from the white men's prison to the royal pavilion. Not to prolong the discussion, which, on the part of his Majesty and court, had degenerated into a challenge, I briefly observed that fasting, as a help to piety and devotion, was in harmony with the practice of the apostles; but such fasts, I added, were different from, nay, opposed to those enforced by the Abyssinian Church, and designed to effect a compromise between sin and good works, as was evident from Isaiah lviii. His Majesty instantly applied this chapter as a censure on his own actions, and I might have had to pay dearly for my temerity, had not, at the very moment when a loud and ominous cry, re-echoed by scores of voices, " Bring Cocab," a counter order of " Tou" (stop), arrested the dangerous command. This discussion, which might have brought the terrible "bedder" stick on me, created, as we were told, a variety of speculations in the army, and it is very likely that the anticipations of an abridged Lent would have been realised, had not the Prophet Isaiah too unsparingly, by his denunciation of injustice and oppression, offended the sensitive Theodore.

The unloved Lent, however, passed away, and so also Easter, the season of pardon and mercy to criminals not stained with blood, and yet there was no indication that our fetters would be loosed or our imprisonment come to an end. And now winter—bleak and stormy winter—charged with misery, wretchedness, and gloom to the captives, stole upon us. The hordes who constituted the tyrant's stay and prop did not admire the inactivity to which they were condemned, nor did the visions of an impending famine improve their temper or deepen their attachment to the king and his throne.

Dissatisfaction among the people, factions and desertions in the camp, aroused all the vile passions of the despot's ferocious heart. The spear, musket, and stick had, however, already lost the dread they were wont to inspire; and the giraff and mutilating knife were henceforward called into constant requisition. On one day, within sight of our prison, forty persons had their hands and feet wrenched off, whilst many more perished under the inhuman lash of the terrible whip.

On the 12th of May—a day which, like one or two more, will never be obliterated from my memory—his Majesty had a boisterous public interview with the "Aboon." Epithets neither becoming the descendant of Solomon nor the successor of the apostles were most profusely interchanged between the head of the State and the ruler of the Church. Once I audibly heard my own name, and two of my fellow-prisoners understood that it was coupled with the concealment of a curtain and taking of notes. Like a flash of lightning it struck me that it must refer to a certain morning when Consul Cameron and myself arranged some money matters with the bishop, which malicious tongues, in this country of inquisitorial espionage, had viciously distorted into an unlawful secret communication. The altercation, which was occasionally very loud, and then again more subdued, lasted about an hour, and, from the deep silence which prevailed, it was evident that the army did not approve of the quarrel. His Majesty, weary with the contest, abruptly mounted his horse, and, followed by a vast concourse, dashed furiously across the plain.

Conjecture was now rife among us about the probable issue of the dispute, in which one, if not more of us, were certainly involved. We were not long permitted to indulge in these gloomy musings. The tramp of feet, the hum of numerous voices, and the tinkling of church umbrellas, announced the approach of an extraordinary procession. Suddenly there was a rush of slaves through the palisaded doorway which led from the camping-ground of royalty to our prison, and then followed a mass of turbaned priests, proud chieftains, and high State functionaries. The Primate, clad in his simple Egyptian garb, with a black silk scarf negligently thrown over his head and face, led the van. There was a boisterous call for "Cocab" and the "Frendjoj." Precipitately we rushed out of our tent, and, in a most deferential attitude, confronted this formidable array of Church and State dignitaries. The royal notary, a tall, sleek personage, now opened a small parcel, and, taking out a portfolio that once belonged to me, he thrust his unwashed fingers into a packet of greasy papers, and took out the document that contained the charge garbled from my pilfered notes, and the letter of Mr. Rosenthal. These were then read amidst a profound and death-like silence. The notary having performed his task, Samuel, the courtier, advanced, and, in a persuasive strain, more entreated than commanded that we should state the parties who had been our informants. Rosenthal, who, as Samuel well knew, had no communication with the bishop, in a few brief sentences, satisfied the inquisitor. Samuel then turned his villanous countenance full upon me, and requested that I would state the source from whence I had obtained the statements embodied in the books and papers found in my possession. Fully aware, from the character of the king, that the examination was a serious business, I turned to M. Bardel, and inquired whether he objected to my denying the correctness of the translations. M. Bardel rejoined: "No, I only read the English; Birrou, Samuel, and the debterahs are responsible for the Amharic."

Relieved from the apprehension of incurring the reproach and abuse of a fellow-prisoner, or the responsibility of adding to his troubles, whether merited or not, I turned to Samuel, and, in unsparing severity blended with becoming meekness, deprecated the malice of those who, without any provocation, had sought my destruction by attributing to me language not to be found in my

papers. Then, addressing the whole assembly, I said: "What offence have I committed? That I said the king had pillaged certain provinces was no libel, for I saw it myself. That I stated a number of people had been executed at 'Dubark,' the skulls scattered over the plain attest the fact. That I was misinformed about his Majesty's descent, I must blame the late Mr. Bell and the Negoos' own speech at the capture of a chief, recorded in the history of his accession to the throne, and at present in the possession of the king himself. That I was not impelled by any ill-feeling towards the Negoos, my book incontestably proved, for the very mistake about his origin was an honour in Europe; since beyond the great waters, not a man's glorious ancestry, but his own deeds, shed lustre around his name. The bishop," I continued, raising my right hand, "I honour as a friend, and were he even my enemy, neither diversity in our religious sentiments, nor the dread of danger, nor the hope of favour should make me swerve from the truth."*
Samuel now interposed, and hypocritically remarked: "We do not wish that you should utter a false-

---

* Captain Cameron, in a letter to Dr. Shaw, the late Secretary of the Geographical Society, which I saw on my return to England, says: "On the morning of that day (May the 12th) there was a public interview between the king and the Metropolitan, who had always been our fast and open friend, and a Billingsgate scene between the heads of the Church and State ensued, in which the representative of the State taxed the other with having given the information to

hood, nor does any one feel disposed to contradict your assertion that you had no design to misrepresent the origin of the Negoos; but there are different ideas in Europe, America, and Asia; and this," he added, emphatically, as if anxious, by a biting sarcasm, to vent his rancorous hate, "this, you know, is Africa." The bishop, who, during the whole of that time, sat like an unconcerned spectator on the bare ground, now started up, and, casting an oblique glance of sympathy towards his white friends, poured forth a torrent of abuse on the king and the whole army of sycophants who swarmed around the throne. "Guards, receive your prisoners!" shouted Samuel, and instantly we were driven into the tent; whilst the Primate and his cortège retraced their steps through the fence by which they had entered.

Enfeebled by a serious illness, from which I had not yet quite recovered, the exciting conference, I expected, would bring on a fatal relapse. A gracious Providence, however, strengthened, supported, and sustained me.

I was destined to confront still greater trials and to encounter still heavier afflictions ere the

Mr. Stern on which the charges against the latter had been founded. The bishop denied, and, I suppose, expecting Mr. Stern's acquiescence, the king sent him down, and confronted him with Mr. Stern, who acted like a thorough-bred gentleman and bold-spoken man in denying anything like collusion."

dark and narrow passage of woe and misery through which I was passing revealed the gates that led to freedom and liberty. It was a critical moment. The king, exasperated against the bishop, whose proud spirit would not bend to the tyrant's lawless demands, artfully sought to find pleas to palliate his unjust proceeding. He had trumped up a variety of charges against the Metropolitan. His morality was impugned, his honesty suspected, and even his orthodoxy aspersed; but the natives and army ridiculed the mean artifices of the despot, and secretly sided with their oppressed and persecuted Primate. Theodore was fully aware of the odium he had incurred by his relentless severity towards the bishop. This, however, only intensified his resentment, and he was determined to continue the contest till the successor of Fromentius cried *peccavi*, and proclaimed every act and deed he had perpetrated, whether in his private or public conduct, whether in despoiling provinces or robbing churches, as proceedings sanctioned by the Church, and in conformity with ecclesiastical canons. To effect this, he suborned witnesses, invented trumpery charges; nay, even attacked the honour of the partner who, during her short and stormy life, had severed every tie of kindred and home to screen and to guard the unworthy object she had unfortunately clasped to her affectionate heart. My well-known intimacy with the bishop led him to believe that the terror of his wrath would frighten his white captive, and induce him to confirm some infamous charges against the man he esteemed. My positive refusal to share in the royal plot I felt sure would involve me in further troubles; but, confiding in the guardian care of Him who is the refuge of the oppressed, I cheerfully said to my companions in misery, "I have hardly eluded the shafts of the angel of death, when I must prepare for foot-chains." No one, I believe, had the remotest idea of what was impending. All conjectured that the king would be angry, and that probably his passion would evaporate in threats and vile abuse.

About sunset his Majesty came galloping over the plain, and, bounding up to his pavilion, he asked some questions, and then there was a sound like the rush of a mighty torrent that had suddenly burst its pent-up limits, and was rolling on in unchecked impetuosity over the ruin and desolation created by its onward progress. M. Bardel, who was outside the tent, explained the cause of the commotion in the brief sentence, "The king is coming." "Dog! Falasha! scoundrel! tell me the name of the man who reviled my ancestors!" shouted the enraged tyrant, "or I'll tear the secret out of your 'hailanya'" (stout heart). I attempted to reiterate what I had said to the delegates in the afternoon; but, ere I could finish a sentence, I was blinded with buffets; whilst, at the same time, several fellows violently seized me by the hand, and began to twist around my arms hard, coarse ropes, formed of the fibres of the Doloussa tree. Rosenthal, simultaneously with myself, experienced a similar treatment. His poor wife, thinking that our last moments had come, distractedly ran into the arms of Captain Cameron. The latter, who also believed that all were about to be butchered, called out to me, "Stern, we shall soon be in heaven!" This exclamation the savage king quickly interpreted into an exhortation that I should not compromise the prelate; and, as if glad of a pretext, Mrs. Rosenthal, under a shower of blows, was driven with her babe into our tent, and then into her own, whilst all the other prisoners, with the exception of Mr. Kerans, who was suffering from a dreaded disease, were thrown on the ground and pinioned.

Generally, criminals under torture are only tied around the upper part of the arm, but the white miscreants were deemed malefactors unworthy of such leniency. From the shoulder down to the wrists the cords were rolled fiendishly tight around the unresisting limbs. This being still regarded as insufficient, the swollen, throbbing hands were bound together behind the back, and then other ropes were fastened across the chest, and that, too, with a force that made one gasp for breath. Writhing and quivering in every nerve, we lay in agony on the hard, bare ground. Some prayed; others groaned; here one, in excruciating torments, rolled about; there another, in desperate frenzy, knocked his reclining head on a loose stone, as if determined to end by suicide his career of suffering. The crescent moon, shining through a white canopy of clouds; the stillness of the guards, broken by the howling of savage dogs as they careered in quest of prey through the camp; and the moans and sighs of the tortured, formed a scene that beggars language to describe. His Majesty, immediately on the application of the ropes, quitted the spot, and repaired to his tent. Samuel, his face concealed under a black hood, every few minutes made his appearance, and inquired whether I would confess, and on not receiving a satisfactory reply, whispered to the guards, "Give him another rope round the chest." Three times he repeated his visits, and three times a couple of soldiers jumped on me, and with ardent delight, as if they felt pleasure in torturing a white man, executed the royal command. To contract the bark ligaments, the executioners now and then poured a profusion of cold water down our insensible backs. "Speak!" once more repeated the muffled royal messenger; a command which Captain Cameron seconded by shouting, "Stern, Stern, say what you know!"

The maddening torture had now lasted about three-quarters of an hour, and still there was no sign that the tyrant would relent in his cruelty. Physically and mentally prostrated, the hand of faith in the birth hour of eternity held confidingly on the Eternal Rock, and prayerfully sighed for release from these earthly pangs and woes. The Negoos, probably suspecting that we should succumb beneath a protracted torture, and so elude the clutches of further revenge, ordered the ropes to be removed. Promptly, a score of black hangmen were bending over us and unfastening the cords. This process caused excruciating pains, for the hard bark ligaments rebounding from the stiff, marble limbs, tore away skin and flesh in broad gory shreds.

Infidelity, scepticism, sneers, and scoffs, were now all merged in one deep and pathetic cry of anguish, fear, and despair. In compliance with the requests of my fellow-sufferers, I poured forth the despair of our hearts to Him who "heareth the sighing of the prisoners, and delivereth those that are appointed to die." Our guards, who, on the approach of the king, scowled on us like fiends, now, in a most sympathetic spirit, so characteristic of the transient emotions of the barbarian and savage, rendered us every aid in their power. My own "kuranyee," the man to whom I was chained, a kind Galla from Enarea, arranged the pallet on which I slept, and also gently swathed my wounded arms in the soft folds of the shama.

A harassing and anxious night was followed by a cheerless and desponding morning. Nervously we anticipated some new harrowing message from the king; but, to our delight, he rode out, and the forenoon wore away in silence and stoical apathy. Towards noon, the chief of our guards came into our prison, and, after some desultory remarks, urged me to satisfy his Majesty. "Tell those who sent you," I returned, "that I have spoken the truth; and if the king does not believe me, I can swear on this book"*—the Bible, which I raised aloft on my palsied and swollen hand—"that the bishop never spoke to me about his descent." "Well," was the laconic retort, "you will all get ropes again, and that, too, much severer than last night." Uncertain about our fate, moments, minutes, and hours passed away in torturing suspense. Near evening, Samuel, that messenger of evil, again obtruded his hated person upon us. He crouched down near Consul Cameron, and with the utmost assiduity tended his

---

* It did not then occur to me that the only binding obligation in Abyssinia is an oath "by the death of the king," or the excommunication of the Aboon.

wounds. His affability and condescension emboldened me to ask him why the Negoos, after granting me a full pardon, again revived the old affair. A withering scowl gathered over his brow at these words, and, as if panting for breath, he glared at me a few seconds, and then poured forth a volley of frightful abuse. "Dog! Falasha! Villain!" &c., "how dare you criticise the king's actions, and defy his authority? Look here, and behold the sufferings you have inflicted on your brethren. This is poor M. Bardel; and do you know who lies here?" (pointing to the consul). "This is Victoria." Shattered and prostrate as I was, my whole frame shook and trembled at this unmerited rebuke. Samuel, I think, noticed this, and, bending down to me, he whispered confidentially, "Come out; I want to speak to you." Once in the open air, the raging courtier subsided into the smooth, flattering knave. Placing his hand affectionately on my aching shoulder, he said, "Don't think that I am angry with you; on the contrary, I admire you; but what possesses you that, for the sake of the bishop, who is neither your countryman nor of your belief, you incur the wrath of the king, and expose your person to suffering? He is my Aboon (he forgot that he had often told me he was a Protestant), but you are my friend; and I don't care what happens to him if you only (whose money I have eaten), by obliging the Negoos, win honour and favours." I shook my head; and the foiled inquisitor hastened away, muttering no very charitable benison on my devoted head.

The shades of night had by this time gathered dark and thick around us. The guards took their station, and the white prisoners, after committing themselves to the guardian care of a Divine Protector, composed themselves to uneasy slumbers. The sudden whisper of voices, and the sound of approaching steps, made us start from our leather skins. "Cocab! Rosenthal! Makerer!" roared several voices at once. Leaping mechanically on our feet, we were in an instant out of the tent. Several dark figures in a trice encompassed me, and with ruthless fury dashed their horny hands in my eyes and face. Blow after blow, in quick succession, descended stunningly upon me, whilst at the same time the ropes were rapidly rolled around my wounded and lacerated arms. "Tie his legs, too, if he does not confess,"* rang in deep but distinct accents from the royal pavilion, and was re-echoed from the lungs of three other beings, who stood at measured distances to send back my reply. My eyes, dimmed by buffets, started almost out of their sockets; my veins began to swell, and throbbed as if they would

---

* This fiendish device, which entirely arrests the circulation of the blood, few persons can long resist without succumbing.

burst; and my heart, compressed by the inhuman tightness of the cords, almost stopped its pulsations. Despairingly I raised my inflamed eyes towards heaven, and prayed that the bitter cup might either pass away from me, or, if I was to drain it to the dregs, that the agony might not be protracted. In less than five minutes my head became dizzy, my eyes dim, and my mind confused, bewildered, and mad. "Samuel, Samuel!" I shrieked, in frenzied agony, "what do you want? what do you want?" "Tell Janehoi all you have been told by the Aboon," was his calm response. "Oh! my God! my God!" I mentally ejaculated, "have I still longer to endure this wasting martyrdom?" and, seized by a fit of delirium, I vociferated in a hoarse, suffocating voice, "Yes! the Aboon often told me that the king was more dreaded and possessed more power than any of the former sovereigns of Ethiopia, but that his ambition and cruelty had depopulated the country." "Untie his ropes!" commanded a clear and distinct voice, that rang appallingly far above the cooling breeze, as it swept in refreshing gusts over the torn and bleeding limbs of the sufferer; "untie his ropes, and ask him if he is not a merchant of insects." *

I hesitated to affirm this palpable falsehood; but

* I had a large collection of insects, which shared the same fate as all my other property.

Samuel, with clenched teeth, muttered, "Dog! do you want a fresh trial of the ropes?" Again roared from a succession of voices, accompanied by a slap in my bleeding face from the chief gaoler, "Ask him whether ladies in England do not eat rabbits and mice." Promptly my interrogator, who evidently now pitied me, responded "Yes." "Ask him whether the Queen of England does not sell thread, needles, and tobacco at Massowah?" returned the dismal echo; and before the sound had died away, there was a wild, merry shout, accompanied by the gay chuckle of some of the royal ladies. "Ask him whether it is lawful for an Aboon to commit ——." Frantic, and almost raving, I vehemently roared out, "No, no!" The ropes were now entirely removed from me, and also from Mr. Rosenthal, whom, contrary to orders, the guards, in the exuberance of their zeal, had also tied; and poor M. Makerer was questioned about certain language insidious malice reported that he had uttered at Massowah. Elated with his success, although it must have been obvious to every rational being that I could not for days and days be the guest of the Primate without conversing on the pillage of different provinces, among which Genda, the domain of the Metropolitan, formed no exception; yet, as he had extorted a reluctant confession, harmless as it was, the triumph afforded him satisfaction, and a liberal supper of bread, hydromel, and arackee was promptly ordered for his wretched victims. Supported by two executioners, I tottered back into the tent, where I sank, more dead than alive, on my painful couch. Immediately on my entrance, Consul Cameron, in that perfect absence of mind by which all the events of the outer world are excluded, abruptly called across the tent, "Stern, throw me over the tobacco pouch." And he might have added, "a star, or the crescent moon, to light the pipe;" for the one would have been as possible for me as the other.

Samuel, accompanied by a Galla slave, charged with a formidable horn of potent arackee, in less than half an hour's interval, stumbled into our tent. His looks, gait, and tongue betrayed that he was already elated, and that probably before long he would be altogether in a state of alcoholic ecstasy.

Our prison at that moment presented a sight Pandemonium alone could have equalled. There, guarded by a band of dark savages, and chained like untamed wild beasts, were huddled together in a wretched tent a party of white captives, in whose forlorn looks, sorrow and suffering, trouble and care, had written their indelible lines. In the centre of their frail tenement squatted several ragged savages around a flickering, unsteady taper, with their dilated eyes wistfully directed to the operations of a smooth-faced Galla lad, who was pouring out of a gigantic horn a strong-smelling liquid. A grinning figure, girded to the waist, received the cup, and handed it, bowing obsequiously, to the criminals, who, with formal etiquette, quaffed the potent draught. The agonising groans of some, as with their tortured arms they forcibly raised the proffered cup to their feverish lips, and the boisterous shouts of others, as in "Rule Britannia," and "Cheer boys, cheer," they sought to drown reflection and sorrow, imparted to the *tout ensemble* an aspect no language can depict or pencil portray. As I was unable to move, Samuel, with great tenderness, held the cup to my parched lips, and in sympathetic tones said, "Drink, if only a few drops, to evince your regard for the king." Covered with bruises, sores, and scars, I did not know how to lie or sit without enduring the most excruciating tortures. Some one proposed that we should take opium, and thus elude the tyranny of the despot, and close our career of misery. My giddy and whirling brain rapturously caught the suggestion, and had my fingers been able to perform their wonted functions, I should, unless a gracious Providence had restrained me, have opened my small basket, and partaken, in the frenzy of the moment, with some or all of my fellow-sufferers of the fatal drug. Mrs. Rosenthal had a similar craving for laudanum, and, as she afterwards told me, she considered it quite a mercy that the dangerous phial was not within her reach, as in the complete prostration of mind and body she might have terminated her own and her poor babe's troublesome existence. The horn was gradually drained, the voices of the singers hushed, and the ghastly visions of executioners and ropes shut out from our view in a dreamy, unrefreshing slumber.

At dawn the sinister visage of Samuel reappeared at the door of our tent. "Cocab," he commenced, in a hollow, sepulchral voice, to which the previous night's debauch, more than the message of evil he was about to deliver, lent a fearful solemnity— "Cocab, his Majesty knows that you are not afraid to die, but don't think that he intends to kill you; on the contrary, he will preserve your life, and torture you till the flesh rots on your bones. That this," continued the truculent delegate, "is not a vague threat, the last two nights, and many similar ones still in reserve, will prove. Do, therefore, satisfy the Negoos, or, by ——, those ropes will soon extort by force what you now deny as a favour." The sight of the torturing instruments, which lay in a heap in the corner of our tent, caused a dizziness in my head, and, raising my racking frame, I said: "Samuel, I told you last night my conversation with the bishop, and if that does not satisfy you, God's will be done. I won't tell a lie." The implacable inquisitor, touched by my sufferings, paused a moment, and then resumed once more: " Let us admit that the bishop did not furnish you with the false account of his Majesty's lineage; still, as he has proofs, you will never persuade him that the statement did not emanate from some of his priests or domestics." I now remembered that one of the Aboon's shums, who was then safe from the myrmidons of tyranny, had, many a time in the presence of strangers, given me episodes out of the Negoos' singular history, which evil tongues might have perverted to effect their own nefarious designs. I said, "Yes, Gebra Egziabcher often spoke to me about the exploits of the king, and at my request also gave me a few details about his birth and education; but never did he utter a word derogatory to his Majesty, for he knew that in Egypt and in Europe, where he had been, a man was respected on account of his actions, and not on account of his origin." "I will report this to the Negoos," was his laconic reply. Slowly the weary hours of terror and dread rolled on. Our nerves were horribly shattered, and our minds, too, would have been unhinged, had not religion, with her solacing influence, soothed the asperities and hardships of our existence. The Bible, prayers—a morning and evening exposition of an appropriate passage—were the exercises in which we regularly engaged. No bitter gibes, no harsh expression, no unbecoming word, characterised our intercourse; religion formed a wonderful bond of harmony, and when I looked on the devout countenances that then hung over the inspired page as I commented on the selected text, I cherished the pleasing hope that the clouds, so big with wrath, had been charged with showers of everlasting mercy.

Our affairs, to our infinite satisfaction, suddenly ceased to occupy the royal mind, and few incidents occurred to interrupt our sad tranquillity. One afternoon there was a suppressed cry : " The king ! the king !" which caused quite a panic in our tent. His Majesty, accompanied by a shield-bearer, it is true, had strayed into our prison premises, but for what purpose remains a mystery to this day. On another occasion Basha Engeda, on the guards being changed, pointed me out as a special object of interest, a distinction I did not much appreciate.

On the 24th of June, 1864, twenty-two days after our torture, and the Aboon's confinement, his Majesty, moved by unmistakable symptoms of dissatisfaction in the army and church, after a long consultation with his great chiefs, sought to regain the primate's friendship, which he had so scornfully spurned. The latter, wounded in his pride, honour, and dignity, refused to receive the messages which were conveyed to his guarded domicile. " Go and tell the king," were his orders to the long lines of turbaned priests, "that I am not afraid of his anger, nor solicitous to win his favours. He has been cruel to me and tyrannical to the church * entrusted to my charge, but God will judge between us. These words you will report to him verbatim; and if you come back with a troop of executioners I shall bless you; but if, on the contrary, you bore me with audacious proffers of reconciliation, I shall excommunicate you." The frightened ecclesiastics hastened back to the royal council, which was assembled in the open air not far from our canvas prison, to report their unsuccessful negotiation. There was some bustle and commotion. The king was indignant, the chiefs sad, and the priests alarmed. Once more the priestly procession, under a pouring torrent, moved up the hill close to the Islam Beit, where the Aboon had his quarters. A few brief sentences were only interchanged, and then the white bands, thoroughly drenched, which gave them a most ludicrous and undignified appearance, retraced their steps to the al fresco parliament. "Back again to the Aboon," rejoined the impatient monarch, to the cold shivering ecclesiastics, "and tell him that I deplore our misunderstanding, which never would have taken place, had I not for nearly

* The bishop referred to the sequestration of ecclesiastical property.

a month been continually drunk." Such an apology from a man like Theodore, even an Aboona Salama could not refuse to accept, and to our delight the occupant of the episcopal chair in a few minutes more was seen on his white mule threading his steps down the hill towards the camp, where, amidst the prostration of delighted hosts, the king and his nobility most meekly and penitently received him. This hollow and insincere peace between the Negoos and Primate gave rise to various conjectures among the prisoners. One evening a young lad in the service of the consul, who, together with other servants, had again returned to his master, crept down near me, and adroitly conveyed a small piece of paper into my dead and feelingless hand. I hastily put it into my Bible, thinking it was a letter from a European—a mistake which the Arabic character soon exposed. The note was from the bishop, and commenced: "To my brother in Christ, servant of the apostles and prophets," &c. &c. It then adverted to the sufferings all, and especially myself, had endured on his account; and quoting certain appropriate passages of Scripture, it concluded abruptly with a remark about money. By the dim glimmer of the guard's light, it occurred to me that the Aboon expected that ere long I should have to endure a fresh ordeal of the Negoos' retributive vengeance, and that, doubtful about the issue, he wanted me to send him an order for the money I owed him. This warning, for such my warped imagination fancied it to be, gave me a momentary shock, and grasping the ill-boding missive between my numbed fingers, I held it clandestinely to the light, and to my satisfaction discovered that instead of an order for the money I had borrowed, it was a generous offer to advance me more. This incident, trifling as it may appear, inspired me and my fellow-captives with a vague hope that the reconciliation between the Negoos and the Aboon would effect an improvement in our position—an anticipation which might, perhaps, have been realised had the susceptible monarch's offended pride been appeased by the timely arrival of the long-expected despatch from England.

CHAPTER VIII.

Winter—Unsheltered Prison—Foot Chains—Religion subdues the Temper—Prison Diet—Small-pox and Famine—Exchange of Fetters—An unhappy Couple—March of the Army—Revolting Sights—New Prison Ground—Deluging Torrents—Prison Rations—Cruelty to Prisoners—Gondar—Exorbitant Fines—Designs of the new Metropolis—A partial Amnesty—Festive Day—Exhausting March—A Wet Night—Advance to Ferga—Consul Cameron and M. Makerer—Remedy against Stoicism—Better Diet—Alcoholic Influence—Promised Release—Artful Rumour—Resignation—Departure to Magdala.

"KEREMT," or winter, as the rainy season is emphatically designated, was now rapidly approaching. Almost every noon the sky became darkened, and lowering clouds, amidst the reverberations of the thunder, poured down deluging floods. Our frail cotton tent, which had already for more than four months resisted the wear and tear of guards and prisoners, sun and wind, notwithstanding the skilful patching of Pietro and Makerer freely admitted the pelting torrent. During the day the horrors of the tempest were still mitigated by the scanty coverings in which each could muffle his shivering frame; but by night, when wedged between suspicious guards, who tremblingly rose at the slightest clang of the heavy chains, one was forced patiently to press the inundated couch. The king twice or thrice in riding out, gave a musing glance across our fence, which led us to anticipate that our wretched apology for a shelter would soon be exchanged for some more substantial covering—an expectation that was never destined to be realised. Condemned to wet and filth, our misery was intensified by the foul aroma of the coarse guards, who in crowds obtruded their offensive persons upon us. Goaded to desperation, we sent one afternoon to Samuel, and requested him to regulate the watch. Samuel mentioned it to the king, and the reply was, "If they don't like to come in contact with my people, give them foot-chains, and let only two soldiers watch in the tent." This unexpected infliction of fresh suffering gave us an unmistakable cue to his Majesty's sentiments towards us; but, without allowing such an ebullition of hatred to depress our spirits, we determined henceforth passively to endure every hardship that might still fall to our lot.

Bad food, heavy fetters, together with the troubles to which we were continually subject, did not, strange as it may seem, impair our health; on the contrary, our appetite increased as provisions diminished; and I believe that, had not the spirit of religion prevailed amongst us, our millet cakes would more than once have been swallowed with a condiment even hotter than our peppery Abyssinian sauce.

Thus day after day was buried in the relentless womb of time, and still our position remained unimproved. Hope, that greatest blessing of man, almost ceased to irradiate the gloom of our captivity, and, in a state of apathy bordering on reckless indifference, the sun rose and set upon the isolated captives in wild Africa. Our mornings generally commenced with the dawn, when all, except the consul, who indulged in later hours, had a small tin of black, bitter coffee, and a piece of wheaten bread. About ten we had Divine worship, which consisted in reading the Psalms and a chapter out of the Old and New Testament, an exposition, and extemporary prayer. Mid-day, a dirty basket, containing five or six half-baked teff, or mashilla flaps, followed by a sooty saucepan, containing some boiled lentiles, was brought into our tent. An ebony-coloured woman—a curious specimen of the Shankgalla race, formerly in the service of Consul Plowden—instantly bared her arm, and dashing it up to the wrist in the uninviting decoction, threw piece after piece of the soaked cakes into the basket, around which the prisoners, with becoming gravity, were squatted. Mystoura, the cook, a liberated Galla slave, occasionally varied the bill of fare, and we had sun-dried flesh, called quanto; or a very limited quantity of fresh meat, transformed into a stew; or, if she was in a very good humour, which could not have been very often the case, she sent us a mess of paste, a wretched imitation of macaroni. Consul Cameron fared somewhat more luxuriously, and Mr. and Mrs. Rosenthal dined in private, in a small tent that was assigned them as a special favour. Towards sunset we again had prayers, and then a second sumptuous repast, after which each one tried to woo sleep to his eyes. The king, to our infinite satisfaction, no longer took any notice of us; and, had it not been for the annoyances of the insufferable tabaguees, our life of misery would have flowed on in an even, uniform course.

That terrible scourge, the small-pox, which had already for more than six weeks ravaged the camp, in the absence of every precaution to arrest its progress, spread with increased virulence through the crowded lines of tents, hurrying promiscuously men, women, and children to an untimely grave. An incipient famine accelerated its devastations, and multiplied the funeral processions, which, amidst the melancholy chants of priests, and the wail of mourners, everywhere traversed the gloomy camp. His Majesty, to dissipate the panic which prevailed through the thinning ranks of the army, interdicted the usual lamentations for the dead; but the voice of nature could not be stifled by royal edicts, so that, in defiance of the whip and stick, the shriek and lament of the bereaved rang day and night in wild cadences over hill and dale. Prompted by sanitary motives, on July 5th the camp was removed to Assasso, about three miles west-south-west from Gondar. To our surprise, we received no official intimation that we were to change our abode, and it was quite a relief to our eyes to gaze on the stockaded acclivity above our prison without dread of beholding the despot or his myrmidons. On the 6th, towards evening, Basha Tecka, the commander of the fusiliers, paid us a visit, and ordered our foot-chains to be removed for hand-chains. The operation of unriveting the massive irons required the efforts of eight powerful savages, and even these had to exert all their strength to accomplish the feat. We were immediately linked together in pairs, by shackles fastened around the wrists. The wonted insolence of the conceited Ethiop, which had been often enough exhibited towards us, was on the present occasion not omitted; and many a vile sarcasm was, during the hammering of the irons, expended on the defenceless white prisoners. On the following morning, a formidable guard came to escort us to the camp. Consul Cameron and myself, who, at our own request, were chained together for the ride, formed the most unhappy pair. Enervated by suffering and sickness, I was in no condition to manage the young and untamed mule which I received orders to mount; nor was my companion, whose nerves and mind were dreadfully shaken, better fitted for the novel exercise.

Seizing the restive animal by his clumsy bridle, I vaulted into the saddle, and, with my unfettered hand, sought to adjust my shama, when Consul Cameron, unmindful of his black Arab cloak and European cap, moved in front. The unruly animal instantly commenced his mad pranks, and, ere I could firmly grasp the crupper, I was dragged sideways by the short chain, and fell bleeding on the hard ground. We now, in opposition to the imperative commands of our guards, determined to accomplish the journey on foot, but a boisterous "min abadu" ("who is their father") obliged us to desist from our resolution. The road for a short distance led across a stony, undulating tract, and then gradually declined into a rich pasture land, intersected by numerous streamlets and torrents, where every step was difficult and dangerous. Notwithstanding my accident, we jogged on tolerably well; nay, had not Consul Cameron frequently become oblivious of the present, and allowed his mule to make a circuit around the head of his neighbour, the trip might have proved beneficial to our depressed spirits.

The rabble camp, which, at rest, had still a martial aspect, *en route* presented a picture of ragged confusion that baffled all description. Horse and foot soldiers, great ladies on gaily-caparisoned mules, and greasy, unwashed servants, groaning under monstrous burdens of pots, pans, pipkins, leather bags, and other household utensils, struggled along pell-mell between droves of beeves, bands of prisoners, and swarms of loathsome beggars. Here a young lad, famished and exhausted, had sunk on the grassy bank of a streamlet, where, denuded of every rag, his inhuman master or parent abandoned him to languish and die. There another little creature, fleshless and emaciated, lay roasting in the hot sun, covered with flies and insects, without any other sign of life except a few audible gasps for breath, which showed that, even in the hour of release, it still strove to protract its wretchedness and misery. A few steps further reclined a young woman, in whose vacant stare, quivering lips, and shrunken limbs, hunger and destitution had written lines which unerringly indicated that her sufferings were drawing to a close. Such and similar objects of horror, besides the maimed, blind, and leprous, everywhere shocked the sight, and forcibly recalled the words of Sacred Writ: "The dark places of the earth are full of the habitations of cruelty."

On arriving in the camp, we were conducted up a rugged ascent, on the summit of which, exposed to the cool and refreshing breeze, stood the royal tents. A strong palisaded enclosure prevented any encroachment on this forbidden ground. We were commanded to alight close to the rigorously-guarded entrance, where, together with distrusted peasants, thieves, murderers, and other criminals, we had to await the mandate for our location. At last the order came that we were to march to the part of the camp occupied by the chief of the fusiliers. Ever since the imprisonment of the consul we had always a spot for our tent within the royal fence; but as each indignity to the detested "Frendjoj" was supposed to enhance the glory of the despot and the lustre of his name, we were no longer deemed worthy to enjoy the not very enviable distinction conferred on the more exalted native offenders. Our fragile prison, which the journey had not improved, was at last, with difficulties that appeared almost insurmountable, lashed to the pole, and then, to secure this unsafe abode, an impassable fence was raised around it. All the other prisoners, above three hundred in number, among whom were not a few who had more to deplore the caprice of the law than the perpetration of crime, were shut up in an enclosure separated from our own by a thin acacia partition.

Black masses of clouds, which for hours had been hanging on the eastern horizon, as if waiting till we were housed, now began to discharge their deluging contents. Our unfortunate tenement, instead of affording any protection against the rattling rain and hail, mockingly collected the cold water into the bag-shaped tatters, ere it came in

KING THEODORE'S HOUSE AT MAGDALA.

torrents on our careworn heads. Indifferent to the mad fury of the elements, we lighted our pipes, and, in a stoical attitude, watched the efforts of the tabaguees to preserve the royal property from being swept away by the hurricane. The shades of night had by this time fallen thick and dark around us, and still our usual ration of twenty millet cakes had not made its appearance. Happily, we had some flour, and this, boiled in water and garnished with a small quantity of rancid butter and hot pepper, formed a most grateful repast. The next day the Purveyor-General sent us about nine pints of dried peas, and upon our manifesting some reluctance to accept this niggardly pittance, we were told that if we refused what was offered we might starve.

No funds, no provisions, in the midst of a tropical winter and an unfeeling race, were matters that made us a little anxious about the future. In this emergency, I applied to our constant friend, the bishop; and, to our delight, he sent me forty dollars, nearly all the ready cash at his disposal. The misery, want, and abject despair of our neighbours in the uncovered enclosure reconciled us—nay, diffused a feeling of contentment and gratitude over our wretched home. Reduced to hapless destitution, and maddened by gnawing famine, these forlorn victims of arbitrary power and uncurbed passions, from evening till morning, by their shrieks and funereal dirges, rendered abortive every attempt to get a few hours' sleep. The brutal guards every few minutes energetically wielded their clubs and sticks to suppress the moans and cries that made the very hills and cliffs plaintive of pain; but their violence only intensified the agonies that sought relief in peals of anguish and despair. Three, four, and even more succumbed every night to their hard fate, without a ministering hand to assuage the fire of their fevered lips, or to alleviate the pangs of dissolution. Hardened and steeled to human sorrows and woes, the savage soldiers, jocund and jeering, moved amidst these appalling scenes, where hunger, torture, and death reigned with undisputed sway. Our proximity to this abode of horror had a deadening effect on our feelings; and the sufferings of others soon became merged in consideration of the doom in which we were ourselves involved. Providentially, nothing occurred to excite our fears beyond a few imaginary alarms, exaggerated by a morbid imagination. On August the 19th, 1864, we heard that the long-expected letter from her Majesty had at length arrived, and that the Negoos had sent for the Europeans at Gaffat; then again we were told that the order had been countermanded; and again that they were on the road. These contradictory rumours were not quite unfounded. A letter, it is true, had arrived from the coast, but it was not the document that the king expected, and the Gaffat *employés* had also been requested to come to the camp and settle our affairs; but the vacillating tyrant, probably at the instigation of Samuel, once more abandoned his generous designs.

Gondar, the capital of Abyssinia, owing to its sympathies with rebels, never enjoyed the particular graces of the monarch. The population, confiding in the number of their churches and the wealth of its merchants, quaffed their hydromel and indulged their vicious passions in heedless security. Their fatal dream of undisturbed repose was, however, destined to experience a grievous reverse. A complaint that the bread and mead provided by this town was bad in quality and limited in quantity, afforded the despot a favourable opportunity to satisfy his long-cherished hatred. An exorbitant fine was immediately imposed on the mistaken inhabitants, and on making a slight opposition to this ruinous demand, the whip and rope were energetically used to enforce compliance. Despoiled and pillaged, the wretched populace deceived themselves with the illusive hope that the heaviest calamity was past; but they had not yet sounded the depth of their sovereign's vengeance, and only felt its full weight when they saw their homes on fire and consumed by the devouring flames. The old metropolis, with the exception of the churches, being reduced to ashes, his Majesty, to perpetuate his Neronian achievement, proclaimed Assasso the new capital of the empire. To outdo his predecessors, all sorts of grand plans were projected to embellish the royal city. Churches, palaces, workshops, and gardens, vying with each other in matchless splendour, had already been assigned their appropriate spots. These imaginary schemes occupied the dull brains of the whole army, and led every one to believe that the camp would remain stationary for many months to come. Surrounded by everything revolting, we still preferred our offensive prison to travelling in chains.

About the beginning of September, 1864, the visions of a new capital, which had for some time delighted the ragged hordes, was abandoned, and the camp removed to Mansaroh. It was now universally supposed that the Negoos would proceed to Debra Tabor, the abode of the white *employés;* but, without harassing our minds with probable contingencies, or borrowing troubles and anxieties from the future, we acted on the Scripture rule, and patiently endured the present hardships, of which we had more than enough each successive day.

Nearly the whole army had already quitted Assasso, and still we and our native companions in prison were left in the quiet possession of our respective enclosures. Winter, that trying season to the free, and emphatically so to the captive, had by this time yielded to the more genial influence of spring. Pasture and meadow, hill and dale, hedges and trees—in fact, all nature, clad in smiling green, looked happy and cheerful; only the abodes of the ill-treated objects of King Theodore's wrath were shrouded in desolation and gloom. As the days rolled on and the new year advanced, hope once more began to shed her radiating beams over our charnel-house. The 9th of September,* an auspicious and welcome day to captives, at last broke upon us, cloudless and serene. Early on that benign morn an unqualified amnesty arrived for all prisoners except those stained with the crime of blood. We expected that in this general jubilee the white prisoners would not be forgotten; but morning and noon passed, and still the heavy manacles hung around our aching ankles. Towards evening a division of the rabble hosts, who form the boasted army of the Great King, assembled on the declivity of a hill opposite our prison, and, amidst wild war whoops and a *feu-de-joie*, saluted the new year.

The next day was spent in feasting and gluttony. Beeves plundered from helpless peasants, and mead brewed by kidnapped slaves, were the luxuries in which chiefs and their retainers rioted to excess. On the

* The beginning of the Abyssinian year.

morning succeeding the saturnalia, we were informed that the king had ordered the plundered arms and other property belonging to the white prisoners to be collected, and that after their restoration we should be set at liberty, and allowed to leave the country. Frequent disappointments had taught us not to place any trust in reports, which, in the end, only mocked our patience and fortitude. The few detachments of the army which still remained at Assasso day after day took their road to Mansaroh, till the late camping-ground, a short time before so animated by the hum of troops and the glitter of bristling lances, was almost utterly deserted. On the 17th of September, the imperial blacksmith, accompanied by a score of menials, came to relieve us of our foot-irons. As we were to start the same forenoon, celerity was indispensable; and the important functionary, assisted by his servile subordinates, manipulated most dexterously the chains on our legs and arms.

Shackled in couples around the wrists, and guarded by a band of armed fusiliers, we were now led out of the narrow enclosure in which we had been closely confined for more than two months. The king, more intent on torturing than on destroying the hated and envied "Frendjoj," had given orders that we should be provided with mules; but the escort being well aware that prisoners are not objects of much consideration, did not feel quite disposed to comply with this high behest. The ride from Gondar to Assasso had not increased our relish for bestriding a mule in fetters; and at my suggestion, all, except Mrs. Rosenthal, who had a baby in her arms, consented to try the strength of their legs. The soldiers highly approved of this resolution; and after Mrs. Rosenthal was mounted, we set forward in a placid if not cheerful humour. Some minutes' walk brought us to a precipice, at whose foot extended far and wide the fertile plain of Dembea. Like children freed from the restraint of the school-room, we leaped and scrambled over dislocated pieces of rock and loose gravelly paths with a recklessness that inspired our tabaguees with the dread that these mad pranks were only artful tricks to cover a secret design to effect a sudden escape. Once in the plain, these terrors were dispelled; and, marshalled between a detachment of troops, we were driven along more like wild beasts than the innocent victims of a rancorous despot. For about two hours we kept up a brisk march, and then our feet began to get sore, and one couple after another slackened their pace. Consul Cameron, supported by the sinewy arms of Makerer, to whom he was linked, was the first who declared himself knocked up and unable to move further. A kind soldier—a perfect curiosity in this land of heartless selfishness—generously offered him his mule to mount, a favour which was gratefully accepted. I felt much disposed to imitate my fellow-prisoner, but as good Samaritans do not abound in Abyssinia, I tried with lively converse to invigorate my wearied and trembling limbs. The plain, clothed in the most variegated vegetation of the tropics, and dotted with copses and brushwood, around which the dog-rose, eglantine, honeysuckle, and an endless variety of convolvuli had woven festoons that defied the skill of the florist, afforded ample materials for mutual converse. Our old friend, Makerer, a soldier by profession, a hunter of the elephant by accident, and now a prisoner by a combination of untoward circumstances, to the surprise of all became suddenly transformed into an amateur botanist and scientific farmer. His chief theme was indigo—a topic on which he grew so eloquent and enthusiastic, that at last all grasses, herbs, and shrubs were one great field of this favourite plant. A drizzling rain and the more rapid strides of Consul Cameron's mule, separated us from our voluble companion, and M. Bardel and myself, guarded by half-a-dozen soldiers, pursued alone our toilsome journey. Luckily, our escort pitied my worn-out state, and allowed us to halt every few minutes, a favour which was not so prodigally extended to our friends in advance. On nearing the camp I exerted all my energies to accomplish the short distance that still lay before us, but my eyes waxed dim, my legs began to tremble, my heart violently palpitated, and I sank repeatedly, faint and prostrate, on the wet grass. This was at the outskirts of the camp, and we had only about ten minutes more to the halting-place, yet even this short distance my aguish limbs refused to perform. The guards in advance anticipated our plight, and, what was a perfect wonder, actually brought us two mules to mount. I expected my companions would overwhelm me with showers of reproach, but excess of fatigue had closed their lips, and I only heard from two an ironical *sotto voce*, "Well, will you walk again?" Meanwhile, our tent arrived, and the tabaguees, anxious to be released, set to work to pitch it. This was no easy job, for the decayed and rotten tatters, too feeble to bear the strain of the ropes, blew away at every pull. By dint of perseverance it at last fluttered in the breeze more like a good old flag than anything worthy the name of a shelter. By accident, Bardel and myself, Kerans and Pietro, occupied the side which still could boast of a few hanging shreds, whilst Consul Cameron and Makerer literally had the earth for their bed, and the sky for their canopy. At midnight, a storm, accompanied by impetuous torrents of rain, burst upon us. The uneven, swelling plain formed, for a little while, a temporary barrier to the noisy floods, but the pitiless tempest ere long overstepped these natural boundaries, and muddy rivulets in tumultuous hurry careered over every part of the imperial camp. We tried to shelter ourselves under skins, but finding these efforts unavailing, we laid down in the rolling and splashing waters, and, what many may think incredible, enjoyed in this position a sound and refreshing sleep. Mr. Rosenthal's fragile tenement was almost entirely swept away by the unsparing nocturnal blasts; and, cold and shivering, he, his wife, and babe, sighed for the dawn of day. Fortunately they had some bed-clothing still left, the *débris* of their plundered property, and these, by patching and stitching, they succeeded in converting into a tolerable covering. We were too many, too poor, and too lazy to make a similar effort; in fact, had we possessed the material and inclination, we would not have improved the old or purchased a new tent, from the well-founded dread that it might attract around us crowds of tabaguees, whose proximity invariably caused us far more annoyance than wind or rain.

At Mansaroh we remained encamped ten days, and then proceeded to Ferga. We were now all mounted, and our progress would have been comfortable enough for prisoners, had not the intermittent spring showers converted the whole country into a vast bog, which made the poor mules splash, shake, and tumble at every step. Consul Cameron, about half way, had a serious and painful nervous attack. M. Makerer, ever intent on maintaining what, according to his peculiar ideas, he considered the honour and dignity of the Europeans, most persuasively entreated his master not to make a scene before the grinning natives. The consul, unwilling and unable to attend to this unsolicited advice, in a calm, indignant voice responded, "Mons. Makerer, vous êtes un âne." Although I deeply sympathised with my suffering fellow-prisoner, yet the manner, voice, and emphasis in which this sentence was uttered, made me involuntarily smile. A vast number of thorns and prickly bushes, distributed at regular intervals along the road, at every plunge of the mule in the heavy mire tore our naked feet and made the blood flow profusely; but, ah! the pain was insignificant compared to that withering despondency which wrung the heart and caused one impassionately to sigh for a resting-place beneath the grassy hillocks which rose, wavelike, wherever the eye gazed. Subject to coarse insults, and knocked about like a thing of nought by cowardly savages, an imperceptible antipathy to man stole upon the heart, and the mind continually required to keep before its vision the thorns, buffets, and cross of the Saviour, not to degenerate into a stoic or perfect misanthrope. A latent expectation that at Debra Tabor our cruel shackles would at least be unriveted, if we did not regain our complete freedom, sustained our exhausted strength. His Majesty, it was stated, had said, and the rumour was true, that on coming together with his European *employés* he would finish our business, and allow us either to leave the country or keep us at Gaffat. The capricious tyrant would this time have kept his word, had not *Mr. Samuel*, by crafty insinuations and positive lies (as we know for certain), neutralised his master's designs.

We remained at Ferga from September 24th to October 14th, and then again set forward. The journey from this to the capital of Begemeder took us fifteen days, of which only three were spent in actual travelling. On reaching Debra Tabor we expected that a messenger from Gaffat would meet us, but in vain we wistfully strained our eyes in all directions to discover the face of a known servant or the white countenance of a "Frendjoj." Probably the majority, if not all, would have gladly gone to see us had they not dreaded the cruel tyrant, whose proximity freezed, if it did not entirely damp and extinguish every feeling of sympathy towards those who had incurred his displeasure. As we did not obtain unsolicited intelligence from the Europeans who were located about two miles' walk from our resting-place, we sent one of our servants for that purpose to Mr. Flad. The messenger returned in the evening loaded with potatoes, bread, milk, and a small note, which contained the tantalising news that his Majesty, during the two or three conferences with the Gaffat white workmen, had always carefully avoided to allude to our affairs. Once during an interview, some one ventured to advert to our position, but the Negoos did not deign to notice his remark on that disagreeable topic. Several days of heartburning suspense had already elapsed, and still there was no other amelioration in our condition, beyond that we had an ample supply of wholesome food from Gaffat.

About the 29th of October we were informed that the king, deeply moved by the *potent hydromel* and arackee, or spirits, made by his foreign *employes*, had, in a fit of magnanimity, urged them to solicit any favour he could confer on them, and that if it was not his throne, crown, or wife, it should be granted, even if they should ask for the liberation of the white captives. Acting on a Scriptural precedent, they are said to have merely expressed their delight at enjoying the royal countenance and favour. Two evenings after, his Majesty again drained a good number of " berilles " of the Frendjoj's generous brew, and, once more exhilarated by the potent beverage, repeated the former request a little more urgently. This time they were more bold, and the opportune moment was seized to intercede in behalf of our freedom. The request was instantly granted, and all were to be released from their chains except the Frenchmen Bardel and Makerer.

This was about the beginning of November, 1864. On the 5th of the same month the cheering tidings were communicated to us that Cantiba Hailu, the late governor of Gondar, a man highly esteemed by the king and the European workmen, had received orders to proceed to the camp, and to conduct us and our French fellow-sufferers free to a new home in the vicinity of our countrymen. We were already in spirit revelling in the luxury of unshackled limbs, when at the very moment that we expected to hear the tramp of our liberators' mules, and to grasp their extended hands, one messenger followed by another came to announce that the humane intentions of his Majesty had been defeated by a report of Samuel, confirmed by Dejatch Barea, the governor of Tigré, that a British general and troops had landed at Massowah, and that another great man, whether French or English was not stated, had also arrived at Senaar, and that both publicly declared that they were determined to move towards Abyssinia, to effect our deliverance either by mediation or force of arms. This unexpected blight of our fond anticipations came upon us like a thunderclap, but the soul, when pressed down by a succession of calamities, either becomes callous and apathetic, or tries to obtain calmness and comfort for the troubled heart in prayer and the promises of the inspired page. This was the case with us. Tried, troubled, and almost worried to the last point of endurance, the mind would have become blunted had it not soared above the woes of life, and in the contemplation of the future sought an antidote against the oppressions and tyrannies of the present. Doubt and misgivings being now removed, we resigned ourselves to our fate, and, in listless indifference or childlike submission to an all-wise Protector, prayerfully awaited the solution of our complicated history. On November the 7th, I got a note from Mr. Flad, which contained the dreadful intelligence that we were next day to be escorted to Magdala, the penal settlement of the "Negoos Negest." During my first visit to this misgoverned country, I was nearly forced to see this uninviting Amba, in order to have an interview with the Aboona, then in disgrace; and although at that time I was free and buoyed up by the cheering prospect of initiating a promising mission in Central Africa, yet I blessed a gracious Providence who brought me in contact with the successor of Frumentius ere I had accomplished my first stage; and now my whole frame shuddered at the idea of a deportation in chains to that very rock which once, under the most auspicious circumstances, I had an invincible repugnance to approach. Mr. Flad, in his missive, laboured to soften the asperity of our destiny by predicting a speedy change; but we felt that, humanly speaking, our fate was sealed, and that only a higher power could and would deliver us out of the hands of a ruthless savage.

CHAPTER IX.

Jan Meeda—Unappreciated Scenery—Strange Companions—Warning Beacons—Descent into the Beshilo—A Feast of Air—Makerer in Trouble — Ascent to Magdala — Forewarning Symptoms—Amba Home—Change of Manacles—Precautionary Measures—Prisoners' Wives—Prison Life—New Dormitory—Limited Space—Nocturnal Squabbles—Sunny Visions Eclipsed—Theodore's Perfidy—Destructive Foray.

On the 8th we quitted Debra Tabor, the goal where we had confidently imagined that our manacles would be removed and our captivity come to an end. Our first place was Jan Meeda, the spot where the late Copt Patriarch, the ambassador of the Viceroy of Egypt, was incarcerated by the artful barbarian, whose smiles and suavity ought never to have duped a white man. Here Mr. Waldemaier, *en passant*, paid us a flying visit. He did not alight from his horse; and the noble steed, as it stood, neighing and stamping the ground outside the fence in which we were shut up, conjured up to our minds visions of freedom and liberty that made the irons burn like fire around the wrists. From this to Magdala is about a hundred and fifty miles, which a native can easily perform in five days; but although we were mounted, it still took seven days to traverse that distance. The mountains, valleys, and deep ravines clad in bright verdure, and exhaling at the slightest breath a balmy fragrance, would, under ordinary circumstances, have ravished the senses; but suffering had dimmed our sight, and thrown a funereal pall over these matchless scenes. Villages and hamlets we saw very few; the puissant King had, since his accession to the throne, changed the aspect of these lovely regions, and transformed plains and slopes, once the abode of comfort and plenty, into wilds and deserts where the lion, leopard, and hyena roam unscared. Our party, which, since the departure from Begemeder, had considerably increased, did not much tend to beguile the fatigue and toil of the route. About a dozen criminals, almost all of whom were in a state bordering on *in puris naturalibus*, with long, heavy, wooden forks around their necks, are not exactly the companions a European in Africa, even in the greatest emergency, would ever dream of being obliged to have for associates, much as he might pity their lot; but the mighty name of Britain, respected as it is through the known universe, constituted no palladium, even to a consul, in the lawless realm of the boasted descendant of Solomon. Our fellow-criminals, for such, whether justly or unjustly, they were "reputed to be," experienced even still harsher treatment than their white companions, and once, after halting, to our horror they had to form an acquaintance—only a slight acquaintance—with the torturing rope.

The Alpine ranges of the Wollo Galla, extending in fantastical and shapeless masses far beyond the verge of the horizon, grew more and more conspicuous on our approach to the flat-topped rock that was the limit of our journey. Blazing watch-fires, those primitive beacons to proclaim the advance of the foe, in eddying clouds rose high in the air, giving the whole scene the aspect of an active volcanic region. Descending 3,500 feet, we crossed the Beshilo, which, after its junction with the Djiddah about thirty miles further south, debouches into the Abai, or Blue Nile. From thence the road lay through a shady defile, flanked on both sides by lofty ranges, which shut out from view every object except the nebulous sky, which, in pity to the worn-out prisoners, tempered the flaming rays of a tropical sun. Gradually the road widened, and a chaos of gigantic piles, heaved up by a terrible convulsion, in majestic confusion stood out in bold relief towards the southern horizon. Threading along a succession of almost perpendicular ascents, we at last reached a broad, grassy terrace, sheltered by the refreshing gloom of Nature's mighty ramparts; and here, to our delight, we were ordered to dismount. Our servants, who had some provisions, not having yet arrived, we were reduced to feast on the pure air, which in fragrant gusts was wafted from the Galla heights across our camping-ground. Mrs. Rosenthal, who was more provident in her *ménage* than her neighbours, kindly sent us a tin of coffee, which, like the loving cup, circulated from hand to hand till it was drained to the very dregs. The following day we remained encamped, and then once more mounted our mules, to scale the steep sides of the lofty Amba. By oversight or design, the guards brought us only seven instead of nine mules, which caused a brief delay in our departure. Basha Sena—the commander of a thousand—a diminutive *café-au-lait* coloured Abyssinian snob, impatient to quaff the good old hydromel, which was profusely dispensed on the royal fortress, took umbrage at this detention, and, raising aloft his formidable stick, he rushed on the poor white prisoners, and dealt several heavy blows on the back of M. Makerer, who was accidentally the nearest. The mercurial temper of the old French soldier caught fire at this unprovoked violence, but the chain, and the many hundreds, nay thousands, of barbarians around us, reminded him that, under certain circumstances, discretion is valour; and so, pulling his companion fiercely along, he merely growled forth, in a voice hoarse with stifled passion: "If I die in this miserable country, I shall transmit the name of that villain to my brother!" Climbing about 1,000 feet more, we came to Salamige, a dell hemmed in to the west by a flat-topped rock, called Salasie; and another, opposite to the south-east, bearing the distinguished name of Amba Magdala. On this spot we found all the state prisoners, in number about two hundred, awaiting the royal mandate to proceed to their isolated Amba home. Placed between files of troops, clad in their holiday garbs, many a painful spasm shot through the heart on reflecting on the past, and in contemplating the future. A group of chiefs in their flaunting rainbow-coloured shirts now came running towards us, and instantly the whole party was in motion. Many a sinister, black visage was turned upon us, and many an ill-boding sentence was uttered against us, as we were driven through a narrow gap up into the dreaded fortress. That his Majesty had been bragging about his European captives, was evident from the deportment of the wild hordes; and this idea, which was uppermost in the minds of a few of us, did not tend to soothe the agony of the lacerated heart. Gasping and panting, we at length emerged out of a rude, strong gateway on the summit of the Amba. Again a short halt was ordered, and then once more all hurried forward, towards a collection of sugar-loafed huts—the dwellings of his Majesty's court. All, in a twinkle, lay prostrate in the dust; but the profound obeisance, instead of meeting a response, remained unnoticed amidst the boisterous shouts for arackee. The malefactors and their servile guards paused; but, as the Negoos indulged in his orgies, we were driven on to our lodging—the prison.

Exiled to an isolated rock, in the midst of a strange people, and in an inhospitable land, our position compelled us to banish all vain regrets in which sorrow loves to indulge. Impatience might have increased, but could not mitigate, our misery; and visions of a happy past would only have deepened, and not softened, the gloom of the terrible present. We were prisoners, and, with all the energy we could muster, we struggled against the troubles and difficulties of our sorrowful existence. The great object which, on nearing our Amba home, engaged our thoughts was the place where we should be confined. In the camp and on the march we had, if not a real tent, something of an apology for one; but now we were to be stationary, and the question naturally enough suggested itself to every one— "Where will be our home?" The common gaol, surrounded by a thorny fence, contained only two circular-shaped huts, and these, it was evident, would barely suffice to accommodate our two hundred fellow-prisoners, even if the fifty who occupied them on our arrival had their vainly-cherished hopes of liberation verified. Intently we watched the proceedings of the chiefs, who, in undeviating order, handed their important charge over to the Amba authorities. Rulers of provinces who had unsuccessfully fought for their independence took the precedence; next followed hereditary chiefs of districts; then obnoxious governors, suspected military commanders; and finally common rebels, thieves, murderers, and all sorts of rabble. The poor Frendjoj, as the lowest of the low, held by their chains, were last of all led through the rickety but well-guarded door. Lik Maquas Gedana Miriam, the commandant of the Amba, and a relation of the king,* gave us a contemptuous glance, on being consigned to his care, and then hurried off with all the great chiefs to announce to his drunken master that the prisoners were all landed, lodged, and safe in the gaol. It is said that there is no pleasure without an admixture of pain, and no sorrow without an ingredient of comfort. This experience taught us during our first night's residence in our new convict settlement. We were vexed and irritated that white men who had committed no offence should be condemned to herd with a lot of hardened native criminals in the cold open air. The account, however, which the

* In April, 1867, he was arrested, and died, fettered, in the royal camp at Debra Tabor.

occupants of the houses gave us next morning of their night's rest removed all soreness and heart-burning, and we were more than content to be ranked with the basest of King Theodore's subjects.

In the afternoon the royal blacksmiths and their assistants came to the gaol, and began their pleasant task of hammering on the foot chains, which on the journey had been removed. Some of the old prisoners on the Amba had fetters both around the wrists and the ankles, which made us fear that this double torture would also be inflicted on the new batch of convicts. Our apprehensions were groundless. His Majesty had not yet entirely thrown off all restraints, and become that merciless fiend into which he degenerated a few months later. He had still a great part of the country, and a large army, whose fidelity he was loth to forfeit by any wanton acts of cruelty towards chiefs who, though they were prisoners, had many powerful friends and numerous adherents. It is true he might have been indulgent towards the incarcerated aristocrat and severe towards the plebeian, but as this would have proved an odious and questionable distinction, all, indiscriminately of rank and crime, had the fetters wrenched off the wrists, and shackles fastened around the legs. The operation occupied three complete days, and even then the task would not have been accomplished, had not a band of volunteers aided the sweating royal blacksmiths.

The arackee and tedj in the royal cellars during this interval diminished considerably; and till the new brew was dry, to use the technical term, it was deemed advisable to chastise the turbulent Wollo Gallas, and to quell a formidable insurrection in Shoa.

It was on the morning of November 25th, 1864, that the army quitted the environs of Magdala. His Majesty started a few hours later. Immediately on his departure a herald proclaimed, close to the gaol, that no prisoner was to have more than one servant, and that all the rest were to quit the Amba without delay. This precaution was quite requisite to ensure the safety of the fortress. At Tschelga, where all the great political prisoners were before incarcerated, assisted by their followers, they created a mutiny during the preceding year; and had they not stupidly set fire to the houses, and so roused the surrounding country, all who were brought to Magdala might have made their escape. To forestall a similar contingency, every one was restricted to one female servant, who had to attend to all her master's wants. Those who were what in Abyssinia is designated married, could have their wives in a hut outside the prison compound, but it was enjoined that they were to

be no servants, nor to perform any menial work—
an order which only a few strictly obeyed. Poor
women! their existence on that rocky fortress deserved the deepest commiseration. Exposed to the
maltreatment of cross husbands and brutal guards,
their physical and mental sufferings must often have
wrung with anguish their keen and sensitive hearts.
Many would, no doubt, have gladly severed the
slender ties which bound them to that arid Amba;
but there was written over that home of sighs and
grief: "Those that enter here never leave again."

The departure of the king removed the air of
depression which had rested on our prison, and all
looked, if not content, yet resigned. Condemned
without law, and incarcerated without any hope of
release, the majority of these victims of tyranny
and oppression tried more or less, according to their
means, to mitigate their hapless condition by pro-
curing those comforts which their circumstances
permitted. Thus, some immediately commenced
building huts; others prepared the favourite hydromel. Here sat a group busily engaged in
mending their tattered rags, which the journey had
not improved; and there squatted a half-score
nimbly plying their fingers to unmat their bushy
wigs, ere the detestable layer of butter glittered
and sparkled on the stiff-twisted plaits. We tried
to imitate the example of our companions;

and whilst some procured materials to build huts where they might pass the day outside the prison, the rest, myself among the number, improvised an awning, which we attached to the eaves of the prison, and there whiled away our time in converse with Ethiopia's most notorious vagabonds and ruffians.

The daring character of the houseless criminals frightened the guards, and, after many consultations—for without counsels and joint responsibility under the suspicious rule of Theodore nothing could be attempted—it was decided to erect another house for the night accommodation of the unsheltered and dangerous class, to which we belonged. With horror we saw the heaps of poles, sticks, and bamboos swell before our eyes. It was bad enough to be in the narrow compound of our uncovered, foul prison, but to be shut up in a close hut, and to be compelled to inhale a pestilent atmosphere, appeared to us the acme of misery. We spoke to our guards, and in most coaxing terms entreated them to exempt us from the horrors of the new dormitory. Two kindly promised to befriend us, but the rest justly remarked: "The Negoos charged us to guard your person, and not to watch over your health and comfort. If you die we shall not be blamed, but if you escape we lose our heads." It was of no use to represent to them that we had no wings to fly out of the Amba, nor claws to climb over perpendicular precipices; they dreaded our skill, and neither entreaties nor arguments were of any avail. In a week the house was finished, and a little before sunset all, not already domiciled, were driven pell mell into it.

Our native companions and associates, in anticipation of a scramble, installed themselves in their different places early in the afternoon, long before the usual hour for muster; and the close quarters they occupied gave us a glimmer of hope that the densely-packed hut, which rendered every accession to its numbers impossible, would be more gracious to us than the guards. We were deceived. Crowded in every nook and corner, the eight Frendjoj, despite all protestations, had to squeeze themselves in among the heaving and fighting, the squabbling and shouting mass. We were now eighty-one prisoners, in a house scarcely large enough to accommodate, with anything approximating to comfort, a fourth part of that number. McKelvey, whom we emphatically designated "*L'enfant terrible,*" gave the key note of a boisterous altercation. "Tabaguee be Janchoi mout" ("Guards, by the death of the king") give us a place where to lie. The embarrassed watchmen did not dare to close their ears to such an adjuration, and indisposed as they appeared to be, they had to attend to the summons. "Move your vile carcase, you murderer; get up, you rascally thief; draw up your knife-doomed legs, you cowardly deserter!" resounded far above the hum and din of the fettered throng, from the stentorian throats of half a dozen tabaguees, accompanied by the rattle of the long, knotty sticks, that fell discordantly on the chains and skulls of the unyielding, closely-wedged crowd. By dint of menace and blows, a small space was at last cleared, which enabled us to squat down. We had now to arrange the position in which we intended to sleep. This was indispensable, to obviate a disagreeable collision.

Some thought that rational beings invariably slept on the right side; others, on the contrary, maintained that since they first opened their eyes to the light of day they had always slept on the left. A little discussion, however, settled this difficulty, and all unanimously agreed to follow the example of the majority. The intention was good, and had it merely depended on immobility, our comfortless nights might have glided on in perfect harmony. Unfortunately, now and then one or the other got tired of that forced method of repose, and, forgetful of the conditions imposed, veered round and rolled on his angry, and sometimes half smothered and gasping neighbour. These incidents produced a little hilarity, but did not effectually mar our unity. Such, however, was not the result of an accidental encounter with the slumbering groups at our feet. Accustomed to a putrescent atmosphere, and indifferent about future contingencies, the poor fellows grunted and snored on their hard stone pillows as if they reposed on beds of down. Disgusted with the discordant noise and the crippling posture, the restless Frendjoj would now and then, to obtain a little comfort, stretch their limbs beyond the legitimate limits of five feet. Instantly there was a shout and a protest, the rattle of clanking fetters, and the sound of a hammering stone. Knocks and kicks, threats and abuse, in boisterous confusion, reverberated through the dimly-lighted prison. In a few minutes the shackled combatants were *hors de combat*, and, at the intercessions of friends, ready to conclude an armistice, which restricted the skull and feet of the belligerents within proper bounds, if not for ever, at least till dawn of day. A fortnight we had endured the horrors of this swarming, suffocating, and loathsome dormitory. During this interval we became intimate with most of the guards, which removed their apprehensions about our supernatural skill; and we obtained full permission to sleep under the awning outside the gaol. This favour was highly appreciated, and, when we had the means, substantially acknowledged. Our hours, days, and weeks, if not broken by an occasional squabble or some other disagreeable exhibition, glided on in wearisome and unrelieved monotony.

Like our native comrades, we often imagined that our shackles would speedily drop, our prison open, and the captive exile hasten away to freedom and home. The sanguine and imaginative Ethiopian, more than the cool, deliberate, and reflecting Frendjoj, was always building castles in the air. For months and months delightful sunny pictures, never, perhaps, to be realised, danced before his eye. Suddenly a whisper circulated through the crowded huts, which shaded every face, and imparted an air of desolation to the careworn, swarthy countenances. The messenger of evil had arrived, and, without any previous intimation, hint, or warning, the deluded "prisoners of hope" were dragged away in dozens, and hurried—for the king's behest must be promptly executed—shriftless and unprepared, into eternity. Frequently did I hear the guilty and innocent dilating, in glowing colours, on the future, when lo! and behold! instead of thongs and poles to wrench off the heavy irons, there gleamed over their devoted heads the sword and spear—the symbols of their woeful doom. Such sad and harrowing sights damped the ardour of the courageous, and filled with dismay the timid. An ostentatious indulgence in meat, drink, and even dress, which before many delighted to display, was thenceforth carefully avoided; and expensive shamas, even if they were the reward of former services, as well as an exhibition of hydromel jars, for a long time after did not annoy the eye of the envious. Seriousness wonderfully increased; the saints quickly rose in estimation; and prayers, in Ethiopic, a language not understood, were, day and night, chanted. A few months without any alarm or panic restored the wonted confidence and serenity. Pleasing shadows once more played on the dungeon's dingy walls; joyous prospects once more loomed in the distance; the conversation, if not gayer, became more animated; the hydromel cup circulated more freely; and most, as if infatuated, gave themselves up to dreams of liberty, rank, and power, utterly forgetful that the sword of an unsleeping vengeance was still suspended over their guilty or innocent heads. A rumour that the king was coming, an order for more weighty chains, or the seizure of an aristocratic prisoner's concealed property—nay, even the torture of one or more of the greatest miscreants, produced an instantaneous change of sentiment, demeanour, and language amongst the medley crowds huddled together in that disgusting gaol. I was myself intimately acquainted with prisoners of rank who, if they had been free, might, in a short time, have raised forces enough either to support or to defy the despot's tottering power;

yet these men, whose very name precluded the remotest chance of their ever regaining, under Theodore's rule, their forfeited liberty, were so regardless of the symptoms which forewarned them of their approaching doom, and so wrapt in fanciful contemplations of battle-fields, victories, and triumphs, that they did not perceive the dangers which thickened around them, till the mutilating knife dimmed their sight and terminated their mortal career. Hallucinations like these might have been taken for madness, had it not been a well-known fact that the ruthless tyrant had obtained an almost undisputed influence over the captive and free, who had alike to dread his ire and vengeance, his blandishments and winning smiles.

The sad history of Imam Ahmadee, and his ill-fated companions, strikingly illustrates the fascinating power the tyrant exerted to inveigle the unsuspecting and confiding into his treacherous net. In the year 1856, shortly after the complete subjugation of Shoa and its southern dependencies, a few Pagan and Galla districts, King Theodore, the crowned ruler of Ethiopia, turned his victorious legions towards the fertile plains and well-stocked pastures of the Wollo Gallas. The proud, martial, and bigoted followers of the pseudo-Prophet, confident in their valour and the unfailing flight of their spears, smiled at a foe who, in his march southward on Shoa, had not dared to linger on their widespreading plain, where, as they presumptuously imagined, their well-trained war-steeds might have trampled in the dust his undisciplined robber hordes. Theodore, by his emissaries, encouraged an illusion which he knew would be their ruin. The war in Shoa was successfully terminated. Hailu Malakot, the king, had sought safety in flight; but, ere he gained the appointed refuge, toils and cares, grief and despair, put an end to his chequered and unhappy career. "Forward to Jerusalem" was the command that now rang along the serried lines of the victor. Amazed and bewildered, the mute chiefs stared at each other in wondering surprise. "March on!" shouted once more the herald's stentorian voice; and, ere the echo had died away, several great military chiefs, weltering in their blood, lay stretched by the tyrant's spear close to his stamping feet. The Aboon, the true friend of the people, rushed out of his tent, and, with an uplifted cross, adjured the king not to touch a man. "Monk!" vociferated the exasperated monarch, "do you wish the cross for ever trampled in the dust, the Saviour's sepulchre for ever defiled, and David's city for ever in the infidel's accursed possession?" "No, let us fight," responded the politic Pontiff; "but do you, and not these men, lead the van." The crafty Theodore perceived that his artful trick to excite the ardour of his forces against the hated Mahomedans, which had already cost several lives, was suspected by the Aboon; and, to forestall an exposure that might damp their enthusiasm, he called out, "My father is right. Let us crush the infidels at home, before we precipitate ourselves on those abroad." Almost spontaneously—and I heard it from the bishop's own lips—every face was turned in the direction of the fated provinces. The doomed tribes, unconscious of the destructive tempest that was brooding over their quiet and peaceful homes, pursued their usual occupations.

It was Tekemt, October, the second month in the Abyssinian spring, that the royal army quitted the lovely, verdant plains of Shoa. The season was propitious. Pastures and meadows, hills and dales, were all smiling in beauty, and blooming in a rich and abundant harvest. Not a field could be seen that did not wave to the balmy breeze its shocks of wheat and barley; not a mountain slope that did not exhibit a variegated collection of sweet tufting flowers and shrubs; whilst the meandering streams, still replenished from the copious torrents of the preceding rainy season, contributed not a little to enhance the lovely aspect of the ever-varying scenes. King Theodore had no eye to admire, and no heart to pity. His mission was proclaimed by his deed, and woe to those who attempted to arrest his destructive, onward progress. The Gallas—by their prowess far more than by their Mahomedan creed—had incurred the resentment of the implacable tyrant, and to annihilate these martial tribes was the longing ambition of his fiendish heart. Animated by a corresponding passion, blended, in the present instance, with an innate desire for rapine and bloodshed, the fanatical Amhara, avalanche-like, descended on the unsuspecting foe, spreading far and wide ruin and desolation, misery and death. Young and old, the strong and the weak, were indiscriminately subjected to a cruel death, or, what was perhaps still worse, brutal atrocities. The villages were burnt, the fields laid waste, and men, women, and children unsparingly butchered, or dragged into irredeemable captivity. Fell vengeance in a few hours had consummated its ruthless work, and the tyrant, elated with his infamous achievement, and accompanied by a weeping and disconsolate multitude of enslaved and helpless creatures, quitted the blood-stained battle-field.

CHAPTER X.

Death of Ahmadee Busheer—Villany Triumphs—Revolt in Shoa—Guerilla War—Disastrous Campaign—Cruel Scene—Vain Negotiations—Prince Menilek—Want of Gallantry—Disagreeable News—Massacre of Gallas—Atrocious Orders—Good Advice—The Negoos and Metropolitan—Defiant Attitude of the Aboon—Unprovoked Resentment—Additional Fetters—Ingratitude—The Penitent Thief—Captured Galla Women—Royal Diversions—Fictitious Victory.

WEAKENED, but not exhausted; prostrated, but not destroyed; defeated, but not vanquished; the Gallas, after this convulsive shock, rose again out of the depths of their humiliation, and, headed by Ahmadee Busheer, a chieftain famous for his valour, sought to retrieve their overwhelming misfortune. The struggle lasted several years, and would have continued, had not a double-bladed lance pierced the brave leader, and forced him to tend the wound, which, to the universal grief of a grateful people, proved fatal to his precious life.

Woizero Worket, in the name of her youthful son, Imam Ahmadee, the hereditary prince, and the nephew of the valiant Busheer, now assumed the reins of government, and, to retain the fealty of the chiefs, prosecuted the popular war.

Unwilling, and perhaps unable, to contend against a foe whom he could not annihilate or subdue, the artful Theodore, in conformity with his usual practice, tried by hollow flattery, and treacherous promises of glory, wealth, and renown, to entice the young prince into his plausible meshes. Restless, bold, and aspiring, the youthful Imam, who was dazzled by the fair speeches of the royal emissaries, and still more by the chivalrous exploits of the dreaded monarch, in an evil hour yielded to their reiterated solicitations, and, together with twenty-four of his great nobles, joined the Amhara's faithless standard. The unhappy regent-mother and her panic-stricken subjects, to forestall a more grievous calamity, in their embarrassing position submitted to the onerous conditions imposed by the crafty Negoos. Concession, extorted by villany and enforced by menace, could not perpetuate peace, or ward off hostilities. Theodore's demands, as in our own case, grew in proportion to the anxieties of the regent, and when it became impossible and ruinous to comply, the prince and his veteran companions were bound in fetters, and thrown into the common gaol.

The revolt in Shoa, and the defections in and out of the camp, ought to have taught the despot a salutary lesson; but propelled by the fury of his passion, he spurned opposition, and madly pursued a policy that shook the whole realm to its very foundation. Impatient to chastise the disaffected provinces of the south, he took his prisoners from Zar Amba, in Tshelga,* and hurrying on to Magdala he deposited them there, and then, with his usual alacrity, rushed on the seditious Gallas.

His plan was feasible, and had he succeeded in subjugating those restless mountaineers, it would have disheartened the Shoahs, and driven them to sue for an ignoble peace. The enemy penetrated his design, and, without hazarding a battle, withdrew to some distant and inaccessible rocks.

Foiled in his expectations, he recklessly pushed across the plains he had more than once before traversed as victor, and in his mind, no doubt, already ruminated on the castigation he would inflict on his rebellious Shoa subjects. Once in the midst of the hostile land, the foe plucked up courage, and, pouring down from their lofty hiding-places, began a destructive guerilla war. Numerous bands, like birds of prey, hovered around the camp when it rested, or assailed its rear when it moved. The entire route along which the enemy marched was stained with the blood and covered with the corpses of the mangled and mutilated Amharas.

Worried, exhausted, and dispirited, the dastardly hordes, who had achieved their former exploits more

---

* This Amba lies between Wochnee and Tschelga, and is the scene of Rasselas' Happy Valley.

by the exhibition of numbers than genuine martial valour, did not much relish the hardships, privations, and perils of the campaign; and the discouraged forces, instead of exposing themselves to the trenchant blades of the Mahomedan Gallas, and the no less true weapon of a rebel Amhara, deserted in whole divisions the Negoos' standard, and went over to the lines of the enemy. The expedition proved disastrous, and the tyrant, chafed and vexed, like a furious lion baulked of his prey, on the morning of February the 22nd, 1864, returned again to his secure and loyal Magdala. Imam Ahmadee and his companions were immediately visited by Ras Engeda and his myrmidons. "Why has your mother risen in arms against her friend, the Negoos?" bawled forth the exasperated commander-in-chief of the royal troops. "I am a prisoner," responded the youthful, undaunted Imam, "and cannot control the actions of my mother, or those under her sway." The ill-fated prince had scarcely uttered these words, when a dozen hands, storm-like, rattled on his own and companions' devoted heads. "Seize their property, arrest their servants, and lead away their wives," were the orders that issued in breathless succession from the Ras' compressed lips. Brave Imam, unintimidated, submitted to every indignity his oppressors could heap upon him, but the removal of his affectionate and tender wife, who clung to him in distracting agony, shook his powerful frame, and he sank, unmanned, on the hard and stony ground. Disconsolate, and almost frantic, the impassioned young creature, in a flood of ardent, wild eloquence, besought the tyrant's minions not to separate her from the only object she loved on that lonely and friendless Amba. The attitude of mingled grief, adjuration, and despair so beautifully depicted in every line of that pale and agitated countenance, as she knelt, with one arm flung around the neck of her husband, and the other raised to the Ras in imploring entreaty, enlisted the loud sympathy of the captive and the free. The Ras himself, hardened as he was to every human sentiment, was visibly uneasy, and he might, perhaps, have yielded to the thrilling appeal of the crouching figure before him, had not the stern mandate of his cruel master steeled his heart, and, in a sharp voice, he called out to two grinning blacks: "Tear that woman away, and, if she refuses to walk, carry her." The grim eunuchs in a moment clutched her in their brawny arms, and, despite scalding tears and thrilling appeals, hurried her away to the royal harem — that dreaded abode of blighted affections and mourning hearts. Severed from the wife of his bosom, stripped of every vestige of property, buffeted, scorned, and derided, the young chief and the sharers of his captivity had, besides all their other sufferings, to experience the torture of the crippling hand-chain, in addition to those around the ankles.

The queen-regent, on learning her son's unhappy position, tried, by bribes, ransoms, and even the offer of an annual tribute, to conciliate the rankling hate of the ferocious despot. Messenger after messenger in rapid succession followed each other with proffers of amity from the Gallas, and exorbitant conditions from the king. "Give up the deserters," was the peremptory order addressed to the regent, "and Imam shall live; refuse, and he shall die." Worket would willingly, had she been able, have sacrificed all the Amharas, to save her own son; but this she could not effect without the consent of her proud chiefs, who unanimously refused to yield up to a capricious and faithless tyrant the men they had solemnly sworn to protect. Baffled in her expectations, she had recourse to fair words, artful promises, and valuable presents, to ward off the catastrophe which might rob her of the very object around which her deepest affections were entwined, when an event occurred that caused every Galla's heart to swell with the mingled passions of anger and pain, indignation and grief.

Menilek, the son of Hailu Malakot, the successor of Sahala Salasie, the late King of Shoa, and heir-apparent to the throne of that province on the defeat of his father, gave himself up to King Theodore.

THE QUEEN OF THE GALLA COUNTRY,
WITH HER YOUNGEST SON AND A MAHOMETAN PRIEST.

Quick, gentle, and unpretending, he propitiated the tyrant's favour, and was honoured with the hand of a royal princess, a daughter of the invincible conqueror. The troubles in his native land, combined with flattering offers of support from priests and military chieftains, revived in his bosom the dormant desire to ascend the throne of his father, the heritage of a long line of puissant ancestors.

Prompted by this proud and ardent passion, he did not long deliberate on the course he ought to pursue. His friends, to whom he communicated the design, gave their approval, and, during a dark and auspicious night, he and his followers, guided by a few glimmering stars, quitted the camp. Afraid to disturb the sleeping hosts, they noiselessly threaded their way across the wide chasm which forms a most formidable barrier between Amba Magdala and the Galla country, and then, pursuing their tortuous path up a steep bank to the south-east, they arrived by dawn of day on the high table-land of the Wollo Gallas.

The camp was astir at an unusually early hour. Bustle and confusion, which never prevailed in the lines of the royal army except under extraordinary circumstances, that morning had reached their climax. Officers, soldiers, servants, and slaves, excited and bewildered, were rushing about in all directions, instituting inquiries, and soliciting information, about the fugitives. The princess, forsaken, and, if the report was true, maltreated, by the spouse her rank had exalted, sat convulsed with shame and indignation in her disgraced pavilion, sighing for the moment that would give satisfaction to her revenge, and quell the tempest of her soul in the torments of the ingrate.

At sunrise, the gates of Magdala were unbarred, and Ras Engeda, the commander-in-chief, followed by a score of nobles and governors, swept through the narrow entrance towards the royal domicile, to announce to his master the untoward event. The tyrant, although conscious that this desertion involved the irretrievable loss of a kingdom, dexterously concealed the wound that bled beneath the white shama in which he was enveloped. Being informed of the direction the runaways had taken, he calmly ordered his telescope, and gazed towards the spot where Menilek was exchanging courtesies and felicitations with his mortal foes. Immovable and statue-like, he sat for some minutes absorbed in the terrible contemplation that tore his heart; and then, turning to his expectant chiefs, he observed, with indifference—the prelude of an atrocious deed: "Worket has found a son who is free; she can dispense with the one who is chained."

These words, notwithstanding the bland accents in which they were uttered, needed no comment to those around him, who so well understood his character; and, almost instantaneously, every one grasped the hilt of his sword, and stood ready to fulfil the executioner's task. Imam and his companions, twenty-five in number, were instantly dragged out of the prison-compound, and, in the presence of the king and his nobles, hacked and chopped into pieces. Not satisfied with the blood that had already flowed, he ordered the execution of all the Christian prisoners on the Amba. Lik Maquas Hailu—the second head-gaoler, and, till his death, which took place two years ago, one of my best friends—presented himself before the tyrant, and, in calm and respectful terms, deprecated the fiendish mandate. "You have executed the Gallas," energetically observed the worthy old man, "because they and their tribes are your enemies; but what reason can you allege for the butchery of a mass of people, whose only misfortune is that you are strong and they weak; you the master, and they slaves; you free, and they captives?" The counsel of the good man would probably have been unheeded, had not the despot shrunk from the dangers and perils which the wholesale massacre of all the great men of the land might entail. The Christian prisoners were spared, but the tyrant's rage was unappeased. He had seen blood flow; he had rioted in the dying throes of enemies; had stabbed a queen-mother through the heart of her son; yet all this did not suffice to allay the evil passions which raged in every corner of his soul. Fiercely and madly his flashing eye roved in eevry direction, to discover some one on whom his torturing vengeance might exert its fury. The bishop, quietly seated in front of his house, was at once singled out for that purpose. Leaping out of his saddle, the infuriated monarch sprang forward, and, with a quivering spear, confronted the calm and undaunted pontiff. "Monk!" was the polite salutation, "why did you not come out and absolve me?" "I saw your face stained with blood," was the laconic reply, "and had no inclination to intrude on your presence." The altercation grew every moment more loud and animated. The king called the bishop traitor, and the bishop the king diabolos. Words led to threats, and threats almost to deeds. Weary of the wordy strife, the brave and fearless primate dashed aside his veil, and, baring his neck, summoned the executioner to execute the despot's fell design. Touched by the sight of their unshaken and death-courting Aboon, who stood before them like a venerated saint of the calendar, hurling heaven's wrath and judgment on scorning unbelievers, the fickle and superstitious multitude, fresh from the field of slaughter, cast themselves before the monarch and supplicated his clemency. Mute with surprise, the baffled tyrant, who expected to see a meek and not defiant churchman, with affected scorn, said, "Well, since he wants to die, let him live; but write down his property, and guard him."

Disgusted with the proud attitude of the Aboon, the irritated monarch cast his vicious glance towards the gaol, where he knew he could, unopposed, extort tears of blood from the victims of his violence. Hitherto, most of the Magdala prisoners, ourselves among the number, had only manacles attached to their ankles; but now, at the behest of his Majesty, the right hand was fastened, by a chain about eight inches long, to the legs, and in this crippled and doubled-up posture all the prisoners were condemned to spend, according to the tyrant's expectation, the remainder of the wretched days of their life. It was at this very time that he received a third letter from Mr. Rassam, in which he solicited permission to visit the Abyssinian court. We anticipated that the reiterated proffers of friendship on the part of her Majesty's representative at Massowah would mollify his wrath, and improve our position. No such thing. The chief gaoler, anxious to know what he was to do with us, as our names were not on the list, asked whether the Frendjoj were to have wrist chains like the rest. "Ahia" (jackass), quickly returned the king, "I impose fresh penalties on my own people, and do you think I allow these hated strangers to escape unscathed?" This happened the very time that Mahomed, a rascally relation of Samuel, reported to Mr. Rassam the well-known story of Consul Cameron's release—a fiction that had not even the faintest shadow of truth for its foundation. Had the king been inclined to practise any deception, he might have released the consul before the messengers were dispatched, and then chained him again after their departure; but King Theodore was above such tricks; he had a lot of hostages in his dungeons, and he was determined not to give to any of them his freedom till he had obtained substantial concessions.

Housed together with a number of people of every rank and grade, from the midnight murderer to the proudest noble, our captivity was continually diversified by incidents that broke the stern monotony of our sorrowful days. We had discussions on religious and secular subjects, on ecclesiastical and civil law, murders and homicides, petty larceny and highway robbery; and when these became threadbare or tiresome, there was, perhaps, a squabble and a fight, a truce and reconciliation. Amongst our numerous companions we had some really good men, and others who were thoroughly bad and irreclaimable. A few of these, notwithstanding their professions of friendship, every night regularly pilfered our bread. As we were generous to all the poor, even if it involved a personal hardship and privation, we thought this a very ungrateful and unbecoming act. We complained to the guards; but as prisoners in Abyssinia are without the pale of the law, they merely rejoined: "We have to watch your person, and not your bread." Determined to detect the thief, Mrs. Rosenthal baked a loaf with a few grains of Tartar emetic in it—enough to make the offender sick, without doing him any actual harm. As usual, early in the morning the bread-basket was emptied. We went to the chief gaoler, and related him our mishap. "You know the thief?" was his reply. "Yes, we suspect him." More considerate than his subordinates, he ordered the culprit to be brought before him. The offender, who felt not the effects of a guilty conscience, but of a powerful medicine, in a whining voice, denied the charge. "Take care," was the reminder, "that you do not enhance the sin of theft by adding to it the guilt of lying." "I am innocent," was the plaintive rejoinder. The fear of detection, blended with the energetic action of the emetic, rendered concealment beyond the reach of possibility. He grinned, spat, made comically-wry faces, and tried, by all kinds of gestures and contortions, to suppress a nausea for which he could not account. Unable to restrain any longer the internal commotion which shook his frame, he cried out: "If I am to die, let me die with the truth on my lips;" but ere the confession could find utterance he lay writhing on the ground, in the wholesome tortures of the emetic. The poor fellow, who imagined that every convulsive start would be his final struggle, with vows and supplications invoked saints and martyrs to carry him through the terrible conflict. Old Lik Maquas Hailu, the second chief gaoler, who knew the trick, requested Mr. Rosenthal to give him an antidote. "This," he added, " will lead everyone to suppose that you can communicate sickness and health, and thus your bread will never again be touched." A few cups of water and the assurance that he would live and not die reanimated the penitent thief, and henceforth our larder was inviolate.

The king, so long as he continued in our vicinity, amply contributed to keep up the excitement among his prisoners. Thus, one day a whole troop of Galla women, most, if not all, young and handsome, were brought to the prison. They had not been kidnapped by the dealers in human flesh, or seized what is termed in fight and open battle. Secure on their native upland glades, and in the homes that had sheltered their infancy and childhood, the defenceless creatures were, in the absence of parents and husbands, who had been summoned to a tribal council, surrounded by some robber bands of Theodore, and dragged into misery and bondage. Their mournful looks, tremulous frames, and piteous sobs, as much as their youth and beauty, ought to have ensured them a generous and considerate treatment. Such, however, was not their unfortunate lot. Driven like a herd of cattle into the prison compound, where ruffianly guards had them at their own mercy, they remained in that foul abode about forty-eight hours, ere they were handed over as lawful property to the tender care of their brutal and savage captors. A raid or two made the Gallas more wary; and outposts were planted on every hill and pass to give warning of the enemy's approach. Driven by want, the king himself made occasionally forays into the adjacent hostile districts, but as they invariably cost him numbers of his people, and brought him no other return than half a score of prisoners, whom he sent to swell our overflowing gaol, he gave up these disastrous expeditions, and contented himself with annoying everyone on the Amba, not excepting his own poor queen, who more than once bled under the application of the terrible giraff or an eunuch's hard fist. His chief place of diversion was, however, the prison. To kill all would have been his delight, but, as already stated, he dreaded the disgust, horror, and consternation the act would excite. In the absence of tens he contented himself with units. Two young men, whose only crime consisted in that they sought to facilitate their imprisoned master's escape, were one morning taken out of the compound, shot, and tossed down a steep precipice. One of them when called was busily engaged in washing some tobacco for Consul Cameron. Seated close to him, I quite accidentally asked him: "What do the guards want from you?" Briefly he replied, as if he had a presentiment of what was impending: "Egziabeher youkal" ("God knows"). It was the last sentence he uttered. On another occasion two soldiers who wanted to desert, after enduring the most fiendish tortures, were executed—one by the hands of the king, and the other by a near relative.

To vary the programme, his Majesty at one time would order a public rejoicing on account of a fictitious victory, pretended to have been achieved by his troops over a powerful enemy; and at another, because he had received positive intelligence that Tadlow Qualou in Godjam, or Wagshum Gobazie in Lasta, had expiated the crime of rebellion by the invisible arrow of the angel of death. Thus, on July 11, 1864, there was music and rejoicing, gaiety and merriment, singing and firing, the greater part of the night, because at Cubreed Amba, near the entrance of Shoa, the royal garrison* sustained

* They were indeed faithful to their king, and only surrendered to the enemy when they saw themselves abandoned by a sovereign whom they had most faithfully served.

a defeat, and not as he, the truthful Negoos, alleged, because they had won a triumphant victory. The prisoners guessed the truth; and the roar of the cannon, the firing of musketry, and the shrill notes of the martial airs were to them, as they secretly expressed, a sure indication of Theodore's waning power and approaching fall. A few days later there were similar rejoicings, to celebrate the death of Tadlow Qualou, the Godjam rebel. He had already been buried and raised so many times, that the most devout friends of the Negoos could not refrain from joining in the waggish joke—"Tadlow Qualou is too bad for the grave, for it always casts him up again."

CHAPTER XI.

Departure of the King—Seeking for Truth—Opposition of the Priests—Triumphs of Truth—Death in Prison—Small-pox—Sympathy Unappreciated—Chains Tightened—The Young Pilgrim—Brief Career—Mournful Funeral—Considerate Guards—Nightly Torments—Incipient Sickness—Colocynth Pills—Sickness Forestalled—Kerans a Dentist—Makerer an Oculist.

ASHAMED of his inactivity, and the unchecked progress of the insurrection, which spread like wildfire from province to province, the great king, to the secret delight of the captive and the free, buckled on his sword, and, with his army, crossed the Beshilo. The departure of the tyrant removed the shades that had rested on each brow, and brought contentment, if not comfort, to the heavy heart. We had now visitors every day. Some came to hear what we had to say about our religion; others wanted an explanation of a Scripture passage; and not a few, among whom were the royal scribes, wished to obtain an intelligent knowledge of that Gospel in which they professed to believe. The guards did not approve of these visits, but by coaxing and cups of strong coffee they were won over to our side; and almost every day my lair was crowded to suffocation by three, four, and sometimes more, honest and candid inquirers after the truth. Our fellow-captives, provoked to emulation by what they witnessed, also began to inquire into the great and overwhelming question which had excited general attention. A vast majority, of course, could not read, but they were so earnest, that many an old man began to study the alphabet; and very often for hours and hours these illiterate disciples drove one mad with their loud, monotonous chants of hissing consonants and deafening vowels.

The light of truth kindled in the hearts of a few soldiers and captives soon communicated itself to kindred spirits and congenial minds. The priests observed this movement, and clamorously raised their voices to check its onward progress. Their opposition stirred up stagnant superstition, and won fresh supporters to the cause of the Gospel. There were meetings and public disputations, warm debates and sharp threats. The champions of truth appealed to the Bible; and the defenders of error to saints and legends of the Church. These contests, which exhibited the worthlessness of monkish puerilities, and brought out in bold relief the pure and soul-saving declarations of Scripture, invariably proved disastrous to the cause of the Church and its untutored champions.

Several of the latter, prompted by a solemn conviction that their creed was not in harmony with the Word of God, seceded from their own ranks and joined the number of their opponents, whose very life proclaimed the pure and ennobling doctrines of their faith. What influence these bands of believers may yet exert on their unhappy country it is impossible to prognosticate. They may, to escape the moral pollution of the world in which they live, seek the retirement of the isolated village and solitary mountain range; and they may also, prompted by a holy and divine impulse, like the messengers of glad tidings who in times of yore planted the standard of the cross on the Abyssinian Alps, go forth, in the full ardour of their young love and zeal, to spread far and wide, over scenes of sin and vice, superstition and ignorance, the saving and enlightening knowledge of the Gospel.

Death, the dreaded enemy of the happy and gay, and the friend of the sorrowful and sad, almost disdained the putrescent gaol, where his visits, if not courted, would not have been unwelcome. We had a little sickness, and a few deaths; but each one, wrapt in profound reflection on his own woes, almost unconsciously became indifferent to the woes of others. Each week, perhaps, one died. The funeral obsequies occupied very little time, and excited very little attention. Freed from the toils and troubles of a harrowing life, the miserable sufferer had scarcely gasped forth his last breath, when half-a-dozen of his fellow-captives lifted up his shackled and still quivering corpse, and laid it on the bare ground under the prison caves. The same kind hands, guarded by gaolers, dug, at some distance from the prison-compound, a hurried grave, whilst others wrenched the fetters from the stiffening and iron-wasted limbs. In about an hour all was over. One or two, to whom the departed was dear, shed a silent tear over his mortal remains, and then, without a ministering priest to say, in solemn voice, "dust to dust, and ashes to ashes," the corpse was put into the ground, the clods were rolled over it, and he had ceased to be numbered among the victims of King Theodore's tyranny.

A sudden outbreak of an epidemic, which prostrated its scores, unlike an isolated death, produced a solemnising, but not, what might have been expected, a desponding effect. Death to most had lost its sting, and his approach was regarded with sullen indifference, if not with gloomy satisfaction. In autumn, 1865, numbers of our fellow-prisoners were attacked by that terrible scourge, the small-pox. The groans, shrieks, and lamentations of the sick and dying wrung every heart with anguish and grief. Removed from friends and relations, whose tender care and assiduity might have assuaged the pangs of disease

and the agonies of dissolution, the shackled and
afflicted sufferers without exception refused to accept
the sympathy and attention which charity proffered;
and, in mournful and pleading accents, they entreated
to be allowed to have a peaceable, and not, as they
prophetically anticipated, a forcible exit out of this
world.

The scourge, which had for many weeks lingered
in and around our prison, gradually abated. A
healthier atmosphere was again breathed, and more
animation and cheerfulness displayed. No longer
was every countenance wrapt in thoughtfulness, and
every eye dull and lustreless. There were loud and
secret speculations on the tenure of the king's power,
and the chances of each rebel's future greatness and
success. Whether these unguarded hallucinations were
reported to the king by his spies, who infested our
prison, or whether they were merely surmises of the
suspicious tyrant, this is certain, that some cause of
irritation must have occurred, for, quite unexpectedly, all the better class of prisoners had their upper
garments, the only dress they could wear, torn in
pieces, and their chains more tightly riveted. We
were exempted from this penalty—a kindness for
which we were indebted to the guards, and not to the
king, who was then at Wadela. Grateful that we
were left in possession of our scanty wardrobes, and
the little money which served to supply our daily

wants, our eventless weeks rolled on, undisturbed by incidents that could either elate or depress.

It was at this very period, when our prison-life was so even and uniform, that death entered our small circle, and created a painful gap. Little Henry Rosenthal, endeared to every one on account of his innocence, infantine beauty, and sweet disposition, suddenly quitted the narrow confines of an African prison for the glorious mansions of the redeemed. The young pilgrim, whose short sojourn in this lower world had been fraught with trials which, happily, seldom fall to the lot even of the beloved ones of missionaries in the most unexplored and ungenial climes, seemed destined to brighten for a short period the dismal life of his father and mother, and then departed for ever.

Born a few months before his parents' imprisonment, the tender creature just began to be conscious of a mother's loving smile, when, driven from house and home, he had to feed on tears, and to repose on a bosom often, very often, throbbing with the anguish of a breaking heart. Like some tender plant, he gathered strength during an interval of calm, and pined whenever there was a storm.

After the departure of the king from Magdala, all the prisoners began to breathe a freer and more invigorating atmosphere. Little Henry, in the placid countenance of an affectionate mother, intuitively perceived that something auspicious had occurred. Better clad, better fed, more of cheerfulness and less of sadness around him, like a bird released from a cruel cage, he was always in motion, running, unhindered by guards, from one white prisoner to another, with a gaiety and playfulness as if he had suddenly been transported from the land where the eye is never dry to a scene where weeping is unknown. Shy, and possessing an innate repugnance towards natives, he yet soon became reconciled to the youthful criminals, who, in the absence of other play-companions, led him round the prison inclosure, rolling about a worsted ball, or plaiting stray grasses, which sprang up here and there despite the tramp of countless feet. Several times he also moved beyond the limits of our gaol, and, by special request, visited the mother of Ras Ali, the late ruler of the Amhara country, and also Aboona Salama. The latter, to win the affections of his youthful visitor, offered him glittering watches, crosses, and a variety of attractive objects; but he gazed upon all with an indifferent glance, as if those gaudy trinkets were unsuited to the child of imprisoned parents. The kind-hearted bishop, on observing this unusual indifference to all these gay and fascinating articles, remarked to his guide, a soldier, and a sincere Christian man: "This child bears the impress of heaven, and will not continue long upon earth."

About the beginning of December, 1865, his rosy cheeks began to pale, and a sombre shade, the herald of death, overspread his ever-beaming countenance. He now no longer quitted the tent, or enlivened by his merry laughter the gloomy court of our prison. Two days before his decease, just as a few of us had finished our usual morning devotion, a piercing shriek summoned me to the abode of my fellow-captive. The infant sufferer was then panting and gasping for breath, whilst his deep blue eyes, in mournful glances, wandered from one to the other, as if imploring help and relief. I prayed, with the deeply-afflicted parents, that if the beloved object of their affection was to be removed, the struggle might be short. That prayer, like many others, as perhaps eternity will reveal, which was sighed out in agonies and tears in that doleful spot by one and the other of the sorely-tried white prisoners, was heard, and the spasms that tore and racked that frail frame ceased. In the evening, as was his custom, he folded his tiny hands together, and, raising his eyes solemnly to that spirit-land where the songs of infinite love, and not the clang of fetters, are heard, he devoutly followed every word, as if he understood the import of that prayer in which a mother's grief-wrung heart sought comfort and support. The next day he appeared more animated, but during the night he had a relapse, and ere the morning dawned his eyes were closed to earth and earth's pains and woes.

The bereaved parents, deprived of all that had tempered the severity of their misery, lay forlorn and desolate on the hard ground of their prison, bemoaning the loss of their first-born. With our left hands (the right being manacled), McKelvey and myself dressed the corpse in white; and, with the aid of some native fellow-prisoners, made a small coffin of reeds, which the bishop kindly sent us. The grave was dug on an acclivity close to our gaol, and to this spot with tottering steps we followed the first and youngest victim of our captivity to his final resting-place. All the guards, and scores of women, had assembled around the grave; and, amidst the wails and sobs of the multitude, to whom the sweet child had endeared himself, I performed, crippled and bent double by heavy shackles, the touching funeral service of our Church. A month later a fresh tomb had to be raised by the side of the departed for his little sister; and once more, midst the rattle of chains and the prayer of hope, was the earth heaped over the second white child's grave on this sterile and isolated Amba.

The spot where the two children lie interred is marked by a tombstone, two feet high, with the inscription: "Suffer little children to come unto me, and forbid them not: for of such is the kingdom of God."

The crippled posture to which we were condemned, the putrescent atmosphere in which we moved, and the bad food which we ate, visibly sapped our health and energies. Some of our party manfully struggled against their hard fate; others, on the contrary, allowed the cruel iron to pierce their soul, till the very excess of their agony brought on a frenzied insensibility. The pain in the spine, of which Consul Cameron and myself suffered most, was very irksome. Happily, we were enabled to open the wrist-rings by night, otherwise we might never again have recovered an upright and erect attitude. Our guards knew the trick we practised, but, as they got now and then a trifling present, they closed their eyes to our nocturnal proceeding. In the day-time, or evening, we could not have ventured to do so, as one or another of the chiefs made a tour of inspection, and the faintest suspicion might have been severely rued. Once I neglected the precaution, and with unfettered hands performed my ablutions. One of the guards at that very moment happened to gaze over the piece of black serge that shrouded my lair from public scrutiny. He noticed my confusion, and, as if undecided what to do, he glanced at my face, then at my hands, and, at last, like a good man, walked away. I never again violated the prison-law during the day. It was a curious coincidence, that during the whole of our captivity I should have had the heaviest shackles on the legs, and the lightest and most easy to open round the wrists. On the day that the latter were fastened on, Kerans, McKelvie, and Rosenthal, all requested to get those that were reserved for me. The guard who had them in his keeping was inflexible, and no persuasion could induce him to part with the easy fetters he had selected for his friend Cocab. I owed this special favour to a copy of the Amharic Gospel, which I had given him a month before.

But it was not the chains alone; there were many other daily trials that tended to brim the cup of gall we had to empty. The days were still endurable, and glided away in converse with fellow-prisoners, soldiers, and guards. Most of my companions, immediately after sunrise, sought the shelter of their huts outside the prison-fence. I never erected one of those tenements, and generally remained within the compound, where scores of criminals did not allow time to hang heavy upon me. The nights were terrible beyond expression. The damp ground, saturated with every kind of fetid and decayed matter, bred, fed, and multiplied all that crept, leaped, and crawled. Torpid and innocuous during the day, they were the more lively and active by night. The weary captive, anxious to seek forgetfulness in sleep, had no sooner wrapt himself in his shama than stings and bites, as if he was in a bee-hive, made him convulsively jump and start. To attempt the destruction of the intruders was perfectly ludicrous. Like a stream, they poured down the walls, bubbled up from the stagnant pools, and tumbled from the putrid roof of thatch. Towards dawn, they were either satiated or exhausted from their toils, and then, if the troops of rats, that disputed every inch of ground with their tinier but more lusty rivals, were considerate, one could get an hour's rest, and if not, one had to fight, kick, and beat, a labour not easy for crippled lumps of humanity, till morning came to the relief. Sometimes, I determined to triumph over these malicious midnight bacchanals, and, for a brief half-hour, succeeded. The shama, in which I was enveloped like a mummy, after that interval, would become too close, and, by some unconscious movement of my hand, it exposed the face, and then unbared the left arm. The villainous rats, attracted by the warmth, would instantly stop their open-air gymnastics, and, with a dash that made the blood run cold in the veins, seek to take forcible possession of the warm folds of the covering. Two or three it was easy to dislodge; but a whole family, with their numerous progeny of children and grandchildren, cousins and nieces, extorted shouts of distress that afforded general merriment.

Sickness, too, began to prostrate our party. Every one had bad eyes: the consul and Mr.

Rosenthal most seriously. I was exempted from this evil, but afflicted with others. We had a few trifling medicines, and these we husbanded most carefully. My own laboratory contained paste of colocynth, opium, and tartar emetic. The selection, if not very choice, was, at least, very potent. Not accustomed to dabble in the healing art, I made experiments on myself ere I tried to tamper with the health of others. My colocynth pills obtained a fame at Magdala that Morison and Holloway might have envied. In-door and out-door patients applied for that wonderful specific against all diseases. I had no objection to part with my pills, but a decided objection to manufacture them. Kerans, who, I believe, had imbibed a profound knowledge of the pill-manipulating process beneath the parental roof, occasionally came to my help, and after we had fabricated two or three dozens, which took about an hour, our hands, and sometimes our faces too, looked frightfully impressed with our profession.

Aboona Salama, much as I liked the kind man as a friend, I dreaded as a patient. Unable to stir out of his house, subjected to a variety of petty annoyances, and stung to the very quick by the perfidy and ingratitude of the tyrant, whom, if he had possessed more sagacity and foresight, he might have chained on that very rock where he was now a prisoner, the poor man, in his despairing ruminations, which keenly affected his bodily health, sought solace in my pills, like a drunkard in his bottle, or the miser in his gold. One day he accidentally heard that I had cured an obstinate case of dysentery with my colocynth and opium. Instantly he despatched his boy with a note to the prison, entreating me not to waste my medicine on bad natives. His missive made us laugh heartily. But, if the worthy Aboona was a little selfish in the matter of my pills, he had imitators in the prison—a spot where charity should have expanded and become diffusive. A certain lady, the wife of an imprisoned chief, who had been long subject to a disagreeable disorder, was happily cured by my uniform specific. Grateful for the blessing I had conferred on the partner of his life and the comforter of his captivity, the affectionate husband came to me, and, in a whisper, assured me that he was a very great man, and would ever be grateful to me if I gave an extra dose of medicine to his wife to forestall a relapse of her malady. This exhausted my patience, and I gave him a long, but I fear unprofitable, lecture on "Charity."

If I devoted myself to the healing of internal complaints, Kerans applied himself to alleviate external pains. The Abyssinians, although favoured with good grinders, are not entirely exempt from tooth-ache. Many constantly applied to us for relief. At first we were nervous in our practice, as we had no royal diploma, and without such a high sanction it was not advisable to incur the risk of a misrepresentation, which a disappointed patient might perchance fabricate against us. This diffidence speedily wore away, and, encouraged by a few incipient successes, we unflaggingly pursued our healing art. Kerans and his forceps, Makerer and his sulphate of zinc, and myself with the eternal colocynth, were inseparables. My pills, as already stated, did wonders; but they were altogether eclipsed by the miracles performed by my two companions. Fellows with eyes glued together as if they were hermetically sealed, had only to submit to Makerer's potent phial, and in three or four days they were cured. Others, with faces swollen, swathed, and dreadfully woe-begone, needed only a touch of Kerans' forceps, then there was a loud crack, a gory tooth, a stream of blood, a polite prostration, and, what was most welcome, a farewell to pain. They had all implicit faith in the skill of the dentist, and no one, that I recollect, would ever push away his arm, or hoist him down from the heaving chest, till the operation was accomplished. These acts of kindness procured us friends, and we enjoyed privileges which, during our second captivity, when we were in what the king termed his elfin, or harem, handsome largesses could not purchase.

CHAPTER XII.

Hope Deferred — Embarrassing Negotiations — Approach of Mr. Rassam—The Artisans' Disappointment—Delightful Message—Removal of Fetters — Strange Sensation — Departure from Magdala—Ominous Intelligence—Arrival at Gaffat—Camp of Mr. Rassam — Order of March—Samuel's Kiss —Theodore's Dissimulations—Malicious Charges—New Garments—Sham Trial—Alleged Offences—Forced Admission—Royal Satisfaction—Solomon's Seal—Suspicious Intimations.

"Hope deferred makes the heart sick." The truth of this aphorism of Israel's wise king we had experienced in its fullest latitude. For months and months we had yearningly waited for the letter from her Majesty the Queen, which we all believed would decide our doom. Time, precious above computation, glided by, and still that document, which we regarded as the charter of our liberty, did not make its appearance. Secret factions in the royal camp, numerous desertions from the ranks, and a general disposition to revolt throughout the whole land, all prognosticated a revolution which would inflict a terrible retributive lesson on relentless despotism, and entail countless sufferings on the tyrant's hapless victims. Delays became every moment more dangerous. The crafty tyrant, in the zenith of his glory, wanted to make capital out of his foreign captives, and, now that rebellion was accelerating his fall, we felt sure that he would either drag us with him into ruin, or seek, by our instrumentality, to raise a barrier between his throne and an enraged people. Mr. Rassam, we knew, had been more than a year in Massowah, waiting most anxiously for permission to enter Abyssinia. He had already written twice to the king, without receiving a reply, and the third letter, to which an answer was tendered, we heard from the royal scribes, was so rude, coarse, and uncivil, that we felt sure it would abruptly suspend all further negotiations.

Political sagacity and diplomatic skill, which hitherto had certainly not improved our position, now threatened to aggravate it. From Gaffat, where the European workmen resided, there sounded the ominous alarm: "If Mr. Rassam does not come you will be lost first, then ourselves." On the Amba the expressions were less emphatic, but the gestures more significant. Dejatch Mered, a Tigré prisoner of note, who was in many of our secrets, as he aided us in keeping up communication with our friends on the coast, repeatedly assured me, that if Mr. Rassam did not comply with the king's request, the fate of the murdered Gallas would be our own. In this critical emergency Consul Cameron wrote to Mr. Rassam, and urged him to come. I also sent him a few lines, which are published in the Blue Book of 1846—1868, but as I was no official, and the causes of my captivity were erroneously, or, perhaps, designedly attributed to sins that would never have caused the chains to rattle around my limbs, I merely told him that if he ventured into Abyssinia, the enterprise was laudable, and God would also bless it.

In November, 1865, tidings reached us that Mr. Rassam was on his march, and would probably reach the royal camp in December. The intelligence thrilled our hearts with delight. In the joy inspired by the faint hope of liberty, some of us did not forget that human efforts, unaccompanied by the Divine blessing, would be unavailing to effect this end. This gave fresh fervency to our prayers, and seldom did humble faith and anxious fear waft a sweeter incense to heaven than ascended in those days from the narrow confines of our Magdala prison.

At Gaffat, among the royal workmen, the approaching advent of the British envoy suggested a variety of speculations. They were all positive that no one would be liberated without their previous advice and assent. This conviction had taken such firm hold on their minds that Waldemeier wrote me a long letter in which he informed me that neither himself nor his brethren would intercede for my release if I had, since my captivity, written against them.* To their vexation and disappointment Mr. Rassam was summoned to the royal camp at Damot, and there and then, without any Gaffat council, the order was issued for the liberation of the captives.†

On the morning of February 24th, 1866, Agha Faree Gholam, and another inferior messenger, arrived at Magdala. With the rapidity of lightning the report spread that he had come to release us. All were instantly in a state of feverish exultation. Many of our friends amongst the guards caught a kind of sympathetic hilarity from their captives, and though they did not display it openly in vehement expressions, one could read in their very looks a contentment and joy that needed no utterance. About four o'clock Consul Cameron, myself, and afterwards the rest, according to royal orders, received a summons to come outside the prison. Most of the Amba chiefs were seated on the south-eastern slope fronting the prison, chatting, laughing, and criticising the fortunes of the Frendjoj.

* This charge referred to an article in the *Egyptian*, on the marriages and lives of these men. The report, it was alleged, emanated from me, and though I repudiated it again and again, they pertinaciously insisted that I was the author.

† The king was informed, whether directly or indirectly, that his white workmen were offended that they had not been consulted on the subject of our liberation. His Majesty forwarded them the following message: "My children, the great Queen of England has sent me a very great man, and I have released the prisoners."

The appearance of the royal messenger put a stop to all talk and merriment. "Consul, Cocab, Rosenthal, &c.," began the subordinate messenger: "The king, my master, has charged me to inform you that he has received a letter from your Queen, through her envoy, Mr. Rassam, and that in conformity with the request embodied in the same, he has been pleased to order your liberation." Painful and inconvenient as it was to prostrate ourselves in hand and foot chains, we managed most gracelessly to tumble down in token of gratitude for the Royal favour. Poles, ropes, and wedges to wrench off the fetters, were quickly supplied by the Amba chiefs. The clumsy operation, as usual, inflicted many a gory scratch and wound, but who cared for physical pain when the illusive visions of liberty, friends and home, floated before the enraptured eye. Our gait on the removal of the manacles resembled that of a thoroughly drunken man. We staggered, reeled, and sank down. All was swimming before the eyes or moving beneath the feet. To make a regular firm step was beyond the reach of possibility. We walked on air. Each one, as the shackles dropped from his limbs, was gently supported by two or three kind friends, but notwithstanding every effort, the frame was too light and the head too giddy to maintain the equilibrium, and we rolled towards Ras Gedana Miriam's house more like revellers from a scene of debauch than prisoners released from their manacles. In the Amba commandant's house we met Agha Faree Gholam, who reiterated the royal message, and then all squatted down to partake of a liberal Lenten repast. The same evening we were to have quitted the Amba for Salamege, but as this would have involved much inconvenience and great fatigue we requested to postpone our departure till next morning, a favour which was readily granted. Most of us did not sleep, nor attempt to sleep, that night. A mingled feeling of happiness on account of our deliverance, and of secret surmises about future consequences, kept us in a state of tumultuous agitation. With daylight we repaired to Salamege, and there we encamped. On the 27th, Agha Faree Gholam made his appearance at the head of a considerable division of the Magdala garrison, who, as the roads were infested with bands of rebels, had orders to escort us down the Djiddah. Our daily stages were long and fatiguing, but what did we care for exhausting marches when we knew that each step diminished the distance that lay between us and those dear faces, in whose smiles, chains and captivity, Theodore and Abyssinia, would be forgotten.

On approaching Gaffat the ardour of our spirits sustained a terrible check. We had received a variety of conflicting news. One day a royal messenger brought tidings to the chief of our escort* that we were to hurry on, as the king wanted to expedite our departure before the rainy season came on; the next, that we were to proceed slowly, as the exertion of fast travelling after the long confinement might prove injurious to our health; and then again, that we were not to leave till the rains were over. Flad, Staiger, Brandeis, Essler, and Schiller, the only Europeans at Gaffat, as the rest, consisting of workmen, had all been ordered to Quarata, the temporary home of the British envoy, wrote to us several times on passing events. Their last missives, however, contained the startling intelligence that his Majesty, under the superintendence of Mr. Rassam,† was going to build a fleet to navigate the Tzana, and that we would all have to fell trees, chop wood, and make ourselves useful in the ship-building line. Staiger, in a letter to Consul Cameron, reminded the latter that if he complied with the Negoos' wishes he had a splendid opportunity to regain his forfeited good graces. Our chief, the Agha

---

* On the whole march we were always surrounded by two or three hundred soldiers, or armed peasants, who watched us with lynx eyes by day and by night. It was pretended that this precaution was requisite, as the country was disturbed; but I believe the precaution was dictated by a suspicious fear that we might distrust the king, and decamp.

† Mr. Rassam was asked some questions about ship-building, but he shirked the question by pleading, what was wise and prudent, utter ignorance of the art.

Farce, got similar tidings. He understood the import of the message, and with an honesty that was a perfect libel on his character, he assured us that we would not leave Abyssinia so very soon.

On the 7th we reached Gaffat. The five Europeans located there met us at some distance from their homes. Our conversation naturally centred on the ship-building question. They could give us no further information beyond that which we had already obtained. It was a shameful mockery of the tyrant to deceive us with promises of freedom, when in reality he only designed to protract our captivity. I tried, and tried hard, to shake off those gloomy fears that obscured with their troubled shadows the bright vista of my future. The effort was unsuccessful, and neither converse nor travel could dispel the vague presentiment of a renewed captivity.

Near Quarata, where Mr. Rassam and his two companions were encamped, messenger after messenger came, in rapid succession, with commands of a very questionable character. All, I believe, issued from Samuel, who, as baldaraba of the envoy, sought to enhance his master's greatness in the eyes of the Abyssinians by imperious commands to his friends or guests. We were to come in European clothing, stockings and boots, and, if my memory is correct, with our faces washed. We were not to ride on pell-mell, but in regular order. Cameron was to lead the procession; close on his heels was to come Cocab—*i.e.*, myself—then Rosenthal, Flad, Kerans, &c. Some strictly conformed to all these behests, and others disregarded them all. I certainly washed my face, but coat, stockings, and European trousers were articles to which for months and years I was a perfect stranger. Two or three hundred yards from the envoy's camp we were met by Samuel, all radiant and beaming. Like, I wanted to say, Judas—no, like the penitent prodigal, he fell round the neck of each, and imprinted a kiss of fraternal affection. The kissing business over, he conducted us, in a stately procession, into the tent of Mr. Rassam, where we met with a sincere, cordial, and hearty welcome. Mr. Rassam did not share my own and Consul Cameron's apprehensions about the successful issue of his dangerous mission. He had hitherto only seen the tyrant in his good and gracious humour, which had imposed on more than one foreign representative.

Theodore was a consummate adept in dissimulation. He had deceived the Copt Patriarch; his successor, Abdul Rachman Bey; the French Consul, Mons. Lejean; the Nayeeb of Arkiko; Consul Cameron; and last, though not least, Mr. Rassam. Flattered by a mission from one of the greatest sovereigns of the universe, it is possible that his intentions on his arrival were more honest than the freaks of fancy or the insinuations of malice allowed him afterwards to adopt. This is certain, that Mr. Rassam met with a reception the most flattering ever accorded to a foreigner in Abyssinia. Not only was Theodore himself all condescension, but his courtiers and people were strictly enjoined to follow the royal example. Every wish of the ambassador's was to be gratified, and every request in her Majesty's letter was to be granted. The captives, or, as the artful despot, in deference to the envoy's sensibilities, courteously styled them, " the Magdalodj," were to be released; the mission was to be treated with royal honours; not the most trivial whim that could minister to their gratification was to be denied to the distinguished guests. Damot, on the borders of Godjam, where "the great men" first witnessed the full blaze of Theodore's magnificence, was, in token of gratitude for their safe advent, or some other equally plausible pretext, plundered of more than 80,000 heads of cattle to furnish broundo for the royal table; and the Island of Dek, according to Dr. Blanc, had to fork out 10,000 dollars—all their earthly possession—to fill the ambassador's money bags.

These acts did more than counterbalance the atrocities of the tyrant towards his unfortunate prisoners, whom he styled ill-tempered, ill-humoured, and mad. He was right; some, perhaps, were mad, but it was the long period of unparalleled misery and torment to which he subjected them that produced it. Mr. Rassam was, however, enchanted with Theodore, and if a suspicion now and then arose in his mind, he did not in word or look betray his surmises. Some of the workmen who were in the royal confidence acted their part well in this horrid farce, which wrung tears of blood from the eyes of the captives, their kindred, and friends.

Our friend Mr. Rassam kindly supplied us with the most needful garments. He had charitably provided himself with a stock of shirts, stockings, handkerchiefs, and shoes, which he generously divided among the prisoners. Coats and trousers were at a premium. Consul Cameron and myself got each a coat from Mr. Rassam. Mine was a little narrow and short, as I am about half a foot taller than Mr. Rassam, but still it was a better fit than Consul Cameron's, who outtopped his brother officer by a foot. Kerans, with the aid of a native tailor, stitched together a few pieces of red merino, and though it did not bear a full resemblance to an over-coat, frock-coat, or hunting jacket, it was nevertheless gorgeous, and he swaggered about in all the terrors of a flame-wrapt spirit. The rest, by a fortunate accident, had either preserved some remains of their former wealth, or they were too fondly attached to the native fashion to adopt so easily another and less convenient mode.

On the 15th, three days after our arrival at Quarata, a grand sham trial of the prisoners was instituted in Mr. Rassam's tent. The officials in their military and diplomatic uniforms formed a striking contrast to the prisoners in their quaint garbs, the white workmen in their flaring silks, and the royal delegates—of whom Waleda Gaber, formerly a servant of M. Barroni, who was a servant of Consul Plowden, a rascal of no mean degree, was the chief—formed altogether a group worthy the pencil of a Rembrandt. When all were in proper trim, Alaga Engeda, the chief royal scribe, read the charges. He commenced with Consul Cameron, against whom a long indictment was preferred. His most grievous offences were that he had neglected the king's letter and gone to his enemies the Turks, where, he was informed, he had lowered and insulted him. On his return, to use the official language of the protocol, "I (the king) asked him, 'Where is the answer to the friendly letter I intrusted you with; what have you come back for?' He said to me, 'I do not know.' I said to him, 'You are not the servant of my friend the Queen, as you had represented yourself to be;' and by the power of my Creator I imprisoned him."

The next charge was against M. Bardel on

the subject of his mission to France, and the last against all the other prisoners, myself included, was, that instead of defending him against the aspersions of his enemies we had joined in abusing him.

We all, as strictly enjoined by Mr. Rassam, acknowledged our offences and humbly craved the royal clemency. This admission was not a matter of choice, but sheer necessity. On my first trial at Gondar I defended myself boldly. This, the European workmen subsequently alleged, closed their lips and neutralised their influence with the king in my behalf. At Zeghee, on the fifth or sixth trial of the unfortunate captives, less than a month after the above judicial mockery, I was the impersonation of humility, and then these very men who, two years before found a plea for their indifference to the cruel position of a fellow creature in his pride, discovered an apposite pretext for a similar unconcern in his own and his companions' excessive humility. Mr. Rassam's presence gave quite a new phase to our affairs. It was henceforth no longer the prisoner's lives alone that hung on a slender thread, but in their fate was bound up the fate of the envoy and his companions. The king was most anxious for a pretext to stir up fresh complications, and nothing would have more delighted his unprincipled spies than to construe a word or gesture into an accusation to effect this object. The prisoners—I mean the principal prisoners—penetrated the designs of the worthy Negoos, and had he charged them with murder, sacrilege, or any other revolting crime, I believe they would, without wasting their breath, have all most tacitly listened to the indictment.

His Majesty pretended to be delighted with the result of the trial, and compliments the most exaggerated and fulsome were exchanged between the camp of the king on the southern extremity of the Lake Tzana and that of the British envoy on the eastern shore. "My children," was one, " I am full of gratitude for what you have done: come to me, I will kiss your hands and feet."

Solomon's seal, with which the members of the mission were to be decorated, now progressed most admirably, at an inverted ratio. The artist who was intrusted with the workmanship was coaxed and flattered, lauded and admired, to accelerate, if possible, the movement of his tools on the flattened precious plate. The Abyssinian lion, I believe, had claws; but, oh! the inscriptions—they were most provokingly slow in starting into existence. I took the most lively interest in the operations going on in the workshop of Zander, one of the king's European *employés*, and although I never went there myself, I heard enough from all the other visitors to make me conjecture that the elaborate decorations would not obtain the finishing touch before the Greek Kalends.

Wearily glided the sluggish hours into days, days into weeks, and at last the welcome intelligence reached the mission camp that saddles, swords, and other trinkets which were, to form a part of the presents for the embassy, had arrived from Debra Tabor. They were blessed tidings. No more delays — no more trials — no more chains. The very thought sent the blood in delicious glow through the throbbing veins. Alas! short is the happiness of frail humanity. The seals, those abominable seals, they were still in embryo, and far, far from completion! I always, notwithstanding his faults, admired the inspired writer of the matchless Book of Proverbs, but regard and veneration were now scattered to the winds, and the wise monarch rose before my mind like a ghastly unsightly spectre. Whether Zander's fingers were palsied, or whether an ominous warning checked the progress of the work is, and probably will continue, a secret to the end of time.

The Solomonic decorations, his Majesty at last declared, were not to protract our stay. Unfinished, unadorned, and unembellished, they were to be suspended round the necks of the honoured ambassador, his two companions, and—if Dr. Blanc is right—

the worthy Bappoo.* We received portentous hints about workmen, compensation, hostages, and other equally significant and vexatious matters. The distrustful prisoners trembled, the less suspicious mission hoped. Theodore had convoked a great council, and debated the question of our departure. The concentrated wisdom of the nation was for our exit, his Majesty against it. The European workmen, whose opinion was also consulted, chimed in with the voice of the multitude. Zander, who had that morning evidently fortified himself with a few extra glasses of potent tedj, proved the adage, *in vino veritas*. He reproached the king with his cruelties and the outrageous tortures inflicted on the white prisoners. "You say these men are badalanyodj" (transgressors) continued the elated orator; "no, you are a badalanyo. You have ruined your country, drenched it with blood, and closed it permanently against all Europeans." The great Negoos, who was also in his cups, retorted: "Let good men only come † and I will treat them well—not men like Cameron, who, to my question replies by pulling his beard;

* This excellent personage was Mr. Rassam's Indian butler. He had already received a silken shirt, which raised him to the rank of noble, and though he bore this dignity with becoming meekness, I question whether the seal of Solomon glittering on his breast would not have produced an opposite effect.

† He forgot that he had Mr. Rassam, whom he styled a good, sweet, dear man.

or that French Consul, who made his appearance on a donkey like a beggar, with a paper in his hand written by a scribe (the French minister); or that man Cocab, the ally of my enemy and traducer the Aboon. Let good men only visit my country, and I will show that I know how to appreciate them."

CHAPTER XIII.

Easter Day—An Ambiguous Compliment—Contemptible Trickery—
The sullen Agha Farce—Delightful Ride—Unappreciated Attentions—Royal Missive—Confiscation of Valuables—Uncomfortable Position—Conflicting Rumours—Comfortless Lodging—
Voyage across the Tzana—The Royal Robber—The Mission Arrested—Diplomacy Foiled—Grand Court—Meekness and Rage—Diplomatic Manœuvre—The Christian Diplomatist—
Gymnastic Performances—Sworn Friendship.

LENT was now drawing to a close, and the long season of abstinence was about to be followed by days of revel and debauch. Our friends at Magdala, when they heard of Mr. Rassam's arrival, congratulated us on the auspicious circumstance that he reached the camp when the king was the greater part of the day sober and amenable to reason, and not, as at other times, drunk and crazy. Unfortunately, incidents, over which we had no control, protracted our stay, and at last the dreaded weeks of festive hilarity and drunken riots, to our dismay, closed in upon us. Our own Easter fell on April 1st, and that of the Abyssinians—who pretend to follow the oriental churches in their computation—the Sunday following. We had on that occasion, for the first time,

Divine worship in the envoy's tent, which the European colony completely filled. Some of us, after service, commemorated the dying love of the Saviour, a privilege we had not enjoyed for nearly three years. It was a sad and mournful band that gathered around the table of the Lord on that distant and inhospitable shore, and in the emblems of a Saviour's suffering compassion sought calmness, strength, and support for their ruffled and fainting hearts.

Easter brought felicitations and compliments, sheep and cows in regal profusion. The released prisoners did not share in these tokens of royal favour. They were still in the shade, and only brought prominently forward when the despot by reproaches and insults wanted to indemnify himself for his condescension towards the envoy. Thus, in an interview with Samuel during the Abyssinian Passion-week, he told that worthy that he wished to see the captives—the word Magdalash was again in abeyance. Samuel, who had changed his tactics since the advent of the envoy, whom he hoped to accompany down to the coast, where he knew good dollars abounded, promptly rejoined: "Has your Majesty not dirt enough, that you want more?" The compliment was rather ambiguous. Samuel, however, meant it kindly. He was tired of his falling master. He had performed many a dirty trick, had betrayed many an innocent man, pressed hot tears out of many an eye, and all that he received in return consisted in cuffs, abuse, and empty promises. Contempt and disgust for the tyrant, together with an alarm for his own life, wonderfully stimulated his desire to win the good graces of Mr. Rassam, and, as this could only be done by accelerating our departure, he exerted himself most laudably to effect this object.

It is said that a ripple on the ocean warns the expert mariner of the impending storm, and this certainly was the case with us at this critical juncture of our captivity. All sorts of sinister and well-founded rumours reached us. It was said that the king had enclosed an empty space with a high fence, that he talked very often about *kasa* (compensation), that he stood in communication with certain spies, and that he was undecided whether he should be kind or severe, pleased or angry, with the Frendjoj. It was at this time that a packet for the coast, containing letters about our release, was twice seized by the king's people, and brought back to the royal camp, from whence it was despatched to Mr. Rassam. This was not only mean, but base and contemptible. He had himself sanctioned the despatch of those letters, and ordered the Governor of Quarata to send one of his own people to accompany the messenger; so that he had not even the shadow of an apology for his dishonourable proceedings. It proved, however, that he was anxious to pick up a quarrel; and, to effect this, he became indifferent to that pride and dignity of which, when it suited him, he knew well enough how to brag.

Our anxiety increased in intensity as the days multiplied. At length, on the morning of April 11th, Agha Farce Gholam; Lidj Abitou, a Belessa chief; Kasai, his friend; and a few other stars of lesser magnitude, made their appearance in the mission camp with orders for our departure. This was the most surprising and agreeable intelligence we had received since our misfortunes. With alacrity we hastened to make the few necessary preparations for our journey. Mr. Rassam and his two companions were not to start with us. They were the dear friends of the king, and, as such, the Negoos could not allow them to leave without a parting interview. The rest, as Samuel designated them, were "dirt," and not worthy to behold the glorious countenance of his Majesty, a privation for which we knew how to console ourselves. Agha Farce Gholam, our uncouth, semi-negro friend, did not share in the satisfaction which prevailed in our small camp. There was a forbidding leer in that one glittering eye, which the small-pox had most ungenerously left him, to fill up, I presume, the black catalogue of pillage and murder entrusted to him by his worthy master, that caused me a pang whenever I glanced at him. He had swallowed down substantial pieces of quivering broundo, drained many a berrile of potent arackee and tedj, and still his spirits were below zero. It could not be an evil conscience that was at work within him; for a man like him, whose very garments were drenched in blood, could not have much of a conscience, and even if he had, it was torpid, or altogether in abeyance. I had no tedj or arackee to offer him; but, instead of these delicacies, for which most Abyssinians will sell their souls, I almost drowned him in excellent coffee. The genial beverage did not melt the ice of his soul, or loose the strings of his tongue. He was sullen, morose, and unsociable. There was something on his heart which evidently troubled and perplexed him. He had a kind of doggish affection for some of us, partly on account of the presents he had received, and also partly on account of the kindness and courtesy he had invariably experienced, and this rendered his taciturnity still more suspicious. Several times I tried to worm out the secret, by questioning him, in a most coaxing tone, about our journey; but, like one of those ugly, squatting, Indian idols, he sat motionless and mute. Once only, in reply to a dubious wish that he might be the chief of our escort, did he yawn forth, in croaking accents, "Koi,

Koi" (wait, wait). He knew that a detachment of royal troops was on the road to seize us, and very likely the secret would not have remained enshrined in his black bosom, had he not justly dreaded the consequences it might involve. In the afternoon, a grand council was convoked at Quarata, which was attended by all the magnates of the place. Samuel was one of the wise men who constituted that conclave, and it does not reflect much credit on the ungrateful courtier, that a cowardly fear deterred him from warning his new master, Mr. Rassam, of our coming troubles.

The following morning, which was to consummate our Abyssinian exodus, we hailed with joy and delight. Mr. Rassam, his companions, and the European workmen, at sunrise embarked in a small fleet of bullrush boats for the royal camp, and about two hours afterwards the late Magdala captives, the three missionaries, and two hunters on parole at Gaffat,[*] in high glee sprang on their saddles and trotted away. Our road lay across rough and uneven paths lined with stinging nettles, and broken by dried-up canals and deep ruts. This, however, we did not notice, our excited imaginations tinted

[*] Mr. Flad was an agent of the London Jews' Society; Messrs. Staiger and Brandeis agents of the Scotch Church; and Messrs. Schiller and Essler were hunters in connection with several German museums. They were not allowed to leave the country, but were not chained up in prison.

every object with lovely colours, and we stumbled over holes and ditches, brushed along weeds and bushes in the delirium of a most ecstatic dream. Our guards never flagged in their vigilance. They were in the rear and in the front, on the right and the left; in fact, wherever we wandered there they hovered around us.

After all, we had misunderstood Theodorus. Did not the very attentions of the guards prove that the reconciliation, at least on his part, was quite sincere? Did not those watchful eyes, that gleamed on us whenever in our rapture we deviated from the right path, show how precious we were to his heart? Did not the solicitude which every soldier manifested for our safety demonstrate how tenderly his late prisoners had entwined themselves around his deepest and best affections? Smite on your breasts, prostrate yourselves on the ground, and acknowledge that Theodore is a grossly injured monarch, and a most amiable and forgiving Christian. Such, perhaps, were the thoughts that floated through the mind of one or the other on that short hour's travel. At the village where we alighted, a whole detachment of troops, without lance or sword, probably in order not to awaken any suspicion, sat basking in the sun's mild rays. We wanted to encamp outside the fence that encircled the fragile tenements of the district governor's abode, but were solemnly assured that this was impossible. "You," we were told, "are friends of the king, and we cannot allow you to camp in the open air where hyænas, leopards, and lions may disturb your nocturnal slumbers." This was kind, provident, and considerate; and, with all our disgust for enclosures which we had imbibed at Magdala, we readily yielded to the commands of these cautious men. When our tents were all pitched, Lidj Abitou and his friend Kasai paid me a visit. I ordered some coffee, but he refused to drink any as he was so very busy in attending to our rations. *En passant*, he enquired whether I or any of my companions had fire-arms. I told him that I had none, and the majority of my companions were also unprovided with arms, swords, or weapons of defence. He chuckled on hearing this, and then walked away, evidently pleased with the idea that the capture of the white men could be effected without any serious resistance. Late at noon we were all summoned into a hut to hear a letter read which it was pretended had that moment arrived from the king. We all thought that it was a parting epistle, embodying the following or similar contents: "I am well, and hope you are well. I love you, and want you also to love me. Send me cannon and gun makers to chastise my bad people, who advised me to chain you. By your favour, and the power of . . . I shall send their bodies to the grave and their souls to hell. Farewell."

The haystack-shaped cabin, on our entering, to our surprise, was closely lined by well-armed troops. We did not exhibit any fear; but, placing ourselves in front of the compact mass of sentinels, with some internal trepidation awaited the issue of these strange and mysterious proceedings. Beitwodet Tadlo, a chief of some note, who perished a year later under the executioner's knife, after putting some questions to his subordinates about our numbers, and whether all were present, unfolded a paper, and, lifting it on high, inquired whether we knew the seal. "Yes, it is the king's," was the simultaneous response. "Guards, seize them!" and instantly each one was in the iron grasp of two or three ruffians. The blow was so sudden that we had no time to reflect or make any conjecture. One or two ejaculated "Are these villains going to murder us?" Quiet and order being restored, the royal epistle was next read. It began, as usual, in the name of the Trinity—the blasphemous despot had learnt to interlard his abominable effusions with Scripture sentences—it then adverted to the friendly feeling that had always subsisted between the king and Mr. Rassam; touched in ambiguous language on an unhappy quarrel that had marred their attachment; and finally closed with an injunction to put us in chains, but not to maltreat us by any other infliction of suffering. Fetters—the heaviest I had yet seen—were soon hammered around the well-trained right and left wrists of each pair, and thus linked together we were driven, well watched, into prison. The two ladies and their children were exempted from this rigorous guardianship, and they had a quiet but sad night in a tent that was assigned for their sole occupation. Our luggage was, of course, strictly examined, and all money and valuables confiscated for the royal treasury. Most of us had some papers and notes we were anxious to destroy. I had nothing that could compromise me, except a few cash accounts from the bishop, to which his seal was attached. I was, however, anxious to consign to the flames every vestige of written paper in my possession, and to do this I got the basket which contained them, and whilst Kerans—my companion —was eating, I consigned one after the other to the flames of the flickering taper I held under the folds of my shama. So long as Kerans' appetite lasted I knew that I was safe,* but I dreaded lest he should stop before I had finished. He had certainly already swallowed bread and pepper enough

---

* Abyssinians never look at a man whilst he is taking his meals, as they dread the influence of an evil eye.

to cloy the appetite of any reasonable being, and still there I was toiling and sweating over my candle and basket. "Do finish, Mr. Stern, or the guards will see you, for I cannot eat any more," his plaintive voice whispered in my ears. "Take one piece more," I persuasively rejoined, "and then I have done." Again there was a pause for a few seconds, when once more, with a jerk that made the chains rattle, my companion, in louder and less gentle accents exclaimed, "Hang the Aboon and his accounts. I won't eat any more, for I shall get sick." "Don't be churlish, my good fellow," was the rejoinder, "there is no necessity that you should eat to surfeit; chew a rag, and no one will suspect your digestive faculties." During this colloquy my papers disappeared, and I had one care less on my shoulders.

Early next morning we retraced our steps to Quarata. On the road our servants hunted in all directions for news. The reports they brought to us were most conflicting. One had heard that Mr. Rassam was restored to the royal favour; another that he was in chains; and a third that he and his companions had been executed. Judging from the tyrant's vicious temper, the latter story appeared most probable. But what could have induced him to perpetrate such an outrage? Mr. Rassam, we knew, had not offended him; and against the old prisoners, we were certain, he had not any fresh causes of complaint. Our speculations were most painful, and, at the same time most unsatisfactory. Death had lost all its terrors; life alone was fraught with troubles and cares. The executioner's sword would have been merciful compared to the horrid suspense we had to endure. At sunset we were marched into Quarata, and lodged in two separate houses. We had no bedding, not even a hide to sleep on. Our luggage was in charge of guards, and those dastardly poltroons would not allow us a rag without the royal sanction. Condemned to a captivity that appeared destined to last as long as the tyrant's reign, the mind almost revolted from conjectures, and if now and then faith portrayed to the imagination happier scenes than a dungeon and chains, one shrank from the ever-disappointing vision, as the sensitive plant from the finger's touch.

The weary night at last waned, and the grey light of dawn began to be visible through the chinks and holes of our prison. The clanking of chains and the sound of steps roused the snoring guards, who would gladly have slept half an hour more, had their restless charge been a little more considerate. By the time our braves had girded on their unwieldy swords, swathed themselves in their bulky belts, and removed the barricades that protected the doors, orders came that we should proceed to the lake, where boats were ready to convey us to the royal camp.

On our arrival at the beach, we found our acquaintance, Agha Farce Gholam, the "negad ras" (chief of the merchants), and a few other distinguished and exalted personages. Mrs. Waldemeier, daughter of the late Mr. Bell, by his first native wife, was also there. She could not give us any positive news, except that the king was angry because Mr. Rassam had despatched the Magdala prisoners without a personal interview and reconciliation with him. Samuel and Cantiba Hailu, whom she did not particularly admire, she further told us, were in disgrace, and that probably they would have to bear the brunt of their master's ire. The springs of my belief in the king and every one, directly or indirectly, connected with him were, however, dried up, and nothing remained but an unfeigned trust in the promises of Him who could save and deliver his ill-used and maltreated servants.

The voyage across the lake in fragile boats, and in couples closely chained, was not very agreeable. Agha Farce Gholam called Kerans and myself several times along his boat to partake of some of the luxuries with which he had provided himself. Despite the splashing oars, broiling sun, and swollen wrists, we had a good appetite, and the good cheer of our chief was highly appreciated. The most woe-begone of our party were the Indian servants of the mission. Boola, Mr. Rassam's valet, consoled himself in his fetters by a vague Moslem belief in adamantine decrees; but Francis, the Goa Portuguese, who had no such consolation, was pale and livid with contending passions. His whole frame quivered as he held up to our gaze the fetters in which he was tied, whilst his voluble tongue poured forth incoherent English and Hindostanee abuse on the king and everyone else whom he disliked. "Very good king," he shouted across to us. "Plenty dollars—ten thousand to ambassador—fine country—much execution—king fine gentleman, very fine," and then there would follow an outburst in Hindostanee, that must have been unique, for it made even the sedate Boola roar with laughter.

Mid-day we reached Zeghee. Several of the European workmen on our arrival came out of the royal enclosure, but they took no notice of us, nor even sent a servant to inquire after the welfare of their brethren, of whom three were in our party. They were certainly slaves, or, as the king used to style them, most servile and subservient slaves. In getting out of the boats each one was searched, to see if he had any money about his person. This act was not dictated by hostile feeling towards us, but by pressing want. The soldiers were starving, the loyal provinces impoverished, and the exchequer drained and empty. These were contingencies that weighed heavily on his Majesty's mind; and as the wretched Frendjoj had a few dollars, the unscrupulous son of Solomon, who was never particular about the *tuum*, thought he might as well appropriate them to his own use. He had plundered me before of more than two hundred pounds in cash, besides a valuable collection of manuscripts, a watch, clothing, photographic apparatus, &c. I pardoned him those robberies, as he had at least some extenuation in the custom of the country, but to deprive a number of pardoned prisoners of a few paltry dollars was an act worthy of a mean thief, and not of a mighty king.

The "stand and deliver" business over, we were led into the ready-prepared fence, to which I have before alluded, where a small tent was erected for our accommodation. We were scarcely settled in our new home, when bread, pepper, tedj, and cows came pouring into our fence. The royal purveyor who accompanied these bounties, with a glow of pride, told us that he was the slave of his Majesty, and had a message for his children. "Janchoi," quoth the modest slave, who might have spared himself the trouble to announce his character, which was legibly written on every line of his grim face, " has charged me to tell you that he hopes you are all well. He has sent you so much bread, pepper, &c., &c., which you will eat and be merry. May God soon release you." We made a most humble obeisance, and then the whole procession whirled round, and, headed by the big man, the royal slave, marched off.

We had not yet seen any one of the mission, but we got all the particulars of their seizure, maltreatment, and arrest. It did not take so much time, nor were there so many precautions adopted, as with the less dignified and more desperate old criminals. They were conducted to the audience hall, an oblong cabin; asked a few questions about the whereabouts of the prisoners; why they had not come to Zeghee, and who had given them leave to depart; and then three ruffians rushed on each, and declared them prisoners. A whole string of questions were put to Mr. Rassam, to which he gave firm and decisive replies. He particularly insisted that the prisoners had started with his Majesty's sanction, and under the charge of an escort provided by him, and he might have added, that had he brought them to Zeghee, the king would have subjected him to still coarser severity because he had done so. The shameless braggart actually—at the very moment that he informed Mr. Rassam that he had intended to give us mules and money—at that very moment his banditti were rummaging our poverty-stricken luggage bags, to rob us of the little cash in our possession. His Majesty, during the whole of the proceeding, was invisible. This did him credit, as it showed that he was not yet what he subsequently became—lost to all shame.

The following morning there was a grand court within the royal enclosure, to try the prisoners. It was a meagre and beggarly affair compared to the imposing spectacle presented on a similar occasion, a little more than two years before at Gondar. The tyrant himself, if he cast a retrospective glance at the past, must have felt the contrast most dire and rueful. He was then in the zenith of his power. Success everywhere attended his arms, and in the flush of glory the infatuated man really began to think that he was the Theodorus of prophecy. All was now reversed. His army had dwindled down from 150,000 warriors to about 25,000 ruffians. His extensive realm had shrivelled into a few provinces, and his schemes of foreign aggrandisement had become confined to a desperate struggle with home rebels. Had he reflected, he might have remembered that his power began to wane from the very hour that a scarred, lacerated, and bleeding missionary lay insensible at his feet; but he had sold himself to work evil till the bolt of justice put an end to his desolating career.

Driven along like a gang of galley slaves, we hurriedly traversed the camp, from whence, through a wide passage in the royal fence, we were ushered into the presence of the judge, jury, and audience. His Majesty was on an alga or divan; the members of the mission on his right, about ten yards in front; the European workmen about double the distance in the same line; and the rest, consisting of military chiefs, officers, and priests, were ranged in a semicircle, according to their rank. We were placed in a row at the farthest end of the assemblage, opposite the alga. His Majesty asked us a few questions about our health and welfare, which we acknowledged in prostrations so exact and uniform as to do credit to our long training. Consul Cameron, in whose behalf, it was said by high and low, soldier and chief, the mission had visited Abyssinia —a report not at all creditable to those who spread it—was ordered to be released of his chains, and placed near his brother officers. M. Bardel, probably on account of some special service, had the same honour assigned to him; and the rest, who had neither merit nor official position, were obliged to gratify, in their humiliating fetters, the gaze of the assembled multitude. The questions propounded were of the old stereotyped stamp, with a few embellishments to heighten their effect. We were, of course, all meekness and submission. The fiendish malice in the tyrant's eye, even more than words, expressed his disappointment with our conduct. He wanted to find an excuse for his vile treachery and base designs, in the boldness of the captives, or in their defence of paltry charges preferred against them. His scheme failed, and he had to seek some other subterfuge to palliate his past proceedings, and to throw a veil over his well-matured, nefarious projects. "My children," he then said to his workmen, who were called before him, "is it right that I should ask for Kasa" (compensation)? Waldemeier and Zander, in their excitement, said loudly, "Kasa is very good." Perhaps if they had remembered that so many ears were listening with intense interest to every word they uttered, they would have expressed their opinion *sotto voce*, for they were both expert Abyssinian courtiers of the real, genuine, and unmistakable type. The rest were more politic, except Saalmüller, who said distinctly, "No, Kasa is bad." These, then, were the men who, a few days before, had boldly requested the king to sanction our departure? The story is true, but the motives by which they were actuated will remain a mystery. It is most likely that the bold straightforwardness of the native chiefs excited their emulation—an indiscretion for which some at least atoned by a diplomatic manœuvre, that screened them from his Majesty's displeasure.

Before the court was dissolved Mr. Rassam and his party were ordered to rise.

The compressed thin lips and spasmodic contortions of the king's bloated face indicated something boisterous, but he restrained himself, and merely said, "Why did you send the prisoners away before I was reconciled with them? Are you my masters? I want England to be my friend, for we two can make a hedge around Senaar.* Now you remain with me; and wherever I go, you will go; and wherever I stay, you will stay." Mr. Rassam, undaunted by royal rhetoric, like a Christian and a gentleman, in becoming terms, requested our release. His Majesty grinned, and then rejoined, "Enough for to-day."

On the ensuing morning our fetters were taken off, and a treaty of peace, amity, and eternal love concluded between Theodore, Consul Cameron, Cocab, Roos, and all the late captives. The ceremony required a fearful amount of prostration—a task which we performed with wonted credit. Consul Cameron alone made a mess of it. His spine or knees were evidently out of working order, for he

---

* Senaar, the former capital of the Soudan, for centuries paid tribute to Abyssinia. This had been stopped since its annexation to Egypt—an insult which rankled deeply in the tyrant's heart.

neither toppled down nor rose up in conformity with the prescribed court etiquette. The masters of the ceremony were quite in distress, and they had to do their utmost to get him through the ordeal. After we had performed our gymnastic feats, the king played his part in the comedy. He was perfect in the art of dissimulation. There the great Negoos lay on the ground, mild, gentle, and penitent, imploring, in language the most tender and solemn, the forgiveness of those whom he had, under mistaken impressions, wronged and injured. It was a performance no Othello ever rivalled. We would gladly have clapped our hands, and applauded the histrionic artist, but as this was unbecoming in a royal theatre, we contented ourselves by repeated entreaties that the actor should rise. The farce over, we were told to sit down, whilst several documents were read to us for our edification. Our relatives' mournful and affecting petition made us forget the nonsensical ceremony in which we had taken such an active share, and with thrilling emotions we listened to every word of that tender appeal. The tyrant himself, as he said, when he received it about a month before, was deeply touched on perusing its contents, and the seriousness he evinced when it was read to us in English, a language of which he understood not a word, showed that the impression was not entirely effaced.

Harmony and peace being restored, the king dictated two letters—one for her Majesty the Queen, and another for our relations, which were to be conveyed to England by Mr. Flad, who, as he had a wife and three children to leave as hostages, was selected for that post. The one to our friends contained the tidings that for the sake of the Queen of England he had given us over to Mr. Rassam, the other to her Majesty, this significant phrase : " We, the people of Ethiopia, are blind, and we beg your Majesty that you should give light to our eyes;" or in plain language, "we want some more hostages, and then we shall seek to enforce our conditions."

CHAPTER XIV.

Sensation Scenes—Brag and Bluster—Zeghee Pillaged—Cholera in the Camp—Abrupt Departure—The Penitent Tyrant—Death in Pursuit—Raw Recruits—Vice Dangerous—Prelude of Ruin—New Homes—Transient Honours—Royal Craft—Grateful Counsellors—Murder of a Beggar—Doubtful Parentage—Undisputed Claims—Dismal Dungeon—Royal Visit.

THE camp, which was never a very agreeable home, after the blighted prospects of freedom became a perfectly loathsome abode. Those fond of sensation scenes could here have cloyed their strange taste. There at one time could be seen the cracking giraff (hippopotamus-whip, six feet long), as it descended on the bare back, cutting deep furrows with every stroke; next, the knotty stick rattled noisily above the bluster of heaving bands; and then, again, there were executions of every device and cunning, from the severing of the head to the amputating of hands and feet, and from the battering with stones to the braining of a supplicant for justice, with a block of wood, by the delicate hands of a king. But it would be sickening to linger on the diversions of the Negoos, with which every one in the position of a captive became, alas! too familiar and intimate.

Encamped on the confines of a country that had first raised the standard of rebellion and challenged the despot's power, it was naturally anticipated that an order to march against the insurgents would every moment resound through the long lines of black tents by which the king was surrounded. The enemy, undaunted by the herald's vaunting proclamation that ere long a rich booty would fall to each soldier's share, hovered in small divisions around the outlets of Zeghee, killing stragglers, and enticing deserters. Ashamed and irritated, the blustering despot indulged in all sorts of unmeaning brag. "Godjam," he prated—and that, too, in the presence of his foreign guests—"Godjam I shall destroy, and its inhabitants I shall kill." Such were the outpourings of his heart; but, happily, the promptings of his ruthless spirit were not accomplished. His feelings were most merciless, and had his arm been equal to the task, the lion, the leopard, and the elephant might now occupy the homes where busy multitudes of human beings quietly pursue their peaceful and varied occupations. Godjam was spared, but Zeghee had to suffer.

This Kadom (asylum), embosomed in one of the woods that skirt the Maitsha plain, where the Blue Nile, after a graceful sweep through the Lake Tzana, sends its muddy but prolific waters over dizzying cataracts and across fat pastures and dreary sands, down through regions of immortal fame, enjoyed, owing to its superstitiously-sacred character, a kind of immunity from the forays and exactions which so often blighted the prospects of the merchant and the labours of the husbandman in this misgoverned and distressed country.

King Theodorus acknowledged no such privileges, nor admitted any rules which did not coincide with his despotic will. The Church might, indeed, be sacred, but it must be stripped of its wealth; the homes of the peasantry might present charming retreats for an industrious and peaceful population, but they must be rifled and burnt for the benefit of the impoverished king, or the advantage of his hungry and pillage-loving hordes.

His was not a mission to teach subjects to live in the midst of charming bowers; no, they must learn to despise the sylvan beauty of the coffee and lemon-tree, the jasmin and myrtle, and be content with stinging weeds and pestilent wilds. He was, in all that involved ruin and misery, true to his character—a despot and a despoiler. And Zeghee will for years not recover from the horrors of its king's last visit.

Whilst the despot, like a destroying angel, was scattering death and desolation, another, and a no less dangerous and unsparing foe, made its appearance.

For some days there had been rumours that the cholera was in the camp, but superstitious fear foolishly sought to suppress the ugly fact. A sudden death in the royal household, and the unmistakable symptoms that others would speedily follow, awed the tyrant, and induced him to hurry on to Quarata. The insidious enemy obstinately followed the weary hordes, marking the whole way with the corpses of its victims. Agha Farce Gholam, one day, whilst squatting in an easy attitude near me, was suddenly struck by the invisible shaft, and for ever deprived of the abused power of the hangman. The cemeteries round the monastery and churches in and near Quarata were choked with the dead, and still the terrible scourge did not abate in its violence. Everywhere, in the streets, in the tents, and in the fields, in fact, in all the surrounding places, there were heard the plaintive wails of the mourners, and the thrilling shrieks of the bereaved and dying. Few were exempted; hoary age and innocent childhood, the burly warrior and the tender maiden, all were—unmourned, and, I fear too frequently, unforgiven—consigned to the silent tomb. The tyrant, thinking that the clods might soon rattle upon his own coffin, read the Psalms, prayed, and appeared penitent. No longer was the ear startled by the crack of the "giraff," or the vociferous shouts for the Agha Farees. The executioner's post was in reality, what no rational being could have dreamt of, an absolute sinecure in King Theodore's camp, whilst the office of the priest became a most arduous and self-denying task.

"On to Debra Tabor, where the air is salubrious, and the hills breathe the vigour of health!" shouted the royal herald. Instantly tents were struck, horses and mules saddled, and every one scampering away from the pest-smitten spot; but the rider on the "pale horse" was as indefatigable on the march as he was during the halt, and multitudes who in flight sought to escape from his icy grasp were struck down, and never reached the desired goal. The whole road along which the army marched was strewn with the dead and the dying. Those who had no kind friends or kindred to alleviate or lighten their convulsive agonies, tottered along till their eyes became dim, their limbs stiff, and they sank down to rise no more. No sepulchral rites were awarded to their mortal remains; no funeral hymns were sung around their sleeping dust; a few handfuls of earth were thrown over their corpses, and then the indifferent multitude rushed from the exposed village cemetery, or the isolated dell, careless and unconcerned whether before another sun rose the vultures of the air, or the hyenas of the forest, had gorged their voracious maws upon the lately breathing and thinking forms of their companions and relatives. Thus perished many hundreds on that dreary and dismal three days' march.

The epidemic had been most virulent in the army, and how to reinforce its diminished and broken ranks began to be a grave and serious question. Quara and Tschelga, to the north-west, had hitherto been privileged provinces; the former on account of its being the natal home of the despot, and the latter because it formerly contained the State prison, and also offered a formidable barrier to any encroachments from the north-western Egyptian dominion. Necessity, however, admitted no exemption; and, reluctant as they felt, they had to furnish the requisite contingents. The raw recruits, fond of their sunny vales, where benignant nature with the least toil amply provides for every want, did not relish the bustle and excitement, and still less the privations of a camp; and so, without troubling their dull intellects about the king or the condition of his country, they girded their unwieldy swords upon their belts, and, during a bright moonlight night, bade adieu to the chilly upland plains, 'where they had been called to join the

T

army, and returned to their picturesque and fertile lowland homes.

The tyrant, instead of shaking off dull sloth, most recklessly abandoned himself to ease and vicious indulgences. Rebels, with their factious bands, defied him on all sides, and he had only to buckle on his faithful sword and all their contemptible brag would have terminated in a precipitate flight. His *prestige* was still unimpaired, and had he retained a spark of his former daring the spreading rebellion might in several provinces have been nipped in the very bud.

Besotted by an insane belief that his throne was secure, he wasted his days in fanciful speculations on contests, slaughters, and victories. "Let the insurgents get fat during the rainy season, we shall kill them afterwards," was his favourite expression. Impoverished and grievously taxed, Begemeder had during the whole of this time to bear the burden of providing for the king and his army. Military chiefs, governors, and even common soldiers, despairingly shook their greasy bushy wigs. The insurrection in the disaffected provinces assumed a wider range; the dangers far and near grew more and more pressing; and the prelude of impending ruin resounded from voices hitherto duly vocal to the tyrant's praise.

Infatuated by a foolish belief that like the fabled

phœnix he would rise out of the ashes of his empire more glorious and powerful than any of Abyssinia's former sovereigns, he whiled away his time in the diversions offered by an extensive elfin, a good quantity of strong tedj, and the unfortunate white captives.

During the first few days his Majesty was exceedingly courteous and civil towards Mr. Rassam, his two companions, and the old prisoners. We were lodged in the houses of his European workmen; and when the latter on their arrival manifested some displeasure at this not very satisfactory arrangement, we were transferred to abodes not far distant. The mission were accommodated in tolerably good houses, but the rest had holes assigned to them so filthy and swarming, that the "Society for the Prevention of Cruelty to Animals" would prosecute a person, and that justly, if he placed a dog in such a kennel.

I ventured into the one that was to be my abode; but although I had regularly graduated in the common Magdala gaol, I recoiled from the offensive sight I encountered. Debterah Birrou, an excellent Falasha Christian whom I met on my return, stood aghast on beholding the condition of my garments. I gave him my shama to clean, whilst I toiled hard to restore my trousers to something like their original purity. Some of my companions cleared the styes which they were condemned to occupy. I was under no such necessity, as I had a small tent that afforded me, if not protection against rain, perfect immunity from all kinds of vermin.

"Decorate his house, spread carpets, build a fence, do all to make my friend comfortable," were the orders issued by his Majesty concerning Mr. Rassam. Alas! alas! how transient are all earthly honours! how short-lived all sublunary glories! On the 18th, Cantiba Hailu, the governor of Gondar, Kera Meddin, the *negad ras*, or chief of the merchants, and several other persons of rank and dignity, were affixing *gabees* and *shamas* around the walls of the envoy's residence; and on the 25th he and his companions, together with the old captives, were prisoners in a black tent in the royal compound.

This sudden transition, from the height of royal favours to durance vile in a black tent, came upon us like a thunder-clap. We had often witnessed ups and downs in Abyssinia. We had seen rich governors reduced to poor beggars, great military chiefs to low menials, and ancient nobles to the degrading position of prisoners in chains; but we did not anticipate that a favourite ambassador, nor that any one of us, would, during Mr. Flad's mission to England, be subject to those alternations of fortune, which were the inevitable reward of valour and fidelity in the great Negoos' realm.

The cause assigned for this unexpected change in our treatment, was a letter, purporting to have been brought from Jerusalem by a Greek priest, containing intelligence, as it was alleged, that England, France, and Turkey were about to invade Abyssinia. Mr. Rassam energetically protested against this and a few more trumped-up charges, but the Negoos was inflexible, and we were declared *bonâ fide* prisoners.

On July 3rd, his Majesty, who had again assumed a milder and more flattering tone towards his foreign guests, sent a message to Mr. Rassam full of tenderness and affection. "You are my friend, and I love you. If you wish to go out, you are at liberty to do so. With your permission, I now go to Gaffat, to inspect some work of my children, and on my return, or at any time, if you have a request to prefer, or a message to send, call one of the eunuchs, and they will convey it to me without delay."

This was kind and considerate. Theodore could please and offend, be civil and rough, gentle and monstrously cruel. Towards her Majesty's envoy he had for several days been exceedingly affable, for which we were all very grateful, as it indirectly had a reflective influence on our own position. The old prisoners were something like a safety-valve to the mission. If the king was benignant, they enjoyed quiet and peace; and if, on the contrary, he was angry, they had to sustain the whole charge of terrors and alarm. The royal counsellors, who, for substantial reasons, befriended Mr. Rassam, were aware of this; and, as they most justly did not like to see a man who gave them handsome presents exposed to troubles and dangers, they strenuously opposed the king's original plan—to send us out of the country, and to keep only Mr. Rassam, and perhaps one of his companions. "If you let all the old prisoners depart," they remonstrated, on one occasion, as I heard from the very best authority, "on whom will you revenge yourself in case the British Government do not grant all you desire? Against Mr. Rassam you have no personal grudge, which is not the case with the Consul, Cocab, and Rosenthal, &c., on whom you can and should resent any disappointment you may experience."

The visit to Gaffat grievously ruffled the placidity of his Majesty's temper. A beggar, by a fatal mistake, called his children, the European workmen, "Gaitodj" (lords), an indiscretion that cost him his life; next, he was annoyed with some of his own people; then, with two or three of the Gaffatodj; and, finally, Dr. Blanc, but, above all, Mr. Rosenthal, who was by special permission allowed to live unguarded with his wife, came in for a giant share of the royal wrath.

Mr. Rassam, Consul Cameron, Lieut. Prideaux, and myself, were in our prison tent when the despot came back. Ignorant of all that had occurred during the interval, we did not notice his return, till Samuel, in a flurry, summoned us to repair into his presence. The sight of a number of soldiers, who, with their chiefs, were standing in groups all over the compound, indicated something serious. We had, however, no time to speculate, for the fierce voice of the tyrant concentrated our whole attentions. A variety of charges were preferred against Mr. Rassam, the consul, and myself. The stale story about his "pedigree" was the chief crime preferred against me. I tendered my wonted apology for this terrible offence, and he appeared, if not satisfied, at least appeased. His claims on India, Arabia, Constantinople (a name he egregiously mutilated), Jerusalem, and Senaar, were now rehearsed, for the edification of the envoy and the wondering court. Till that moment, I always thought that he claimed his descent from Solomon; but now, for the first time, I learnt that Constantine and Alexander the Great were both to blame for his existence. Mr. Rassam, who was requested to confirm the genealogical fact, extricated himself out of the dilemma by an evasive response. This did not satisfy the despot, and, turning his bloodshot eyes full on me, he said: "*Aito Cocab*, you know history; will you, therefore, tell me whether I have an inheritance in Jerusalem?" "I know that there are Abyssinians living in a convent at Jerusalem," was my response.

Pleased that his claims on the universe, if not fully admitted, were at least not disputed, he suspended the order for chains, and imposed on us the less rigorous penalty of confinement in a black, dismal, dark dungeon. In the evening he honoured our dreary prison with a visit. To enliven our gloom, he brought a formidable horn of arackee for his friends, in which they were to drink his health. The cup that inebriates and does not cheer circulated round most decorously, and, when all with perfect *éclat* had drunk to the tyrant's health, he made fresh artful proffers of friendship to Mr. Rassam, and also told Mr. Rosenthal, and particularly myself, that we should not indulge in harrowing surmises, as he had nothing against us.

INTERIOR OF MAGDALA, WITH SALASIE IN THE DISTANCE.

CHAPTER XV.

Revolt of the Provinces—Sham Campaign—Churches Pillaged—
Retributive Vengeance—Wanton Atrocities—New Prison—Foot
Chains—Domiciliary Arrangements—Despatch of Letters—
Abyssinian Honesty — Our Prison Library — Instruction of
Inquirers — Prayerless Amar — Sundays in Prison — Stirring
Incident—Diplomatic Correspondence—Butchery in the Camp—
Desertions—Reign of Terror—A Midnight Massacre—A Wise
Messenger—The Tyrant Defeated—Cannon Foundry—Unfortunate Fugitives.

THE dangers which had been looming in the distance approached nearer and nearer every day; Godjam, Lasta, Tigré, Woggera, and several other important provinces were in undisguised rebellion against the despot. Dembea, Begemeder, Belessa, and a few small districts, were the only territories in his once extensive realm that still acknowledged a doubtful allegiance to his sway. Roused by these ominous signs of a general revolution, he awoke to a consciousness of the dangers by which he was environed, bade farewell to debasing indulgences, and set out for the south.

It was now thought that the campaign had begun in earnest, and that a struggle, in which the fate of the realm was involved, would ensue in reality, when lo, and behold, the straggling forces are ordered back to Debra Tabor, and the farce terminates by sending eight white defenceless captives to Magdala! Enemies were henceforth secure and friends in peril. Gondar, which more than once had felt the sanguinary violence of the despot, was again to smart beneath his pitiless ferocity. A rebel, whom the few impoverished and half-starved inhabitants were forced to accommodate in their huts, formed the pretext for this outburst. A sharp march of a night and day brought the despoiler to that ruined and ill-fated capital. The people, terrified and panic-stricken, in their confusion raised the wonted "li-li-li" of welcome. This the cruel tyrant construed into a warning note to the insurgents, and instantly every man, woman, and child found in the streets was seized and consumed beneath the burning rafters of the nearest houses. The private dwellings, which had been robbed on several previous occasions, offered no booty to the invaders; but the forty-four churches, which both Christian and Mahomedan marauders hitherto had left untouched, presented attractions not to be despised by the pillage-loving King Theodorus. The command was given, and simultaneously the profane scoundrels rushed into the sacred edifices (which had hitherto been deemed inviolate), and, unheedful of the supplications of the laity, and the deprecations of the clergy, carried off vestments, mitres, crosses, pictures, and chalices; in fact, everything which, on account of its antiquity or value, had for ages been regarded with the utmost awe and veneration by the devout and superstitious. Many of the sacred edifices were wantonly set on fire, and burnt to the ground; and those that escaped the conflagration were vilely desecrated by the miscreants. The news of this infamous spoliation spread rapidly through the length and breadth of the land. "Death to the odious infidels!" shouted every voice but those of the myrmidons of the tyrant. But, although the stir, clamour, and tumult was intense, it all ended in empty demonstration and noise. The tyrant, after this inglorious achievement, returned with his shameless trophies to Debra Tabor, where the gibes and sneers of foes, and the contempt and disgust of friends, stung him to the quick, and raised a tempest in his heart that could only find relief in the wail of misery or the moans of distress. His military chiefs, the abettors of his crimes, in the absence of other victims, were selected to feel the pangs and agonies they had often enough mercilessly inflicted on the helpless and unoffending.

A charge of conspiracy and sedition was trumped up against them, and without trial or inquiry they were stripped, chained, and thrust into prison. An exorbitant fine was immediately imposed upon them, and, when this was not forthcoming, they were subjected to the most excruciating tortures.

The perfidy of the savage tyrant against his chiefs was an unmistakable warning to their people. Confident in the strength of their spears, and the loyalty they had in every emergency exhibited, the threats of their king were recklessly unheeded, and their usual avocations were pursued with unrelaxing industry. The covetous and plundering Theodorus did not admire this tranquillity, as it deprived him of the plea of attacking the peaceably disposed peasantry. Want, distress, and famine, however, broke down the weak barriers, and to the surprise of every one the villages and hamlets in the neighbourhood of Debra Tabor were pillaged, rased, or burnt. The patient and docile people, who had submitted to starvation to feed the robber and his bands, now shook off indifference, and snatching up the weapons, which had hitherto lain concealed, they rose up to defend their rights, their lives, and homes. The beacon of insurrection lighted on the hills surrounding the king's camp met with a ready response from every promontory, nook, and corner of the weary and exhausted province. Frantic with demoniacal rage at this unexpected resistance to his power and authority, the infatuated savage sprang upon the weakest of the seven districts into which the province was divided, and perpetrated enormities not to be thought of without a shudder. The weak and the strong, the aged and the young, all fell beneath the murderous knife or perished in the flames of their burning huts. Prayers and supplications, groans and shrieks, fell alike unheeded on deaf ears; and the cursed blade did not return to its scabbard until, from the Tzana or Dembea Lake up to Debra Tabor, the capital of Begemeder, all that could shelter man or beast was reduced to ashes.

Whilst the king was rioting in carnage and bloodshed, his white victims, to their joy and gratitude, were far away from him, on the world-wide known Amba Magdala. Our journey, which was fatiguing, occupied four good days. Near the fortress we were met by about two hundred men of the garrison; most were old acquaintances, and evidently not displeased to see us again. "May the Lord open you!"—the salutation with which they grinningly greeted us—was the key-note that told of chains and a prison. What the old prisoners most dreaded was, however, not fetters, but the common gaol. Our fears were speedily removed, and to our satisfaction we were, under a strong guard, escorted to a house near the royal fence, formerly the prison of his Majesty's disgraced friends.

We reached the Amba on July 12th, and on the 16th foot chains were hammered around our legs. The commandant, who had received some valuable presents from Mr. Rassam, did not admire this harsh treatment of the liberal Frendjoj, and as he knew that the truth was an ugly fact, he had recourse to the palpable falsehood that chains were the inevitable condition of an Amba residence. It was a well-meant, but ludicrous and stupid lie.

A few days after we were shackled, the Ras, conjointly with his council—for without serious deliberation nothing could be done—enlarged our premises, and we got two huts more in addition to the one we already occupied. The real genuine prison, which faced the entrance to our compound, was assigned to Consul Cameron, Mr. Rosenthal, and myself. Opposite to this was the kitchen, a large rickety circular building; this was given to Messrs. Kerans, Pietro, the mission's Indian servants, and some hangers on. The entrances to the two buildings were in such close proximity, that long before breakfast or dinner was ready, puffs of smoke, redolent with the fumes of seasoned viands, announced the bill of fare. This did not inconvenience us; on the contrary, the smell of roast, curry, and stew, after all the abominable odours we had inhaled in the common prison, was a luxury which our olfactory nerves most keenly appreciated.

Apart from the dwellings of the low and inferior prisoners, about a hundred yards to the right, in isolated grandeur, stood the abode of the envoy—

a hostage, as Theodore himself said, of no mean repute. It could not boast of much architectural beauty or taste, but it was well thatched, clean, and furnished. In a parallel line with "the residency," as in the peculiar jargon of Magdala we used occasionally to designate Mr. Rassam's dwelling, the eye fell on an immense cage, a kind of structure that might have been taken at a little distance for a haystack, and, on closer inspection, for a village circus. This formed the home of his two companions, Dr. Blanc and Lieut. Prideaux. The five old prisoners and the occupants of the kitchen during the night were guarded by soldiers, a nuisance from which the members of the mission were exempted. It was asserted that the king himself had given the order; but as we were more than a week allowed to sleep unwatched, the story lacked even the appearance of probability. Samuel was, no doubt, the contriver of the arrangement, as it enhanced his importance and tended to maintain an invidious distinction between the prisoners. A few months later Consul Cameron, who had succeeded in ingratiating himself with Samuel, got permission to sleep in a hut undisturbed by noisy guards; and in December, 1867, at the kind request of Mr. Rassam and Dr. Blanc, a similar concession was extended to me.

Exiled and banished on a rocky fortress in the heart of Africa, the question which most agitated our minds was the conveyance of letters down to the coast. During our first captivity we sent every month or two some messengers down to Massowah. They seldom met with an untoward accident, and, if they did not quarrel or fight, were almost sure to pass unmolested through the various provinces they had to traverse. Mr. Rassam availed himself of the same agencies, and as he had a whole host of followers, he could select the most trustworthy whenever he had important despatches to forward. The messengers were invariably warned of the dangers they would have to encounter if caught by the king's people—a precaution that kept them in a wholesome tremor till they were far beyond the rocks and ravines that encircle Magdala. It was humiliating to think that in the wilds of Africa a few unfortunate foreign captives should not be able to express their hopes and fears to distant relatives and friends without some risk and danger. The very idea of such a contingency appeared ridiculous; and yet it was not less strange than true, that a simple sentence—and that, too, couched in a foreign language—an evil-disposed European might have perverted into a most wicked, mischievous, and cruel offence. Happily, it only occurred once, and we have to thank our faithful native messengers that it did not occur again. The will existed, but the proofs were wanting.

Our great difficulty very often consisted in concealing letters after they were written. Generally the messengers departed so soon as they were finished, but sometimes it happened that on the very morning when they were to leave, intelligence reached us that the road was unsafe, or that some of the garrison had gone to a neighbouring district. In the beginning, when such an emergency arose, we entrusted them to our native friends on the Amba, but during the last few months of our captivity we concealed them in the bamboos that supported the thatched roofs of our huts.

The journey down to the coast and back to Magdala a tolerable pedestrian could accomplish in two months. Most of the messengers performed the first trip in less time than was expected. The second, however, was not so expeditious, and the third outrageously long. The causes of the delays were obvious. An Abyssinian without money is most obedient, industrious, and frugal, but with money lazy, arrogant, and luxurious. Now, as each man on his arrival at Massowah got twenty Maria Theresa dollars, and perhaps a gratuity on his return, he thought it necessary, after two, or the utmost three trips, to repay himself for his toil by a little indulgence in those gratifications which every Abyssinian village so abundantly offers. Tedj, arackee, and other pleasures did not, however, spoil their honesty, or make them indifferent to what was entrusted to their charge.

U

Our money we got through the same channel; and out of the number that were employed only one man lost about eighty dollars; all the rest brought the sums entrusted to them quite intact. This honesty in our Abyssinians—a race proverbial for their thievish proclivities—frequently amazed us. It is true they could not easily abscond with two hundred dollars, the sum each man carried, as probably the rebels would speedily have relieved them of their dishonest wealth. But these I do not think were considerations that had much influence with them. They had, I believe, a kind of religious terror, blended with a slight attachment to their masters, and these united deterred them from decamping. Had they been rogues, we should have had a terrible existence at Magdala. It was said that the king had ordered rations for the members of the mission. I do not believe it; but even if it was true, they might have perished on the bounties that would have been doled out to them by the royal purveyors. I and my companions had experienced something of this mode of existence. Luckily, or rather providentially, we were seldom long without money, or else we might have gnawed our lips in the grim agonies of starvation.

Wearisome days and restless nights, constant anxiety and everlasting suspense, were a trial of our faith and patience that required more than an ordinary degree of Divine grace to sustain us without sinking into utter abandonment or miserable idiocy.

We had only a few books, and these were neither very edifying nor agreeable reading in a prison. "M'Culloch's Commercial and Geographical Dictionaries," "Smith's Wealth of Nations," besides our Bibles, were, if I am not mistaken, our whole library. I had made myself conversant with every known spot in the universe; and as regards political economy, I could argue on supply and demand with a fluency that was perfectly awful. The Word of God, the comfort and solace, the prop and support of the suffering and sorrowing, was an inexhaustible treasure in the dungeon of the captive. With raptures the eye rested on its soul-thrilling pages, picturing to its view the cross, the emblem of redeeming love and mercy, or wandering, by faith, amidst scenes of glory and bliss, that poured a flood of gladness into the desponding heart. The weakened mind could not, however, for any great length of time sustain the effort of deep thought without serious injury. A religious movement among some of Mr. Rassam's people daily afforded me occupation for one or two hours. It commenced with *Immer Ali*, the dragoman, a Mahomedan, from the coast. He was a good, upright, and honest man. His knowledge was exceedingly limited—a defect which he sought to remedy by an earnest application to the study of the Amharic Bible. His baptism induced six more of his countrymen to put themselves under my instruction. Two of them were serious and earnest men, but the other four I considered very unsatisfactory characters. They assented to all I said with a most provoking quiescence. On one occasion, after a long dissertation on prayer, I asked them whether they ever prayed before retiring, or on getting up. "Naam" ("Yes") was the response. Amar, I noticed, did not join in the reply; so, turning to him, I reiterated the question. He appeared embarrassed, but, after a pause, growled forth, in a harsh, guttural tone: "Ya sede" ("My lord") "what shall I pray for? I have got a good master — plenty to eat, health, strength, clothing, a wife . . ." I never again asked anyone whether he prayed till I had thoroughly impressed his mind with the great truth, that a holy and virtuous life here trains a man for a happy and glorious immortality hereafter.

Our Sundays were to the majority the best if not the happiest days in the week. The old prisoners, who had been robbed and plundered by the king and his people of all that they possessed, were reduced to great indigence in all those articles that adorn the outer man. Mr. Rassam and Dr. Blanc, who had their wardrobes nearly complete, most liberally assisted us, and it was quite a luxury on the morning of the Lord's day to don clean and decent garments. At ten o'clock, we regularly had Divine service in the envoy's hut. Our worship consisted in the reading of the Liturgy, a short sermon, and a prayer adapted to our peculiar circumstances. A prison, and that, too, in Abyssinia, is not the best school for the cultivation of those graces which ennoble nature and refine the heart; nevertheless, we still endeavoured, more or less, according to our peculiar tempers, views, and sentiments, to maintain the decencies of civilised life, and to make quietness and confidence our strength.

Our existence, though monotonous and uniform, was not quite devoid of stirring and exciting incidents. In December, 1867, we heard that Mr. Flad had come back from his mission to England, accompanied by seven artisans and a quantity of machinery. We doubted the veracity of the latter statement, but the king's own communication to Mr. Rassam removed all scepticism. The letter of her Majesty the Queen, of which he forwarded an English copy, was firm, plain, and dignified. We perused it with the deepest emotions of gratitude, and I don't think there was one among the eight captives who did not, with the concluding sentence exclaim, "God bless the Queen."

Theodore did not anticipate such a despatch.

He was himself the impersonation of duplicity and craft, and he judged others by his own principles and actions. His letters to Mr. Rassam were a mixture of meekness and vanity, regret and indignation. He was hurt, he stated, that England had joined Turkey in opposing his schemes and in traducing his character. Had Britain become an ally of Abyssinia all misunderstandings might have been obviated. He was, however, averse to quarrels, and if the Queen would be the Hiram, he would act the Solomon, and wonderful feats might be achieved. The captives he only slightly touched on, and the chains and prison were utterly ignored.

The pith of both epistles might be summed up in this brief sentence: "Procure me the artisans and machinery, those pledges of friendship, and I will prove to you that I am what all know me to be—a clever scoundrel."

In his interview with Mr. Flad he was more explicit. "Why does England not exterminate the Turks? Why did you leave the artisans? Why did you bring me a telescope through which I cannot see?"* Mr. Flad intimated to him that he had powerful enemies, and that it would be for his interest to accept the hand of friendship ex-

---

* General Merewether presented him, through Mr. Flad, with an excellent telescope, but he pretended that it was an insulting and worthless gift.

tended to him, or England would send troops. This roused his ire, and he ejaculated, "Let them come, and if I don't beat them, call me a woman."

The rebellion of Begemeder, the only province that had hitherto continued loyal, ought to have taught the tyrant to adopt a more conciliatory policy. Impelled by the demon of vengeance, he ruthlessly pursued his path athwart smouldering villages and grim and ghastly charnel-houses, the fell work of his own murderous hands. Cowed by the energetic resistance of frenzied peasants, he withdrew from the butcheries in the open field to the less dangerous carnage in his own fenced camp. On the 7th of June, upwards of six hundred and seventy of Wadela, Yedshou, and other troops, under the false pretext that they were to receive their pay, appeared unarmed before the tyrant. "Aha, you vile slaves," was the address, "I hear you want to join the rebels and fight against me. I will feed the hyenas with your foul carcases before you execute your designs. Off with the traitors." In an instant they were in the grasp of friends, companions, and kinsmen, who, strange as it may appear, readily performed the executioner's work.

These wholesale butcheries roused friend and foe to a sense of their danger. Ras Adalou, the chief of the Yedshou troops, on the eve after the massacre of the Wadeleans and their companions, mounted his horse, and calling on his retainers to follow him, they all in a body marched out of the hedged-in camp. Theodore saw them turning their backs upon him, but he had not heart to pursue the desperate bands, who were determined to sell their liberty and lives at no mean price.

The defection of Ras Adalou intensified the rage and despair of the tyrant. Day after day men, women, and children were indiscriminately subjected to the most appalling tortures, or condemned to a horrible death. Within four weeks, according to the statement of eye-witnesses, upwards of three thousand persons perished by the sword, the rope, whip, stick, and mutilating knife.

This homicidal mania became more ungovernable as the victims multiplied. No one was safe. The executioner of to-day bled on the morrow. Accuser and accused frequently perished by the same knife and hand. Near and around the camp all was one large field of death and corruption. The very air was tainted with the poison of the putrescent corpses, and the slain themselves threatened the retributive vengeance which the living were too recreant to inflict.

Terrorism had decimated the camp. The tyrant himself was amazed at the abject servility of the men who, to retain his favour, would betray friends and relations to a most appalling death without remorse or regret. He had effectually crushed treachery and eradicated opposition. To go further he did not deem advisable. The chiefs and their retainers who still remained attached to him, any fresh violence he thought might justly awake from their stupid torpor, and prompt to acts of desperation he shuddered to contemplate. Where was he, however, to find victims to quell the fiery tempest that was devouring his soul?

In the plain of Efag, a day's journey to the north-west of Debra Tabor, nestled amidst groves and a few isolated hills that impart a picturesqueness to the scene, there stood about a dozen villages, which by fortuitous circumstances escaped the general devastation. The infatuated people, confiding in the swiftness of their mules, the weakness of the despoiler, or, perhaps the support of a rebel chief, made no efforts to secure either their property or their lives. The rumoured approach of the tyrant, however, frightened them, and all hurried away in the direction of Woggera, where *Taousie Gobazie*, an insurgent leader, had his camp. Theodore, who was informed by his spies of the emigration of these peasants, despatched some of his chiefs with the most friendly and paternal messages. The insane victims of oppression and tyranny, instead of scorning the treacherous protestations of the false king, listened to them with unsuspecting trust. Back to the deserted homes rolled the tide of the migratory host. Their mules were unloaded; their grain stowed into the empty *godahs;* and their flocks sent to graze on the adjacent rich meadows. No fear disturbed their repose. The solemn declaration of a master who had never kept his promise acted like a fatal spell on the doomed multitude. They spread their hides on the floors of their huts, and wrapped their shamas tightly round—and slept. It was their last repose on earth. The men of violence and blood were upon them, and before another grey dawn had dissipated the blackness of night they were all burnt and charred corpses. A few persons only escaped the fury of the destroyers, and the account they had to give of the scene surpassed in horror the most fiendish massacres ever enacted before. No one was spared; the weak and the strong, youth and age, were all mercilessly consumed beneath the roofs which had given them a shelter and a home. Little children, frightened by the conflagration, here and there rushed out of their huts in the vain hope of escaping the devouring element; instantly a cruel spear tossed them in the air, and they fell shrieking amidst the raging flames. From Efag the blood-drenched ruffianly band hurried on to Derita, a large village of wealthy Mahomedan merchants. Here they intended to perpetrate the same hideous atrocities, but the inhabitants had forestalled them the savage pleasure by a timely flight up the Woggera plateau. It was in this very village that a messenger from Massowah with the ultimatum from England had taken refuge. He evidently intended to execute the errand on which he had been sent had not a wholesome terror of the tyrant's wrath deterred him. We were in raptures when the intelligence reached us. The tyrant was then in no mood to receive menacing despatches. He wanted blood, and the most cautiously worded communication would, humanly speaking, have decided our fate. God was always good and merciful to us.

Elated with his base and dastardly massacre of men, women, and children, the robber chief—he was in reality no longer king—thought that he might again try his fortune upon stronger and more honourable battle-fields. Belessa, two days' journey to the north-east of Debra Tabor, a small mountainous province, abounding in grain, flocks, and herds, offered the tempting bait. Stimulated by greed and rapacity, his pillage-loving bands pressed forward to seize the anticipated spoil. Lidj Abitou, the chief of our escort on the unfortunate day we left Quarata, but then a rebel, together with his father, a former prison companion at Magdala during our first captivity, and the brave peasants, anticipated the bloodthirsty depredators, and boldly confronted them. The cowardly braggart who could riot in the throes of shackled captives and defenceless unarmed peasants, at the sight of a determined foe, poltroon like, shrunk from the contest. His followers, panting for booty, manifested even more daring than their swaggering leader. "Let us advance," shouted a few of the boldest chiefs, "and these rebels will be scattered to the wind." "I know what you want," said the grinning savage, as it was related to us by eye-witnesses, "but you shall not have your wish."

Chafed and galled in spirit, the worthy Theodore, followed by the imprecations and curses of an enraged people, retraced his steps back to Debra Tabor. "Light the fires, smelt the metal, cast the big Sebastopol, and I will destroy my enemies!" were the orders now issued to his servile European workmen, who some time before had been removed from their comfortable homes at Gaffat to the putrescent camp at Debra Tabor. Up circled the flame of the heated furnace; down into the round-shaped form poured the molten metal. Oh! there was a hissing and battering, a whirling and whizzing in that Debra Tabor foundry that eclipsed all that had ever been seen in Abyssinia. The Frendjoj were perfect wizards. It could no longer be denied that they had deserved those dollars which oppressed subjects were so unwilling to resign, and envious soldiers—foolish men—grudged to see so worthily bestowed. There, look at the Sebastopol, that big yawning monster;

and does not the very sight amply repay all that was ever bestowed on its makers? The tyrant was in ecstacy. "Let the wide mouth of that glittering giant only vomit forth its contents, and death and destruction will hurl into everlasting darkness the foes who dare to fight for life and home."

The number of Europeans in the camp at this period amounted to twenty-seven, of whom fifteen were men, three women, and nine children.* M. Makerer and McKelvie, who were formerly our Magdala companions, volunteered to enter the royal service, and this exempted them from chains and a second transportation to the fortress. Messrs. Staiger and Brandeis, the missionary agents of a Scotch Society, and two hunters, Schiller and Essler, after much hesitation and many excuses, were ordered to assist their brethren in the work of the foundry. Weary of a wretched bondage, and perhaps, too, a little apprehensive of coming events, the last four, together with Makerer, resolved to seek freedom and liberty in flight. M. Bardel, who had first suggested the plan, was admitted into the secret, and he manifested the utmost eagerness that its execution should not be delayed. Bardel, Staiger, and Brandeis, were to start together, and so also the rest, to avoid all observation.

* The families of Bishop Gobat's agents are not included in this number, as they were natives and half-castes.

With their money, which was very little, round the waist, and some bread in their pockets, they impatiently awaited the moment fixed for starting. The hour at last approached, and their hearts bounded with joy at the prospect of deliverance. Suddenly there is heard the tramp of feet, the hum of voices, and the rattle of shields and spears. The would-be fugitives turn pale, the cold perspiration stands on their brows, they tremble, nay, almost faint, for the king, with his myrmidons, and their accuser, Bardel, stands before them.

The tyrant's eye vindictively gleamed on the prisoners, while he sternly demanded why they were so ungrateful, and wanted to run away. The reply that they wished to see their country, of course did not satisfy their interrogator, and they were all put in chains. The poor servants, who were utterly ignorant of their intentions, did not get off so easily. Two of them were fearfully tortured, and ere the wounds had healed they were, together with four companions (one a native of Massowah), publicly executed. Their countrymen, and particularly their brethren, of whom four were the king's chief workmen, took not the slightest notice of them for many, many torturing months. They had incurred the royal displeasure, and like the Magdala captives, were to be shunned as if the very chains communicated a dangerous contagion.

CHAPTER XVI.

Hostile Movements—Sham Exploits—Valour at Zero—Plans of Escape—The lucky and unlucky Fugitives—Amba Desertions—Galla Hospitality — Midnight Assassins — Merited Penalty—Death of Abouna Salama—The Apostles of Abyssinia—Spread of Christianity—Truth and Error Blended—Abstruse Dogmas—Theological Squabbles—Indifference of the Laity—Advent of the Jesuits—Laxity of Morals—Protestant Missions—Unsatisfactory Converts—Enlightened Metropolitan—The successful Rebel—Artful Intimidation—Bishop Gobat's Efforts.

Our Magdala home, which, with the exception of the short intervals that it was occupied by the king, always maintained a gravity that was in perfect unison with the numerous unfortunate beings who were lodged on its rocky heights, before the rainy season of 1867 underwent a most indecorous transition. There were exciting reports from the royal camp, from our hostile neighbours the Gallas, and from various provinces in possession of various rebel chiefs. One day it was rumoured that the Wagshum, the acknowledged ruler of Tigré, Lasta, and the adjacent provinces, was moving southward, and would, ere long, besiege our isolated Amba; the next that the king had quitted his fence at

Debra Tabor, and was marching in our direction; and then, again, it was positively asserted that both reports were false, but that it was quite certain that the Galla chiefs had proclaimed a *levée en masse,* and were overrunning every vestige of their spoiler's usurped domain. Such and similar stirring tales of contest and pillage, triumphs and defeats, diffused a wonderful taste for battle and slaughter among all classes, till from the lowest menial at Salamegee, up to the big Ras on the fortress, every contemptible poltroon babbled and chattered as if he were the champion of Abyssinia and the prop of the convulsed realm.

The garrison, confined to an isolated rock, where neither fame nor glory could be won, were most anxious for an opportunity to display their prowess. Their desire was soon to be gratified. I no longer recollect the exact day or hour, nor whether the sky was serene or cloudy, bright or obscure; all I remember is that the occasion was worthy of the men. Without giving the exact day, I can vouch that it occurred in June, 1867. Well, one day in that last month of the Abyssinian highland summer, an officer, or set of officers,* sat gazing on the fissured basaltic cliffs that invest with a gloomy

---

* The king, to compensate the garrison for the pay he could not give, conferred titles and honours on every ruffian on the Amba. His dignities, the ingrates, who wanted bread, did not appreciate.

aspect the wild scenery around Magdala. Something that seemed to move attracted their wistful stare. They looked again, and their sharp eyes discerned distinctly one or more figures threading their way down perpendicular paths into the chasm that separates Magdala from the Galla plain. To be thoroughly convinced that it was no optical illusion, telescopes were drawn out, and wonderful to relate, the glasses were so perfect that their magnifying power exaggerated an old woman and her two children, or, as a malicious wag told me, half a dozen apes, into a great army. A council of war was instantly convoked, and in this wise conclave it was unanimously decided that the garrison must prove their loyalty, and maintain untarnished their notorious fame. Rusty muskets and unwieldy swords, which had never done any great or useful service, were instinctively grasped and ostentatiously paraded before the Amba rabble. Sundown was the time fixed for the march of the expeditionary force. Beitwodet Damash, a consummate bottle hero, was by unanimous voice of the chiefs, appointed leader of the brave band. Punctual to a minute he made his appearance on the open space in front of our prison, where the veterans gave him a cordial reception. He was clad in silks, and adorned with a leopard *lamd* (substitute for a cloak), beneath which gleamed pistols, sword, powder-

v

flask, and all sorts of weapons and ammunition, perfectly innocuous appendages to our terrible neighbour's person.

As it was anticipated, at the sight of the chivalrous host, the poor woman and her youthful companions, or it may be the apes, disappeared, and the whole company, full of glee that the enemy had decamped, came back to their Amba home. Beitwodet Damash and his staff, covered with imaginary laurels, and panting for some potent draughts of arackee,* immediately on their return, repaired to the prison of her Majesty's representative, and partook of copious libations.

The craving for glory which this silly demonstration had kindled in the hearts of our garrison demanded that something more worthy of their prowess should be attempted. The cry that the king's beeves — plundered from the peasants in Dembea and Begemeder — were in peril of being seized by the Wollos afforded the most splendid opportunity. The affair appeared more serious than some of the incredulous Frendjoj were disposed to believe. A real Wollo chief, of Masha, six hours southward of Magdala, in obedience to the behest of his mistress *Mastiad* (looking-glass), had actually

---

* Mr. Rassam is a most temperate man, but as he had always an abundance of *arackee* and *tedj* for every thirsty native who came to visit him, it may easily be imagined that he was never many hours without company.

quitted his verdant plain, and was threading his path down the deep valleys and dells on which pastured the royal herds. To oppose this genuine foe it became necessary that stratagem, valour, and numerical strength should be judiciously combined. More than half the garrison were ordered to arm; and as it was no longer a mere phantom of the imagination they were to encounter, their hot intrepidity suddenly sank far below zero. No deafening war-whoop rang through the air; no shrill, defiant shouts startled the ear; no dancing and capering gladdened the crowd's staring gaze; all, as if engaged in a sad and melancholy funeral procession, marched out of their impregnable fortress. The enemy, who was well aware of what mettle his opponents were made, tried to lure them away from beneath the shadow of their Amba, where they had made their camp; but the braves of Magdala, faithful to their cowardly instinct, would not stray far out of the reach of their safe shelter; and Madame Mastiad's commander, instead of getting, by artful manœuvre, four or five hundred of King Theodore's garrison, had to content himself with *Daunt* and *Dalanta*, of late the granaries of Magdala, which, *pro tempore*, he occupied.

But, it may be said, why, if you were surrounded by such a pusillanimous set, didn't you make an effort to escape? Frequently did we discuss this topic in all its phases. Myself, Dr. Blanc, Mr. Prideaux, and one or two more were quite ready to risk the danger the attempt would involve. Thirty men, friends of Negousee, a sincere and honest Christian, were willing, as he assured me, to second our enterprise, at the hazard of their own lives. Happily, we were not of one opinion; had no weapons of defence; were shackled in heavy irons, and closely watched by vigilant guards. These circumstances united to render the undertaking, if not hopeless, exceedingly doubtful.

At the very time that we were meditating on some plan to escape the clutches of Theodore, two prisoners in the common gaol—one, *Lidj Bacharee*, a Tigré noble, and *Weleda Arogai*, a *Shoa* lad—tried to run away. The plot was well contrived; and had the legs of the elder prisoner been as agile as those of the younger, success would have been the reward of their reckless temerity. They had both succeeded in bursting their fetters, and, dressed in female garb, with water-jars on their backs, were wending their way across the Amba, as if they were going to the springs. The lad, who had only been chained on his ankles, walked firmly and erect; not so his partner in the projected flight. Fettered for many months on hands and feet, his bent frame and stiffened limbs sadly impeded his onward progress. The youth, afraid lest his companion's movements should betray their flight, ran on and escaped. Lidj Bacharee strove hard to follow, but his tottering and limping gait attracted the attention of an ennobled Colonel. The gallant officer, who thought that the staggering fugitive was an elated damsel, on her way home from a drunken bout, approached nearer, and, to his surprise, the gay dame proved to be a runaway prisoner. Well aware that the desperate man would not without a struggle yield himself up to his captor, he shouted with all his strength for help. At the cry of the great man numbers hastened to the spot; and the miserable fugitive, after a most cruel and inhuman treatment, was, bleeding and almost lifeless, borne back to his cell. This important event was, in due course, reported to the king, who ordered that the culprit's hands and feet should be wrenched off, and his body cast down the Amba precipice. The royal command was promptly executed.

The severity of the penalty inflicted on *Lidj Bacharee* did not deter others from imitating his example. On September 5th, 1867, several soldiers of the garrison, and two officials of note—one a guardian of the king's treasury, and the other nominally a member of the council, but virtually a hostage for the good conduct of his family—took French leave of the Amba, and went over to the Gallas. The followers of the Prophet gave a most hospitable and generous reception to the runaway Christians.

Our Amba chiefs were in great perplexity and distress. To retrieve their character with the king, who would hold them responsible for these desertions, they resolved to surprise the village where the fugitives had taken refuge. Four hundred men of the garrison were selected for this arduous duty. They were all, more or less, practised thieves and murderers, so that the errand on which they were about to embark suited their tastes and inclinations. Full of hope that they would avenge the injury done to their king, and enrich their own beggarly homes with Galla slaves and cattle, they started in the greatest glee.

Damash, who was again commander-in-chief, paid a visit to his friend Mr. Rassam. On his approach I crept into my hut, as I had no inclination to admire or to bow before the buffoon, whose fingers ached to murder sleeping women and children. The poor villagers, wrapt in profound slumbers, did not dream of any dangers till the assassins and kidnappers had invaded their dwellings. Quick as lightning spread the alarm to the neighbouring hamlets, but ere help and assistance could be rendered to the surprised, more than a score lay weltering in their blood. The execrable robbers, laden with booty, and about three hundred head of cattle, were most anxious to retrace their steps before dawn exposed them to the spears of the Galla horse. Roused to desperation, Mahomed Hamza, the chief of the invaded village, with a dozen horsemen, charged the contemptible banditti, and for ever silenced many a blustering tongue. By this time about fifty horsemen more had come to join their countrymen, and the small band of brave and fearless men completely routed the dastardly assailants. Many were killed, others seriously wounded, and nearly all deprived of their arms. The news of defeat created the utmost consternation on the Amba. Men, women, and children rushed about in the wildest frenzy. Towards evening the crestfallen braves returned to their Amba. They looked dreadfully woebegone; and as they crept along, bemoaning their own misfortunes, or the fate of a fallen companion, I could have pitied them had they gone out to fight an open enemy in the bright daylight, and not to murder an unsuspecting number of peasants during the murky hours of midnight. Damash, minus leopard-skin, shield, pistol, and gun, was invisible for ten days. He pretended that in the fight he had received a wound; but it was positively stated that in his precipitate flight before the Gallas he had lost his footing, and toppled down the side of a precipice, that brought his skin and dress to grief.

On October 25th, our good friend Aboona Salama, after a lingering illness, breathed his last. The old prisoners deeply lamented the death of their firm and constant friend. Many were his trials and troubles during our chequered captivity; but, whether the king treated him as a friend or enemy, he never neglected an opportunity to ameliorate, at least, our position, if he could not effect our release. Till within a few weeks of his demise he laboured and toiled, formed plans, and enlisted support, to ensure our mutual safety. His measures were well concerted, and, had the blustering rebels seconded the enterprise, the Amba might have ceased to be Theodore's before the close of 1867.

The demise of the worthy metropolitan diffused a gloom over our fortress. Weeping and lamentations resounded from every nook and corner. They were the expressions of honest grief—an affecting tribute to departed worth.

Aboona Salama, the hundred-and-tenth Bishop of the Abyssinian Church, was, like his predecessors, a Copt. The connection of that remote country with the see of St. Mark dates back to those early ages when Christianity, with the vigour of youth and the energy of a Divine impulse, undaunted by obstacles, pressed forward to the conquest of a whole universe.

It was in the year A.D. 330 that two pious young men, the sons of a Syrian merchant, on their voyage to India, were driven by adverse winds to seek refuge on the coast of Africa. Prompted by a laudable ambition of subjugating that remote and benighted country to the sway of the Redeemer, the two exiles immediately applied themselves to achieve this glorious enterprise. The vagaries of an ill-formed Judaism, blended with the polluting system of Paganism, which till then constituted the religion of the land, could not long withstand the simple, pure, and rational creed announced by the pious foreigners. To abandon, however, rites and ceremonies which had entwined themselves around every act of life, and to adopt a belief more sublime and ethereal, did not appear in harmony with the tastes and inclinations of those mountaineers. Fromentius and his companion Edesius, the two devout preachers, perceived the difficulty, and, had their abilities been equal to the task, they might have tried, by humble persuasion and skilful reasoning, to burst the cobwebs of falsehood and imposition woven by clumsy hands; but, unable to cope with the shallow sophistries of the champions of the established religion, they consented to a compromise, and thus some of the institutions of the Jews and the superstitions of the surrounding Pagans became interwoven with the spiritual doctrines of the Gospel.

The conversion of Ethiopia, and the consecration of Fromentius by the hands of Athanasius, the patriarch of Alexandria, brought many able ecclesiastics to the country, who laudably exerted themselves to eradicate error, and to establish an unadulterated Christianity. They translated the Bible, and some of the best works of the most distinguished Greek fathers into Gheez, the sacred language of Ethiopia; compiled a liturgy; established schools, and did all in their power to give life and spirit to the newly-organised church, which, under the good providence of God, seemed destined to be a blessing to enthralled Africa.

The fire of enthusiasm for the new faith kindled in the breasts of the susceptible children of those sunny lands, found sympathy in kindred bosoms, and the sacred sparks, wafted from province to province, spread far and wide, till, from the burnt-up plains of the Soudan, in the north-west, to the picturesque mountain-fastnesses of Gurague, in the south, the anthem of praise floated along scenes hitherto only vocal with the shouts of revelry and the songs of debauchery. This zeal, which derived its impulse from an ardent temperament, and not from the life-giving energy of the Scriptures, communicated its impress to the converts, and they became languid and nerveless Christians. For a time, the fervour of the few truly devout stemmed the tide of corruption that sought to mingle its noxious waters with the wholesome stream that emanated from beneath the throne on high; but that tide proved too strong, and elaborate ceremonies were permitted to supplant the essentials of a saving faith. In the absence of a truly inspired creed, that might have enlisted the sympathies and devotions of the intelligent, pious men worried and perplexed their minds with fanciful speculations and abstruse dogmas. Councils and their decrees formed the themes of discussion, and, when these profound topics exceeded the grasp of their weak intellects, they found food for the indulgence of their infatuated spirits in debates and strifes about meat and drink, sin and penance, saints and devils, till their whole system of theology degenerated into a mazy labyrinth of contemptible and even obscene follies.

The sword of the Spirit was now laid aside, and weapons of another metal grasped. Party was leagued against party, and that, too, with an intensity of rancour that threatened to split the Church into countless sections. Priests, monks, and *debterahs* entered the sanctuary, not adorned with the submissive graces and virtues of the Gospel, but inflated with an unprofitable argument on some senseless tenet. There were men who defended asceticism, and men who opposed it; those who wanted to worship every saint, and those who wanted only to worship the most renowned for their miraculous exploits; partisans for two births of

Christ, and partisans for three; ecclesiastics who maintained that sin is pardoned in this world, and ecclesiastics who asserted that it was in the next; defendants of vice, and supporters of virtue; in fact, these and similar fanciful speculations were debated with such ardour, that the truth was entirely buried under the rank luxuriance of error, and the Church in Africa, around which so many hopes for that benighted continent clustered, became at last a caricature on our Christianity, and a libel on the Gospel.

The theological quarrels of ecclesiastics did not disturb the repose of the ease-loving laity, or undermine the unity of the church. Fond of pleasure, the licentious Ethiopian had no inclination to worry his dull brain with questions that were confined to an arena on which he never ventured. He kissed the cross, worshipped the rude pictures of Mary and St. George painted on the mud walls of the church, strictly observed the numerous prescribed fasts, repeated certain prayers in an unknown tongue, and if all this did not atone for lying, stealing, drunkenness, fornication, &c., he gave an extra jar of honey to the father confessor, and the compact between his low inclinations on earth and his promised hope of heaven was inviolate for ever.

The advent of the Jesuits and their unhallowed proceedings inaugurated a new era. Useful as allies against the abhorred Mahometan invaders, but suspected as promulgators of doctrines opposed to the established belief, the foreigners met with a doubtful reception on the Abyssinian Alps. Their efforts to wrest a legitimate dependency of St. Mark, and to annex it to the see of St. Peter, roused the fiery passions of the indolent highlander, and at the behest of the priest he unsheathed his rusty sword in defence of the Church. Had the emissaries of the Pope restricted their labours to mere teaching, the disasters that befel their cause might have been warded off; but stimulated by pride and arrogance, they commanded where they ought to have entreated, and used coercion where they ought to have applied persuasion; hence their failure and defeat, exile and death.

The religious war in which the white strangers had plunged the nation did not improve their minds or enhance their moral and religious character. Elated with their unexpected success over men who, whilst they professed to proclaim the message of love, wielded the sword dripping with blood, the whole nation abandoned itself to a rapturous jubilee. Priests relaxed the discipline of their flocks, and their flocks closed their eyes to the frailties of the priests. Gross immorality and debasing corruption broke down the feeble restraint which a few undefined religious ideas had erected, and the most scandalous saturnalia were sanctioned, if not actually licensed, by an indulgent Church. "Give! give!" was the motto of the spiritual father, and so long as perfect Maria Theresa dollars dropped into his hand, and jars of hydromel ornamented the walls of his home, every sin found a pardon and every excess an excuse. The Aboona might have done much to check this shameful laxity of discipline; but, indifferent to his charge, ignorant of the language, and very often, if not generally, a stranger to the saving truth of the doctrines he pretended to guard, his vast revenues occupied more of his time and attention than the welfare of the diocese committed to his trust.

Within the last half century a solicitude for the regeneration of this remote and isolated land awoke in the bosom of some generous and benevolent gentlemen connected with the Church Missionary Society. Several missionaries promptly volunteered to embark on this noble errand. Their zeal, combined with considerable abilities, adapted them for this arduous task. Immediately after their settlement on this new and untried missionary field they began to sow the spiritual seed, which, if it had taken root, might ere now have clothed those mountains with a fairer crop than even beneficent nature so spontaneously supplies. Not to shock the prejudices of the natives by a precipitate attack on their deformed Church, they confined their toils to the circulation of God's Word, the writing and translation of useful books,* and friendly social intercourse with the people. Their exemplary life, meek deportment, and unostentatious piety won the affections and removed the prejudices entertained against white men. The contrast between the doctrines promulgated by the strangers and those inculcated by their own priests enlisted attention and excited inquiry. These symptoms of a change in the sentiments of some of the people caused an alarm in the stronghold of superstition, and measures were quickly adopted to arrest the obnoxious movement. Had the Word of Life penetrated the heart, the assault made on it would no doubt have imparted to it more strength and a deeper root; unfortunately it had only affected a few minds, and those not the most honest and upright, and consequently the faintest clamour excited their fears and made them recoil from the unexpected danger they had provoked. Political designs and other odious intentions were now imputed to the missionaries, and though the charges were disproved by the exaggerations of the inventors, the rulers willingly lent their ears to the stories, and the messengers of the cross received peremptory orders to quit the country.

About this period the episcopal chair, which

* The Rev. Mr. Isenberg, of the Church Missionary Society, wrote and translated several excellent works.

for several years had been vacant, was, after much trouble and heavy expense, again occupied by a Coptic priest. The new primate, who had reluctantly accepted the exalted post to which he was elevated, entered upon his vast diocese at a time most propitious to his high and lofty aspirations. Dejatch Oubie, of Tigré, had crushed every pretender, and was firmly installed as the sole ruler of the whole country that stretches from the rugged mountain ranges through which the Tacazze forces its noisy passage down to the sultry plains that skirt the blue waters of the Egyptian Sea. Ras Ali, the voluptuous governor of the Amhara provinces, was quietly pursuing his peculiar pleasures at Debra Tabor, glad enough to bless Tecla Haimanout, or Mahomet, as the whim dictated, if neither rancorous priests nor restless chiefs marred the coarse revels in which he found his delight. Dejatch Goshou, the martial, brave, and generous prince of Godjam, who could boast of a noble line of ancestry, was content with the patrimonial domain and an occasional foray into the adjacent Pagan Galla territory; and Sahala Salasie, the sovereign of Shoa, though anxious to acquire fame, had his ambition curbed by the turbulent Wollo Gallas, and was obliged to seek for laurels on the dreary field of priestly polemics and absurd monkish discussions. Admired and venerated, the youthful Aboona (he

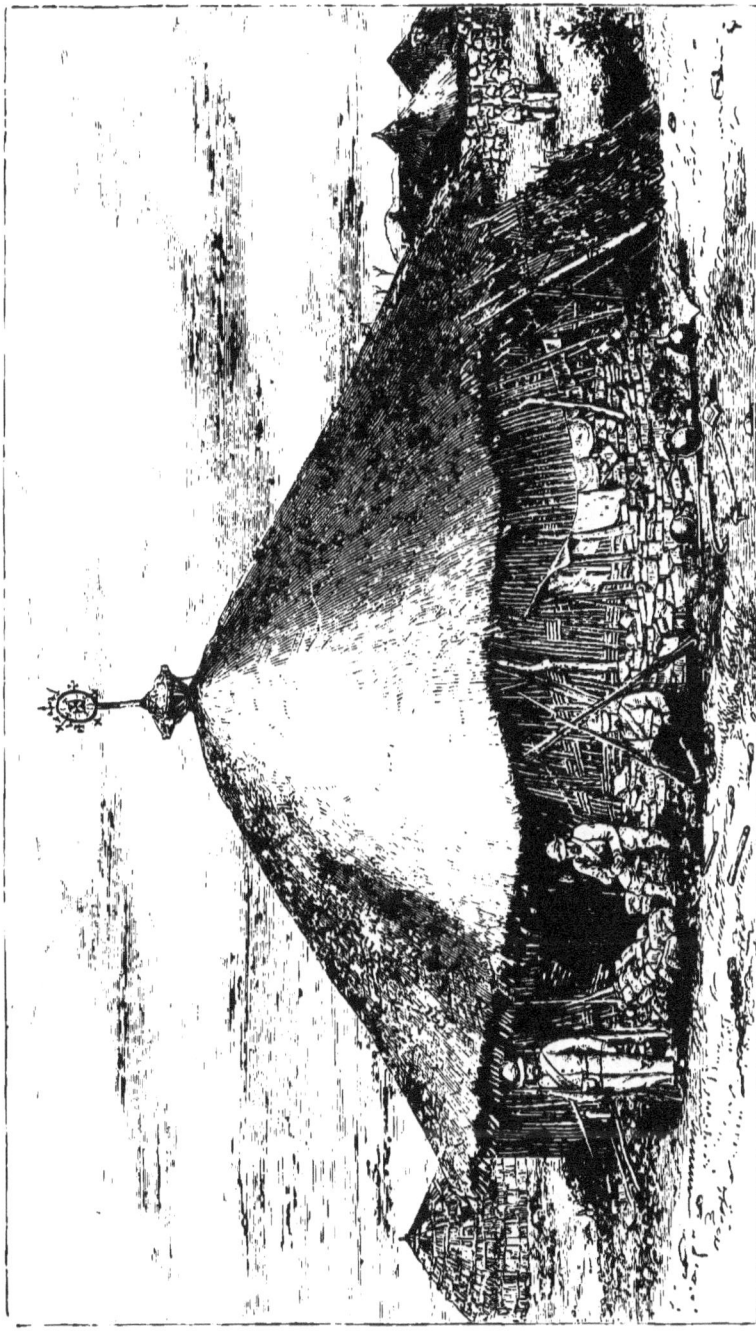

was then about twenty-two) had only to exert his influence, and to apply his energies, and he might have achieved a work equal to, if not more glorious than that of his namesake, the founder of the Christian Church on the Alpine scenery of Abyssinia. God had to some extent, as I often told him, prepared him for that work. Well versed in the Bible, and tolerably conversant with the doctrines of the Reformed Church of England, which he had imbibed in the missionary school under the late Mr. Lieder, at Cairo, the ardour of his temper needed only the live coal from the altar above, and the darkness in which the Church is shrouded would, like the vapours which during the rainy season spring up in the morning from every valley and ravine, have disappeared before the light of truth and the communication of the Gospel message.

His first object was to stifle puerile debates and glaring abuses, and when he saw that these efforts were only productive of bluster and noise, he intended, as I heard from his own lips, to change his tactics, and seek, by such means as the establishment of schools, the encouragement of learning, and the diminution of the swarms of lazy priests, to sap the Jewish and Pagan element which had disfigured the Christianity of the Church. His intentions were good, but the means he used worthless. He wanted to improve, and not to renew; to uproot, and not to plant; hence he provoked violent agitation, but did not develop any regenerating influence. He roused vehement hostilities, but did not initiate any permanent reform. Failure and disappointment might, perhaps, have ripened his judgment, and taught him to leave profitless speculations to the lovers of such themes, and to occupy himself with the Word which reveals life and immortality, but unfortunately the history of Abyssinia assumed a new phase.

Kasa, the future conqueror of the dismembered empire, at this very crisis had already, by his prowess and daring, elicited the applause and admiration of the multitude. The conquest of Tigré and the captivity of its chief completed the triumph. Aboona Salama, the friend of the deposed ruler, was unfavourably disposed towards the impetuous victor, and presuming on his position, he did not even attempt to conceal his dislike. Kasa knew this, but as it was his interest to cultivate the friendship of the primate, he disguised his rankling resentment beneath the bland smile of meek submissiveness.

The sword had prevailed, and Tigré, Amhara, Godjam, and the independent kingdom of Shoa, unanimously declared Kasa the invincible successor of Menilek, and restorer of Ethiopian glory. The incense of adulation, so profusely offered by an enthusiastic nation to the popular hero, did not soften the Aboona's prejudices, and he hesitated to pour on his head the sacred meron, the symbol which would constitute him the anointed of the Lord, and the chosen monarch of the realm. Artful intrigues, which often did him more service than the sword he then so adroitly wielded, here also came to his support, and the bishop, as already stated, received an intimation that if he refused to anoint the descendant of Solomon to be king of Ethiopia, there was another Church dignitary in the kingdom, the head of the Romish mission, who would not scruple to perform that solemn rite. The terrified primate, who in imagination already saw the Church reft into hostile camps, and the country drenched in the blood of a religious war, at length yielded to the universal request, and to the delight of myriads, who lived to curse the fatal day, Kasa was crowned by the pompous name of Theodorus, *negoos negest*, King of Kings of Ethiopia.

The crafty monarch and the intrepid prelate were now apparently reconciled, though it was easy to prognosticate that the pretensions of the one and the spiritual authority claimed by the other would in a very short time lead to a serious and perhaps permanent rupture.

Had the Aboona possessed all the virtues that

can adorn the Christian's character; had he joined to the meekness of a child the spotless purity of an angel; nay, had his life been a mirror of all that is ennobling and sublime, even then it would have been impossible for him to avert the struggle in which, for years, he was destined to be engaged with the capricious monarch.

King Theodorus was firmly seated on his throne. Falsehood, intermingled with some truth, united in proclaiming his fame. He was represented as a mild, just, and affable ruler; a friend of foreigners, and a protector of the rights of the people. Christian philanthropists again turned their compassionate gaze towards Abyssinia, and under the auspices of a sovereign so lauded, anticipated that their benevolent labours would this time not disappoint their fondly cherished expectations. Bishop Gobat, who was tolerably acquainted with the country and its inhabitants, promptly embarked on this charitable enterprise. Now, as all previous attempts for the conversion of this people undertaken by ordained missionaries with superior abilities had failed, it was deemed advisable to try a different plan, and to send out artisans to instruct in the truths of the Gospel, to circulate the Amharic Scriptures, and if necessary, to teach a useful trade. The Chrishona near Basle provided the men, and the Jerusalem Diocesan Fund the means of their support. The rugged, up-hill path of the missionary was, however, soon abandoned by these men for the more remunerative and easy service of the king, and all, with the exception of Mr. Flad,* whom I engaged to labour among the Falashas, became royal workmen.

The incipient efforts for this long-neglected and almost forgotten tribe were attended with more than ordinary success on the wide field of foreign missions, whether among Jews or Gentiles. Schools were founded, Scripture-readers appointed, preaching tours initiated, and in a very limited period, upwards of fifty individuals formed into a nucleus for a future reformed Church in the heart of Abyssinia. Some of the persons who were baptised after my first departure from the country, candour compels me to confess, were neither enlightened nor conscientious Christians; but if a small number did not shape their actions and conduct in strict conformity to the Gospel, there were not wanting others, and they constituted the majority, whose private and public life might have challenged the most rigorous scrutiny.

The introduction into the Abyssinian Church of a body of men who would combat error and satisfy

* Mr. Flad accompanied me on my first missionary tour as assistant and interpreter, and before I left Abyssinia, I engaged him to labour conjointly with Messrs. Bronkhorst and Josephson among the Falashas, in connection with the London Society for Promoting Christianity among the Jews.

inquiry was, under existing restricted circumstances, the best leaven to move an idolatrous, corrupt mass. The experiment, though precarious and unsafe, could not be condemned. Here was a band of believers baptised into a fallen Church, and yet not absorbed into that Church—virtually adherents to the creed of the Protestants, and yet nominally attached to what may be termed the religion of the Abyssinians —avowedly followers of an infallible and Divine Revelation, and yet apparently leaning to erroneous and human traditions. These were certainly paradoxes, but paradoxes capable of an easy solution. The Aboona, tossed about on a sea of doubt, fear, and uncertainty, was not hostile to the spread of the Gospel, but solicitous to prevent stormy combats and violent agitation. He was desirous to uphold the power of the hierarchy, without obstructing the few rays of light which might have tinged, but not irradiated, the clouds of ignorance in which that body was enshrouded. He wanted to graft a few good twigs on the decayed rotten trunk, but did not wish that it should resuscitate and vivify the whole tree. What our labours, under all these difficulties, would have achieved, had not more serious impediments obstructed their promising progress, is beyond the reach of speculation.

The light of Divine truth, diffused over many

a hill and dell, had already dispersed much mental darkness and spiritual night. It had taught the Falasha to reject the childish tenets and unauthorised requisitions of fanatical dreamers and self-righteous ascetics, and turned their inquiry to that Word which neither burdens reason nor enslaves the soul; it had infused its life-giving energy into the mind of many a Christian priest, and unveiled to his astonished gaze the heaven-revealed wisdom which theological disputes and passions had most effectually obscured; it had penetrated half a score of schools for the young, and led the pupils to pity that credulous simplicity which trusts in a silken cord fastened round the neck, or a parchment charm pendant over the bosom, and not in the all-prevailing merits of a compassionate Saviour. A day of grace had evidently dawned for some districts, and it required only, humanly speaking, a little more of the Spirit's impulse, and the dismal shadows of superstition and idolatry would have fled before the illuminating beams emanating from the sacred Scriptures. Unhappily, events occurred which put an end to our mission, and the hopes which clustered around it. We need not, however, mourn over the waste of labour and toil, health and strength, which were expended in its prosecution. A deep impression has been made on the minds of a vast number of individuals, which will not die nor become obliterated. The Abyssinians are a reflecting people, and the lessons they have been taught, the Scriptures they now possess, as well as the splendid example of Christian charity and forbearance so nobly displayed by the conquerors of King Theodore and the destroyers of his impregnable fortress, will, for years to come, form a theme that must keep alive a spirit of discussion, and exert a salutary influence on the whole land.

CHAPTER XVII.

Royal Messengers—Samuel's Terrors—Antidote to Fear—Letter from Menilek—His Approach—Sham Bravery—Jealousy among our Guards—Hostile Demonstrations—Perplexing Conjectures—Cowardice of Menilek—Schemes for Escape—Good News—Painful Suspense—Theodore's Mad Rage—Men Hunters—Royal Duplicity—Reward of Fidelity—Christmas Day—The King and the Peasant—Submission to the Tyrant—Flattery and Treachery—European Artisans in Disgrace.

The disastrous foray in the Galla country imparted for about two months a quiet and repose to our Amba that was perfectly tantalising. Once every fortnight or three weeks, when a royal messenger arrived, we had an exciting day. "Who is the messenger? What orders has he brought? Are his instructions verbal or written?" About two hours after his advent, we generally knew the errand on which he was sent. Mr. Rassam most adroitly managed to enlist every courier in his service. They were well paid, and richly deserved it. They had particular instructions not to convey any command, whether embodied in a letter or verbal communication, that affected the lives of any one of the white captives. Their promises did not, however, quite assure us, and, whenever it was whispered that a *melakdenya* had come, our hearts palpitated, our faces paled, and our limbs shook. Once or twice it was reported that a messenger with the death-warrant for the Frendjoj had really been despatched, but that the rebels tore the despatch and killed the bearer. This, I suspect, was not true. The positive orders of the king were: "If the Amba is beseiged by a rebel, kill the white men."

Besides the intelligence we obtained from the camp, Mr. Rassam was in correspondence with Wagshum Gobazie, the most puissant rebel in our neighbourhood. His missives were invariably confident, defiant, and brave. "That enemy of God and man shall never come near you. My soldiers will frown at me, my wife will spit at me, the peasants will laugh at me, if I do not destroy the monster. Let him only approach, and I shall crush the serpent beneath my feet." His words were bold, and had they been followed by equally bold deeds, the tyrant would never more have gazed on his beloved Magdala. These effusions, which were dictated by resentment and not valour, vanity and not courage, unsettled our minds, but did not inspire much confidence. Samuel, who was never very bold during the Magdala confinement, changed into an abject coward. His imagination, which was always ruminating on some dismal subject, kept him in a perpetual fever of terror. We always guessed when there was something wrong in the wind, from his conduct. When all proceeded in its wonted even tenor, he was placid, smooth, and cheerful; but when any inauspicious report reached him, he looked wild, gruff, and irascible. The arackee bottle, to which he was at all times devoted, became then his inseparable companion. "Drink, for it drowns care and expels fear," was then his motto. The copious alcoholic libations brought on a slight attack of delirium tremens, which lasted three or four days. During that period of mental derangement, it was dangerous to come in contact with him. On one occasion, just as the delirium was coming on, he had a quarrel with Consul Cameron. The latter, in the heat of the debate, said something about the king, which Samuel misunderstood, or misinterpreted. Instantly, he sent for his servant, and ordered him to go to the Ras, to fetch hand-chains to tie the consul. Lidj Engeda Work, the son of the commandant at Geshew, Dr. Blanc, and Mr. Kerans, succeeded in appeasing him, otherwise the consul, and probably all the old captives, would once more have had a double portion of fetters. His wives, and the poor servants in our prison-compound, shook and trembled whenever that drunken mania came on. The whip, whilst the fit lasted, was his delight, and woe betide the man or woman who incurred his displeasure. Mr. Rassam, and also myself, frequently besought him to give up a vice that disqualified him for the various duties which, as the medium of communication between the envoy and the messengers, he had to discharge. "Yes, I shall do so," was his response; but an hour after he had forgotten his promise, and was again quaffing glass after glass of the intoxicating spirits.

"The king has left Debra Tabor, and Menilek is in the Galla country," were tidings that reached us simultaneously. We had been so often deceived by such reports that their import no longer interested us. A letter from Menilek, the rebel king of Shoa, however, made our hearts throb with the most joyous anticipations. The epistle was conveyed to the incumbent of the church in Salasie, and through him to the *Etcheque*, who forwarded it to Mr. Rassam. It was short, but resolute and decisive. He was sure of taking the Amba, by storm, siege, or treachery. All he wanted was one or two secret partisans among the chiefs, and, if Mr. Rassam could render him that service, his task would be easy. Our freedom and departure for the coast were, of course, bound up with the struggle, which was sure of a successful termination.

On the morning of November 30, clouds of dust and smoke on the Galla plain, south-east of Magdala, announced the approach of a real monarch, and not a dastardly, bragging rebel. Trains of sumpter-mules, followed by squadron after squadron of horse and foot soldiers, in an incessant stream, came pouring down the undulating plateau, and encamped on its utmost verge. It was a beautiful and exhilarating sight to gaze, even stealthily (for we were not allowed to move about our prison-compound), on those wide-stretching lines of black tents which, in another day, would send forth thousands and thousands of brave warriors, "to proclaim liberty to the captives, and the opening of the prison to them that are bound."

The presence of a real enemy diffused a feverish animation and bustle over our Amba. Soldiers and chiefs, priests and monks, armed with shield, lance, and sword, were rushing about in sham fury, breathing vengeance and death against the disturbers of their peace. Queen Trounesh, who, I believe, wished the tyrant at Jericho, thought it politic to encourage these boisterous demonstrations. Poor woman! she had scarcely enough to live upon herself; yet, to avoid odious remarks and insidious accusations, she was obliged to beg for a few *gumbos* of tedj, and some baskets of bread and pepper, to feast a number of despicable parasites. The *addrash* (repast), though not very sumptuous, pleased the guests, and stimulated their devotion to Theodore. As if to make up for the limited quantity of their favourite and exciting beverage, they worked themselves into a state of artificial frenzy with war-songs, riotous shouts, and firing of muskets and pistols. It was amusing to listen to the prate of loyalty from the lips of men who were plotting the blackest treason. Two of the most treacherous chiefs, our friends Damash and Beitwoted Hailu, were the loudest in their perfidious professions.

The majority of our braves, notwithstanding the bluster and hubbub in which they indulged, secretly longed for a change of master. To Theodore they could not be faithful. Had he not destroyed their country, pillaged their homes, and, in numberless instances, murdered their parents, sisters, and brothers? All they wanted was a leader, or bold conspirator, and the gates would at once have flown open to admit Menilek. The absence of all confidence, unfortunately, paralysed every arm, and imposed an unwilling silence on each tongue. Soldiers distrusted their chiefs, and chiefs their soldiers. The predominant desire was to outwit each other in intrigue and craft, and, though nothing beyond a silk rag or a profitless title could be gained, it satisfied that base spirit of revengeful jealousy which rankles in the heart of every Abyssinian; and this, more than anything else, fostered suspicion, and checked every attempt to throw off the tyrant's hated yoke.

The camp of Menilek lustily responded to the riotous revel of the Amba. Muskets were fired, cannons discharged, troops paraded, and gorgeous tents displayed, and, no doubt, a mighty amount of wild and tumultuous clamour (which the distance did not permit us to hear) enjoyed. The martial display of the bustling hordes augured well for the success of their enterprise. The true hero, we thought, had at last appeared on the battle-field. The fate of Magdala was about to be decided. Our brave liberators, as we credulously believed they would prove to be, after this gallant demonstration, like nature after a storm, sank into a happy and peaceful repose.

The following day, of course, nothing could be attempted, as it was the Christian's Sabbath, which the Shoas would not desecrate by any private or public toil. From the hostile camp, a reflective calm was wafted across the broad chasm, on our Amba and prison, which proclaimed the beneficial influence of the Gospel even in lands where its spiritual character is least understood. I was in raptures; and, to communicate something of my own exuberant feelings to half-a-dozen unimpressible Mahometans I was instructing, I spoke to them on Abyssinia's future destiny—the triumph of Christianity—the immunities and felicities of the millennial kingdom —and a variety of other grand and sublime topics, quite incomprehensible to their dull intellects — when Dr. Blanc came to the door of my hut, and, in a great flurry, exclaimed: "Mr. Stern, our friends are moving down the chasm." The gladsome anticipation of a speedy release from a horrible captivity dispelled all the glowing visions of the prophetic future which I had pictured before my mind's eye, and, dismissing my catechumens, I limped, in defiance of guards, as fast as my chains permitted, to the entrance of our prison-compound. A small detachment of the enemy's horse had, indeed, quitted the camp, and were, as it appeared to us, going to reconnoitre, but, to our regret, it subsequently proved that they had been despatched on a less important errand. Thus, between hope and fear, conjectures and speculations, the Lord's day glided by, and night, bright and brilliant, spread its magnificent star and planet-studded canopy over the captive's home and freeman's tent.

With dawn the prospect of liberty revived, and our eyes were again clandestinely strained across the intervening space towards the Galla plain. There was still the same vexatious immobility as on the preceding day. Perhaps, we whispered, they will move at noon; no, not at noon, but during the night, they will take their position, and invest our fort. We were right; they did not move during the day, and, stranger still, neither did they move in the night. Unable to interpret this mysterious, death-like quiescence, we consoled ourselves with the fanciful illusion that, notwithstanding our long captivity, we were still novices in the tactics of Abyssinian warfare. Amidst such unsatisfactory conjectures Monday and Tuesday rolled away; and then there came Wednesday—the feast of Tecla Haimanot, the great patron saint of Shoa.

The sun, on that morning, rose in its wonted splendour, and, after dispersing the white vapours, which in those altitudes generally hang over the landscape the first hour of day, revealed to our joyous and sparkling eyes great commotion and activity in the *negoos negest's* camp. "Now they are coming! Now the prey will be wrenched out of the clutches of the destroyer! Now our shackles will drop! Now our prison doors will burst!" Such and similar ejaculations broke from our lips, when lo, and behold! to our dismay and horror, the swaggering hordes veer round, and positively refuse to come to the Amba, because the Amba obstinately refuses to come to them!

The motives the fat king* assigned for this abrupt departure from the scene where he was to achieve such glories were not quite satisfactory. In a message to Mr. Rassam, he alleged that famine in the camp compelled him to quit our neighbourhood; but as the Gallas, who were his allies, could easily have supplied his wants, it was

---

* It is said that he is very corpulent, and on a march exhausts six mules every day.

the general opinion that the approach of Theodore had driven him back to his Shoa plains.

I had hitherto some respect for these blustering rebels, but the conduct of Menilek altogether changed my sentiments. They were, without exception, a gross, dissolute, cowardly set, who pretended to love order, whilst they created confusion; proclaimed that they sought their country's weal, whilst they plundered defenceless peasants; and most boisterously deprecated anarchy, whilst they everywhere introduced a perfect reign of terror.

The imbecile proceeding of Menilek, the absence of all intelligence from the coast, and the distracting conjectures about the advent of the king, painfully jarred on nerves already sufficiently shattered by years of suspense, fetters, and confinement. Shadows, gloomy and dismal, danced on our prison walls, and floated before our eyes. Death, of whom several frequently spoke with a most disrespectful familiarity, entered the abodes of the happy and contented, but would have nothing to do with the miserable and wretched. There was some talk of forcing the Ras on one of his diurnal visits to Mr. Rassam, to join our friends in an open insurrection. Then again we discussed the feasibility of making our way down the Amba by ropes; and, perhaps, a day or two after we debated the success of an attack on the powder-magazine, which would frighten the garrison, and, whilst the panic lasted, intimidate them from opposing our escape. Such and similar topics were for weeks on the tapis; and though we knew that the faintest attempt to carry either of them into execution would cost us our lives, still we loved to dilate on schemes and plots which kept the embers of hope alive in our breasts.

On Friday, December 13, we had a happy day. Messengers from the coast arrived about noon; but it was not before evening that the letters were smuggled into our prison. There were, as usual, none for me. A kind of fatality hung over my letters. My friends wrote, but of the scores which they forwarded not a tithe ever reached me. Vexed and annoyed, I snatched up a fragment of Guizot's "Histoire de la Civilisation," which Mr. Rosenthal had secured during his stay at Gaffat, and began to study the influence of monasticism on the moral and social condition of Europe. A summons to come immediately to Dr. Blanc's hut was significant of good news. The clapping and cheering of several of my companions confirmed my anticipation. "Cheer up, Stern!" exclaimed the doctor. "Good news! Troops are coming! Colonel Merewether has landed! Hurrah for old England!" The budget was worthy of the plaudits it elicited from the captives. Oh, it was a happy evening, that 13th of November! Gloom and despondency had entirely vanished. No vacant glance, no dejected countenance, no shaded brow was visible among the eight victims of Theodore's tyranny. Our chains were light, our hearts merry; we were in a transport of delirious joy—a sensation to which the majority, for more than four years, had been perfect strangers.

British troops and King Theodore were now both on the road to Magdala. But who will arrive first? Will our expected liberators forestall our dreaded captor, or will they allow him to inundate the Amba with blood ere they make their appearance? Such and similar reflections forced themselves very soon on our minds, and filled us with intense anxiety and suspense. Never were the chances of freedom and death so equally balanced; never were the steps of friend and foe so eagerly watched. We were approaching the goal of our suffering, the crisis of our fate. A tranquil confidence that the days of banishment and exile were drawing to a close, however, dissipated those gloomy forebodings, which horrible tortures, ten times worse than death, conjured before the mind. We felt, at least most of us felt, that God had been and would be with us, and this conviction shed a peaceful serenity over our dismal prison home.

The king, serpent-like, continued to crawl on. At Tshetshaho, a broken, volcanic district, which forms the boundary line between the south-eastern plateau and the central province of Begemeder, he encountered a formidable opposition from the insurgents. Too timid to meet him in an open engagement, they harassed him in the front and rear, on the right and left, till, driven to desperation, his maddening passion vented itself in most awful maledictions on himself, his people, and the whole human race. In ascending the steep path that leads to the plain of Zebit, his rage, as I was told by eye-witnesses, resembled the fierce fury of a demon. The insurgent hosts, posted on most favourable positions, from covert and hill, hollow and rock, poured lance and stone, abuse and contempt on the panic-stricken royal bands, who, in a compact mass, without even the faintest effort to repel the assailants, pressed on to reach the plain. Numbers were killed, others wounded, and not a few crushed under the feet of the scrambling and pushing host. Poor Mrs. Rosenthal, in the bustle and confusion, nearly lost her babe. The king, who, accompanied by a strong guard of chiefs and musketeers, had ascended the plateau before his camp broke up, on beholding the terror and dismay among his people, and the boldness and daring of the rebels, lost all self-control. He stamped on the ground, tore his hair, yelled forth fearful oaths and raving curses; in fact, his whole deportment was that of a man either bereaved of reason, or possessed by a legion of fiends. "Why does God not kill mé if I am bad? And if I am better than my people, why do his thunders not burst forth and destroy them? No, justice is asleep in heaven, and till it stirs I will reign, and execute vengeance on earth." Such and far more revolting phrases were now perpetually on his lips. He had become what his own followers termed a complete "diabolos;" and blood only could temporarily allay the fever that burned in his veins. "Go and kill every man, woman, and child you find: for a dead body you will get a white shirt; for a live prisoner, a silk one," was the order given to his followers. A similar mandate was issued a few months before at Debra Tabor, but few of the wretched man-hunters returned from their revolting sport. The peasants everywhere watched for their approach, and before they could level their muskets a stone or lance stretched them on the ground. Two only were successful in their inhuman chase, and these excited not a little envy among their comrades. "So-and-so has been very lucky to-day," they would tell the prisoners whom they guarded; "he brought some one (woman or child, as the case happened to be) into the camp, and got his shirt; whilst I, with my good gun, have not been able to gain a shirt. God must be angry with me."

From Zebit to the descent into the bed of the Djiddah the tyrant met little or no opposition.

His cumbrous cannons, which he hugged with an affection that made even his soldiers style them the "*Taout Amlack*" (the idol gods of Theodore), were never out of his sight either on the march or in the camp. On the plain of Wadela he expected an encounter with Wagshum Gobazie, but this blustering rebel chief, though he bragged more than all the rest, was afraid to measure his strength with an opponent whose marvellous engines, it was rumoured, mowed down, as the ripe harvest before the reapers, whole lines of hostile troops.

Once near the Djiddah, messenger after messenger in rapid succession visited our Amba. Mr. Rassam also renewed the interrupted correspondence with his Majesty. The letters that passed between them were unique specimens of diplomacy on the one side and of craft and duplicity on the other. The king was all courtesy, devotion, and love; Mr. Rassam all deference, regard, and esteem. One of his messages was—"My children, you will be glad to hear that I am well, and by the power of your prayers advancing towards Magdala. Business will probably detain me here some time, but don't be sad, we shall meet ere long." I am certain that our prayers had nothing to do with his southward movement—a fact of which he was fully cognisant —but it suited his purpose to flatter till he positively knew the object and design of the expedition.

Mr. Rassam's task was not easy. He had to flatter, to praise, and to admire the man whom I believe he cordially hated and despised. His most delicate business, however, was the epistolary intercourse. Those who have waded through the Abyssinian Blue Book may perhaps remember the peculiar style current in that distant and barbarous land. Mr. Rassam in a very limited time most successfully mastered it, and his epistles displayed a tact and ingenuity that won him the admiration of every one with whom he came in contact. Like all his diplomatic predecessors, he misunderstood Theodore. His apparent purity of life, his pretended religious impressions, and the perpetual brag that the weal of his people, though unappreciated by the ingrates, were the objects for which he lived, imposed on Mr. Rassam, as it had imposed on every one else. A gracious reception, fair speeches, and a prompt compliance with the request embodied in Her Majesty's letter, naturally removed all suspicion from the mind of England's representative, and King Theodore was, if not a considerate, a most injured monarch. The crafty request for artisans and machinery, to a limited extent revealed his sinister aim, and disclosed to his astonished guest something of his innate treachery. To refuse then the demand might have been construed into a serious affront, and to accede to it might have, as was obvious, only conjured up fresh embarrassments. Mr. Rassam, I know, tried, and tried hard, to escape the dilemma in which he was entangled, but all his tact and skill proved unavailing. The wily unscrupulous barbarian had wisdom enough, and foresight enough, and experience enough to perceive in the desertions of his troops, and the ever-spreading insurrection among the peasantry, that the ground was crumbling beneath his feet; and to avert his inevitable, though lingering doom, he held Mr. Rassam with iron trammels, in the stupid belief that the retention of such a great man would ensure him from England the most extravagant concessions. No diplomatist of the most versatile genius, no officer of the most exalted rank, without a force at his back to strike terror into the dastardly heart of the lawless despot, could have escaped fetters and captivity.

Mr. Rassam, by using well-shaped sentences and hyperbolical expressions of friendship, blended, on two or three occasions, with soft phrases of indignation, saved us what a bolder tone might not have effected, from incarceration in the crowded common gaol and the crippling torture of chains around the wrists, in addition to those on the ankles, a boon which merited our acknowledgment and gratitude.

The Negoos always professed the most unbounded regard and esteem for Mr. Rassam. Sometimes, when his rage and passion burst forth in savage fury about some imaginary or feigned grievance, the old prisoners generally came in for a profuse share of vile abuse. Not so Mr. Rassam; he was always a good man and a devoted friend. Usually, and the last year of our captivity demonstrated the fact, the most faithful adherents to the tyrant's ruined cause in his jealous mood were despatched to a region where love cannot cool nor adversity mar the affections of tender hearts. Mr. Rassam formed an exception to that established rule—a mistake, a happy mistake, which the despot keenly regretted, and it was said that his last moments on earth were expended in bitter imprecations on his diplomatic friend.

Christmas, that season of joy and gladness, had now set in. The expeditionary forces, to our disappointment, we heard the evening before, had not yet quite landed, whilst King Theodore, whose advent we dreaded, was persistently threading his way through bristling lines of cowardly insurgents towards our Amba. Our felicitations on the morning of that happy day were not much associated with the glorious events it is designed to commemorate. Our minds were occupied with King Theodore and his movements. Various conflicting reports had reached our Amba, and they formed the themes of general discussion. It was said that *Daunt* and *Dalanta*, two rebel districts that occupy the plateau between the Djiddah and Beshilo, had accepted the royal amnesty, and made their submission; then, that three hundred rebels had been caught, and roasted alive; and lastly, that his Majesty, in the profound consciousness of the inviolability of the law as a warning and example to his faithless subjects, had immolated on a flaming pyre, Ras Meshasha, the prince imperial. These rumours were followed by others of a less appalling import. A large proportion of the Daunt and Dalanta peasantry, it was true, had made their submission to the king; a few rebels had also been executed; but the story about the royal prince was what we ought to have suspected, a most unworthy libel.

Among the rebels caught by Theodore's hangmen was a blunt, honest, and upright peasant, a *rara avis* in that country of duplicity and falsehood. The sturdy fellow, on being brought before the king, was asked why he and the rest of the people had risen against their anointed and lawful sovereign. Undaunted by the dangers which menaced his life, he promptly rejoined to the question addressed to him: "We have thrown off our allegiance because we believe it is sinful to pay obedience to an excommunicated monarch." "And who excommunicated me?" returned the king. "Aboona Salama," was the response. "Why, then, did he excommunicate me?" "The reason is obvious," retorted the candid Wadelean. "You plunder the country, burn the villages, kill the people, and do many other things which are opposed to the laws of God." "Mention one of those many transgressions which you consider heinous offences," replied the interrogator. "Why, you are married by the Corban (sacrament), and yet keep sixty wives." "Right," returned the calm and placid despot, "I have sixty wives, and want sixty-one; and you must, therefore, bring me your own, who, I hear, is hidden in a cave not far from here, or you die at once." The bewildered peasant had to go with an escort to the spot where his partner lay concealed, and on their return both were torn and hacked into pieces.

Our anticipations that Daunt and Dalanta would continue to form an impassable barrier to the king's progress were disappointed, and day after day we heard that he was advancing nearer and nearer to our rocky home. The road was still a serious obstacle to his onward movement; but with the assistance of the peasantry, who had returned to their allegiance, basalt rocks were blasted and levelled, trees cut down, and every impediment in his march removed. To hurry on the work, the Lord's-day rest, which had hitherto been respected, more from sheer necessity than any religious scruples, was now suspended; and Europeans as well as natives had to ply the axe and hammer on the Christian's Sabbath.

The stupid and infatuated peasants, to compensate for their late defection, exerted themselves to the utmost to retain the favourable opinion of their capricious, whimsical, and faithless master.

At his own particular request the chiefs remained in the camp, while the people carried his baggage, assisted in making the road, and, together with his ragamuffins, *alias* soldiers, dragged his unwieldy cannons up to their own verdant plain. Praises the most lavish and profuse were abundantly bestowed on the good and loyal Dalanta peasantry. They were liege subjects, excellent fathers, and most exemplary men—nay, on the last Sunday before the Abyssinian Lent, during a *broundo* (raw meat) feast, he assured the village authorities that they and their descendants, and the district entrusted to their charge, should, to the very end of time, enjoy immunities and privileges the most glorious and distinguished a monarch could bestow.

Thinking that his wily smiles and glib tongue had dispelled every apprehension of treachery, he gave secret orders to his banditti to fall, before the dawn of day, upon the sleeping peasantry, and to despoil them of their property. The plan was well conceived, but not so easily carried into effect. The slumbering though surprised people were not quite unprepared, so that the ruffians, before they could execute their fell purpose, had to struggle, and that most fiercely, with their stout-hearted, obstinate victims. Numbers of the king's people were knocked down by the heavy, knotted clubs of the vigorous peasantry; others were brained by the infuriated women; and not a few, even in the camp itself, were stretched upon the ground, never to rise again, by the frantic chiefs whom they sought to make their prisoners. The Daunt, and scores of the Wadela people, on hearing the war-whoop, hurried (an unusual thing in that reft and selfish country) to the assistance of their neighbours, and by their united efforts drove the bragging and treacherous robber chief behind the shelter of his artillery.

This last defeat made him conscious of the utter helplessness of his position; and, like ourselves, he was anxious for the approach of the British troops, whose advent he knew would terminate the destructive and unequal conflict in which the captor and captured, the spoiler and spoiled, were mutually involved. Now and then he indulged in a little harmless brag about Pharaoh and the Israelites, David and Goliath, Sennacherib and Zedekiah, and on one occasion he spoke of himself as a man who, like Simeon in days of yore, was waiting for help, deliverance, and redemption.

EUROPEAN ARTISANS IN Disgrace

Towards his European workmen he began to manifest an unwonted severity. The motives for this sudden resentment against his obsequious white slaves were, of course, shrouded in some obscurity; but it was evident that an undercurrent of suppressed anger had long lurked in his heart against them, and that policy, and not regard, had induced him to maintain a sham friendly intercourse with them. One day, on the plain of Dalanta, he was exceedingly indignant against them. Old Shimper, who, for some special services he had rendered, came in for a considerable share of abuse, on beholding the lance in the royal hand quivering before his eyes, already imagined himself a dead man, and in his terror, or perhaps to avert the catastrophe, apparently tumbled senseless on the hard ground. Only a few weeks before, when the rest got gorgeous tents, which they were to pitch and not to occupy—probably to excite the jealousy of the soldiers against them —he was, by some oversight, forgotten. To twist the mistake into a well-shaped compliment, he told the king that he did not require a tent, as every one knew that his Majesty's vast and generous heart was his shelter and home. Poor sycophant! he was ungraciously rewarded for the incense of flattery he undertook to lavish so profusely on the Moloch he pretended to adore.

CHAPTER XVIII.

Theodore reaches Magdala—Change of Guards—Release of Dr. Blanc and Lieut. Prideaux—Royal Promises to the Envoy and his Companions—Change of Sentiments—Bardel's Warning—Mr. Rassam and Theodore—Prisoners Released—Faith and Trust—Summons to the Royal Camp—Gracious Reception—Harmless Brag—The Despised Letter—Seven Executions—Revolting Massacre—Providential Escape—Return to Prison—Battle of Arogie—Diplomacy in Requisition—Lord Napier's Firmness and Courtesy—Theodore's Confession—Suicide Prevented—Suspected Treachery—Sympathy of Natives—Audience Refused — Contradictory Commands—Royal Designs — Divine Interposition—Arrival in the British Camp—Delicious Sensation—Easter Sermons—Theodore's Despair—Visit to Magdala—The Dead King—Success of the Expedition—Thanksgiving Service.

On March 25 the gay and merry li-la-la-lil of the women, and the excitement and bustle of the men, announced that King Theodore had reached Salamegee. Mr. Rassam, whose fetters had been taken off a week before, sent a messenger to felicitate him on his arrival. He was not in a very gentle temper, and it was generally expected that it would require a considerable number of executions to appease his wrath. The messenger with the congratulations met with no very gracious reception, and he was glad enough to get safe and sound out of his presence. The next day he visited our fortress. He was violent, coarse, and savage. Some of the Amba chiefs had ruffled his temper, and as he could not well afford to have them all butchered, he contented himself with bespattering them with volleys of the vilest epithets. More than half the garrison and all the chiefs were removed to the camp, and new men appointed to their posts. We did not like the change; for the old chiefs, bad as they were, had already become familiar with us, whilst the new ones were strangers to us, and of a reputation that made even Abyssinians afraid to come in contact with them.

Our new commandant had an inspection of his prisoners before sunset; and about ten in the evening we were ordered into two huts, which were strictly guarded by a set of coarse ruffians, in whose very countenances vice and malice had traced their most revolting lines. They mustered at least a hundred, a large number to guard only eight prisoners. This solicitude for our safety was not a very satisfactory and auspicious indication. Most of us, however, no longer troubled themselves about good or evil signs. We were impervious to troubles and trials, dangers and difficulties. Our long captivity had hardened us. We sighed for freedom, without perplexing our minds in what shape it would be effected. Life had almost lost its fascination, and death its sting. Liberty alone was the word that haunted us by day, and occupied our dreams by night. A few more unpleasant shocks, a few more ugly encounters, a few more trying episodes we were prepared to sustain ere rest in heaven, or freedom on earth, would bring our misery to a close.

On Sunday, March 29th, the king, accompanied by his ragged chiefs and the European workmen, visited Magdala a second time. A large scarlet tent was erected in the open space fronting our prison; carpets were spread; the troops ranged in a crescent form; and all sorts of preparations made that prognosticated something grand and imposing. We were agreeably mistaken in our conjectures. His Majesty, for the nonce, abstained from enjoying the pleasure of a fresh trial of his white captives—a self-denial, no doubt, painful to his heart; and, to our delight, he contented himself by indulging in a long confabulation with his friend Mr. Rassam, who was summoned from his prison for this very purpose. As usual, he poured forth whole torrents of impotent brag. His subjects, his priests, the late primate, with whom, as ever, he associated my name, came in for a profuse share of abuse—the usual method in which he vented his rage on those whom he had most grievously wronged. To Consul Cameron, Mr. Rosenthal, and others he also adverted, and that too, in no very gentle terms. Towards Mr. Rassam he was all smiles, devotion, and love. At the special request of the latter he removed the chains from the legs of his two companions. From his message to them it was evident that he would not have complied with that request, had he not regarded them with something approximating supercilious indifference: "You are neither my friends nor my enemies. I do not know who you are."

The operation of wrenching off the shackles occupied some time; and then, in conformity with Abyssinian court etiquette, they were conducted into the royal presence to acknowledge the favour that had been conferred on them. The king was all condescension and benignity. "I chained you," he said, "because your people believed that I was not a strong king. Now that your masters are coming, I release you, to show them that I am not afraid. Fear not; Christ is my witness; and God knows that I have nothing in my heart against you three. You came to this country knowing what the consul had done. Do not fear; nothing will happen to you. Sit down." He then adverted to the original quarrel, and, amongst other things, said: "When Consul Cameron came to my country I treated him well. On his departure I entrusted him with a letter to the Queen. He came back a second time, and on my asking him, 'Where is the reply to my letter?' he answered: 'I have not got one.' I then beat

Stern. I know," he added, "that Stern praised me in his book, and said I was a wonderful man. Well, I must prove that I can fight; for if I don't, he will write another book, and call me a coward. I will, however, make him stand near me; and if I am wounded in the left arm, I will wound him in the right. You, my friend (addressing Mr. Rassam), and your two companions, have nothing to fear; your lives are sacred."

This effusion of love, devotion, and attachment to Mr. Rassam was not of long duration. Theodore was as fickle in his affections as he was capricious in his hatred. He had no heart. He was guided by impulse. One moment he would solemnly vow eternal friendship, and the next moment he would forget his oath, and deliver the object of his tenderest regards into the cruel hands of the executioner. Thus, on the Amba, Mr. Rassam was so dear to him that he would not injure a hair of his head, even if he knew (to use his own words) he would kick his lifeless corpse, and deny it burial; but no sooner did he reach the camp at Salamegee than he began to prate about killing Mr. Rassam, as he had brought enemies upon him.

The next day we heard that M. Bardel—the Frenchman, whom, with scarcely any exception, every one dreaded—had become seriously ill. Only about a fortnight before, he wrote an epistle to Mr. Kerans, in which he said, in a tone of triumph, "Kerans, my boy! drink your ink! drink your ink! and don't write religious or political pamphlets. I have seen a pamphlet written by Stern, in which he describes his own and his companions' sufferings, not omitting the straw and the condition of the beard. There is a gentleman here [the king], if he knew of it, would give, not the pamphlet, but the writer's wrist, a red ribbon [cut off my hands]. Drink your ink, my boy! Drink your ink!" My companions, most considerately, wanted to keep the whole story concealed from me; but, by some accident, I heard of it, and then Mr. Kerans showed me that part of the letter which referred to me, the rest my fellow-prisoner told me I should not peruse, as it was too indecent. From the quotations, I suspected that the story of the pamphlet, of which I never before heard a word, was a fabrication; still, it gave me a shock, and some anxiety. Death I did not dread; but the faintest anticipation of torture made my heart palpitate, and my blood run cold. King Theodore, I knew, would not pardon any statement of his proceedings towards us, or any one of his prisoners, however cautiously it might have been worded; and, if really my friends had published some of my letters in a pamphlet, and a single page (which was not likely) had come back to Abyssinia, my doom was sealed. Dr. Blanc, in ciphers, kindly informed

General Merewether of M. Bardel's threat, and the danger to which I was exposed. His sickness allayed all surmises about the ropes, whip, and mutilating knife, which, ever since the arrival of the letter, most persistently haunted my imagination.

Early on the morning of April the 2nd, Mr. Rassam and his two companions received an order to repair to the royal camp at Salamegee. We did not know what the summons indicated, but we felt certain that it prognosticated nothing very dismal or inauspicious. Mr. Rassam still enjoyed ostensibly the favour of his Majesty, and, so long as that was not withdrawn, we felt certain that our heads, humanly speaking, were safe on our shoulders till the approach of the expedition. I certainly, during the last eighteen months, as all my letters, many of which appeared in the public journals, testify, never doubted that God, in His mercy, would deliver us. I prayed for freedom, and I believed that God would also grant it. The king might, perhaps, work himself into a state of frenzied passion; but I knew there was One above who could restrain his wrath and curb his violence. My expectation was not disappointed. King Theodore was, in the beginning of the interview, gruff and sullen; but gradually, Mr. Rassam told me, he became calm and affable. During the conversation which ensued, he dilated on his faded greatness, the ingratitude of his people, and the ungracious repulses he had experienced from foreign potentates. The Emperor Napoleon, he asserted, had taken his envoy, M. Bardel, by the neck, and turned him out of his palace. Consul Cameron had offended him by coming back without bringing an answer to his letters; and the rest had all been guilty of some offence worthy of chains and a prison. Mr. Rassam, during his long interview, most considerately availed himself of an auspicious moment to solicit the removal of the fetters from the limbs of his five companions on the Amba. The request, which was readily granted, afforded great satisfaction to our native friends, and several at once hastened up the Amba to bring the *mesratsh* (happy tidings). Young Desitah, one of Mr. Rassam's interpreters, whom I had for several months under regular Christian instruction, outstripped his companions in the race. He was quite breathless when he came into my hut; but, from the joy beaming in his sparkling eyes, I could perceive that he had no disastrous intelligence to communicate. It took more than an hour to wrench off the fetters, which, for twenty-one months, without a single day's release, had encircled our legs. We dreaded the homage we might have to render for the clemency we had experienced; but, to our satisfaction, his Majesty was too busy with his big mortar to trouble himself about a few prisoners, who, notwithstanding that they were freed from chains, were still as much as ever in his dungeons and grasp.

Slowly the hours of our captivity rolled on. We knew that in less than a week our fate would be decided, and our wretched existence either close in death or liberty. Every incident was now of great significance, and every word the king uttered of momentous import. From four to four years and a half the old captives had lingered in chains and a gaol, and, as the crisis of our sad history approached its climax, it was natural that we should feel a deep and overwhelming anxiety about the issue. Some of our party, myself among the number, were animated by the most sanguine hopes; still, we could not divest ourselves entirely of those fears and doubts, dread and horror, which our position inspired. My confidence and faith in our ultimate release had, during our second captivity, been only once or twice a little shaken, and I was determined, in the final crisis, to continue with unyielding trust to cling to Him who is emphatically the refuge of the oppressed, the strength of the weak, and the help of the destitute.

About sunset, on the 6th, we received an intimation that, on the following morning, all the prisoners, Europeans and natives, would have to repair to the royal camp. We did not much appreciate this impending change from a dingy prison-hut to a tented camp confinement. It was a sad exit that awaited us next day. We had a considerable number of friends on the Amba, and many of these repaired at an early hour to the open space in front of our prison, to see us taking our departure. They all looked sad, disconsolate, and sorrowful; and it was evident, from the sighs and irrepressible tears of the multitude, what doom they imagined would be our lot. The native prisoners, between four and five hundred, who, owing to their hand and foot chains, in a bent and stooping posture shuffled on in our rear, heaved the deepest and most heart-rending groans and sighs. Their eyes were riveted on us with an agonising interest, for they knew that the reception accorded to us would be the verdict of their own fate. To the joy and delight of our friends, and the numerous victims of lawless tyranny, his Majesty gave us a most friendly salutation. On perceiving my long hair, which I had allowed to grow unclipped as a protection round the neck from heat and cold, he smilingly turned his eyes on me, and said: "O Cocab, why have you plaited your hair?" Samuel forestalled my response by replying: "Your Majesty, it is not plaited; it falls naturally over his shoulders."

The bustle and tumult, din and confusion, which prevailed near the spot where we were standing, induced the king to move out of the heaving and toiling multitude by whom he was encompassed.

The officials followed, but the rest of the captives kept at a respectful distance. His Majesty was exceedingly affable, courteous, and polite. He dilated on all sorts of topics, but the tenor of his conversation was so incoherent that his efforts, and he was a master in disguising his real sentiments, failed to conceal the conflicting thoughts that occupied his mind. After an hour's interview, he ordered us all to repair to a gorgeous tent which, in the absence of Mr. Rassam's, had been erected for our accommodation.

After this interview with his white captives, he compensated himself for the little self-denial his courtesy had imposed, by a good deal of bluster and brag on the victories and triumphs he was about to achieve. Amongst other things he said: "The English, ever since the time of Noah, have cast cannons, and manufactured guns and powder, whilst we only commenced yesterday; but don't be afraid, we shall strip them of their arms, and you will be clad in their gay and gorgeous garments." Such and a variety of similar effusions came flowing from his lips, in smooth and well-shaped phrases, till weary with the effort, he dismissed his bands, and mounting his mule, proceeded, accompanied by his European workmen and several chiefs, up to the summit of Salasie, from whence he had a full view of the onward movement of the expeditionary force.

Next day a messenger brought a letter from Sir Robert, now Lord Napier of Magdala. The road to the very camp being infested by robbers and insurgents, it was necessary to stitch the missive in a seam of the bearer's ragged inexpressibles to ensure its safety. Theodore was quite indignant at receiving a small note, instead of a large letter. He was told that it was not disrespect, but necessity, that had compelled the commander-in-chief to send such an epistle. "It is true," he responded, "the road is full of thieves and robbers, but who is this man that addresses himself to me? I wrote some years ago to his Queen, and she did not answer me; does he suppose that I shall enter into a correspondence with him? Take the paper away, I don't want to see it." This was, however, merely bluster, for when the messenger and his own chiefs had retired, he sent for Samuel, and requested to know the contents of Lord Napier's despatch.

In the afternoon of the same day he was angry, passionate, and savage. To quell the fury of his wrath, it was necessary that blood should flow. He had not yet decided on the massacre of his prisoners, but to appease the demon that devoured his heart, a few victims had to be sacrificed. Seven individuals were immediately selected for a holocaust to pacify the blood-thirsty Moloch. Among the innocent sufferers was a young woman and her infant, the wife of the fugitive Becherwand Confou, who had decamped in September last. Ever since the flight of her husband, she had been a prisoner, and probably the long reprieve she had experienced led her to cherish the pleasing illusion that her young life, and that of her babe, would not be sacrificed to the despot's resentment. Poor woman—like hundreds more—she dreamt of life, freedom, and happiness, till the executioner dragged her and the innocent creature clasped in her slender arms, to a horrible and cruel death.

These incipient butcheries were merely a prelude to still greater atrocities and more extensive massacres. In the afternoon of the next day we were suddenly startled by the sound of an intermittent musketry. I looked out of the tent to see whether the king was *fackering* (bragging). The rush of armed soldiers from every part of the camp, indicated that something serious and disastrous was taking place. All was hushed, as if the silencer of all sounds had suddenly traversed those lines of huts and tents in which noise and clamour perpetually reigned. The rattle of musketry blended with the yells of despair, and the shouts of rage fell, however, with an ominous and appalling horror on our ears. "What is the matter?" I inquired of my neighbour. "Hist," was the response, "the king is killing all the prisoners." These terrible words diffused an aguish chill through my very heart. "What!" I involuntarily ejaculated, "killing his prisoners—men whose only crime consists in their having served, and served faithfully, too, a tyrant to whom they ought never to have tendered allegiance?" Most of the sufferers were our former companions in the common gaol, which deepened the sympathy we felt for them in their last mortal struggle. The sun had already disappeared from the horizon, and twilight spread a dismal, dusky hue over the scene around, and still the firing continued unabated. With night it gradually diminished, and then only isolated shots reverberated across the panic-stricken camp.

The slaughter lasted about three hours, and during that interval three hundred and seven human beings were, unwarned, and perhaps unprepared, hurled into eternity. Some of the prisoners did not unresistingly yield to their woeful doom. One, Immer Ali, a native of Ferga, near the Tzana Lake, formerly a chief of consideration in his province, in spite of hand and foot chains, with a convulsive grasp dragged his executioner towards the precipice over which he was to be hurled. The hangman, who dreaded the doom which he intended to inflict on his fellow man, shouted for help. On hearing the cry the tyrant, tiger-like, sprang forward and with his gory sword literally hacked the man to pieces. One victim after another lay writhing and quivering in the last pangs at the foot of the dizzy precipice, and still the tyrant's rage was unappeased. "Bring the white men, and let their blood flow, mingled with that of my own subjects," was the order that fell from his lips. Already, we were informed, whole bands of ruffians stood prepared to seize the intended prey, when several chiefs, no friends of the foreign captives, stepped forward, and requested that our execution might be deferred till next day. "Your Majesty," they respectfully remarked, "the white men do not deserve the easy death of the sword and bullet; no, keep them till to-morrow, and then let the slow torture of a flaming hut put an end to their existence." "You are right," was the response.

We were not unconscious of the perils by which we were encompassed, still we could scarcely realise that our lives were suspended on such a slender thread. One minute's silence, one repressed sentence of the chiefs, and the gulf between time and eternity would have been crossed. When the above fact was narrated to me by one of my companions, I was utterly lost in bewildering amazement. Our Heavenly Father, I knew, had more than once interposed between us and a violent death, but such a visible display of his guardian care and protection overwhelmed me with a feeling of awe akin to that which the high priest must have experienced when he entered the holy of holies, and stood in the immediate presence of the Shechinah.

The following day was Good Friday, which the Abyssinian Church most strictly observes. The tyrant, though a perfect fiend and coarse blasphemer, repaired, from a superstitious impulse, at a very early hour to church. On his return he sent word to Mr. Rassam that we should without delay repair to our Amba prison. It was a delightful message, and I believe no prisoners ever returned to their dungeons with greater joy than the white captives did to their huts on the fortress of Magdala. The very walls of those dismal abodes, which before imparted a desponding melancholy to our minds, on that very morning beamed with a peace and serenity that sent back to our cold hearts a warm tide of gladness and joy to which, for a long, long time, they had been perfect strangers. It was a perfect bliss to quit the royal charnel-house, and to breathe once more, if even for a few hours, an atmosphere not impregnated with blood and death.

In the afternoon of the same day we heard that a division of the expeditionary force had approached till within two hours of our fortress. Some of our servants who had followed us came every instant into our huts with some intelligence about the dress, looks, and attitude of the soldiers whom their piercing glances detected on the heights around Arogie. Samuel, who was justly afraid lest their observations should be reported, and draw on us the tyrant's resentment, ordered none to move out of their tents, if they dreaded the whip.

Between three and four P.M., the boom of a distant thunder, which the rocks and cliffs reverberated for miles and miles around the isolated Amba, made us all start on our legs. "Was that rattle a peal of thunder or the roar of cannon?" formed the question of every lip. Again and again the sky above awakened the sleeping echoes of the surrounding scenes, intermingled apparently with other sounds than those created by the shadowy and hazy clouds that hung pall-like over our homes.. It was now no longer doubtful that the royal artillery was in full play, and that the king was either bragging or engaged in a regular fight. We could not believe that he had ventured to measure his strength with disciplined troops, and the victorious li-li-lil, which floated from the royal camp up to the fortress, where every woman and child repeated the shrill notes, till their throats were hoarse from the exertion, rendered the very thought ridiculous and absurd. At ten o'clock in the evening, Messrs. Flad, Waldemeier, and several of the king's servants, came to our prison to announce to us the cheering intelligence that a fight had taken place, and that his Majesty's troops

MAGDALA IN FLAMES.

had sustained a most signal and fatal defeat. The crest-fallen tyrant who, only little more than eighteen months before, claimed the universe for his realm, had learnt a lesson from the destructive contest at Arogie which, had it been administered to him a few years before, might have spared Abyssinia an incalculable amount of bloodshed, misery, and desolation. "Once I thought," was the message to Mr. Rassam, "that your people were women, and could not stand before me, but I find that they are men. I have been beaten by the *fit aurari* (advanced guard). My musketeers are dead. Prove that you are my friend, and reconcile me with the man who is stronger than I." Mr. Rassam returned a polite and most judicious reply. He informed the king that the object of his mission had been the re-establishment of peace between England and Abyssinia, and that although he had failed in achieving this end, he was still as friendly disposed as ever, and if his Majesty was inclined to listen to his counsel, he would advise him to give up to the commander-in-chief all the prisoners. Not to irritate the chafed lion he, however, proposed to send Lieut. Prideaux as his envoy to Lord Napier, if his Majesty consented to send one of the Europeans and some of his own chiefs to accompany him.

Excited by drink, his Majesty, when the delegates returned, had become oblivious of the errand on which they had been despatched. Towards dawn the fumes of the alcohol evaporated, and the messengers received instructions to depart for the British camp.

Lord Napier was exceedingly attentive and courteous towards the native envoy, Dejatch Alamie. His affability did not, however, modify his demands for the surrender of all the Europeans, and the unconditional submission of Theodore to the Queen of England, who would award him honourable treatment.

Persuaded that all negotiations would be futile if these conditions were not promptly complied with, the delegates hurried back to the royal camp. During the interval King Theodore dictated a semi-defiant letter to the commander-in-chief. "You," he wrote, "have prevailed against me. . . . . Believing myself to be a great lord I gave you battle, but by reason of the worthlessness of my artillery, all my pains were as nought. The people of my country by taunting me with having embraced the religion of the Franks, and by saying that I had become a Mussulman, and in ten different ways, provoked me to anger against them. Out of what I have done evil towards them may God bring good. . . . . Since the day of my birth till now, no man has dared to lay hand on me. Wherever my soldiers began to waver in battle, it was mine to arise and rally them. Last night the darkness hindered me from doing so. . . . I had hoped, after subduing all my enemies in Abyssinia, to lead my people against Jerusalem and to expel from it the Turks. A warrior who has dandled strong men in his arms like infants will never suffer himself to be dandled in the arms of others." This document, together with a letter he had received from Lord Napier, were handed to the messengers. Before, however, finally dismissing them, he inquired what honourable treatment of himself and family signified, and on not receiving the desired explanation, he turned to those who surrounded him, and ironically remarked: "Does the man know anything about my family that he speaks of honourable treatment? Has he counted the number of my wives and children?"

Impassive to a degree that rendered us almost if not altogether impervious to those fluctuations of hope and fear, which, under ordinary circumstances, might have agitated our whole being to a feverish pitch, we passed our forenoon in comparative peace and tranquillity.

The messengers had been gone about two hours, when the king, goaded to despair by the mad fury that burned in his heart, seized a pistol, and dashing the muzzle into his mouth, wanted to put an end to his own existence. Several of his chiefs promptly wrenched the weapon out of his hand. In the struggle the pistol exploded, and inflicted a wound on the royal ear. The chiefs, who were all deeply affected, urged him to shake off all despondency, and to prove himself worthy of the name he bore. "Our lives are yours," they said, "and we will fight, and if necessary, die with you. Let us bravely defy the Frendjoj, and if they venture to approach, they shall have dead and not living captives." To this honest remonstrance—and it was honest, for they fell fighting at his side during the capture of Magdala—he deigned no reply, but turning to Betwodet Hassanei and Ras Bissawur, he ordered them to go to our prison and inform us that we were free, and could go to the camp. I could scarcely believe the import of the message, so utterly opposed did it appear to reason, common sense, and the usual tactics of Theodore.

We instantly got ready to obey the royal behest, the most gracious he ever issued, when another messenger arrived to inform us that it was probably too late that day to reach the British camp, and that we should postpone our departure till the next day. As we all harboured a vague dread that our exit was a mere blind to give *éclat* to some base treachery, we did not regret another night's reprieve. After waiting an hour, more peremptory orders were conveyed to us that we should start. As we emerged out of our prison we encountered many faces bathed in tears. It was touching to see that even at Magdala there were hearts not indifferent to the foreigners, or unconcerned about our freedom and release. The kind and sympathetic groups, like ourselves, imagined that the march into the royal camp was a short funeral procession to execution and the grave. Near the gates of the fortress we met Messrs. Meyer and Saalmüller, two of the European artisans, who were to escort us into the British camp. "Is there any treachery?" we anxiously inquired of our appointed conductors. "We are not aware that there is," was the response. "We know for certain," they added, "that a little while ago the king intended to commit suicide, and had he succeeded in his design, you and every European in the camp would, ere this, have fallen beneath the lances and swords of the enraged chiefs." That the restraint imposed on the tyrant's violence should, humanly speaking, prove the safeguard of his captives, seemed to me an interposition so miraculous and Divine, that I dismissed all apprehensions, and rapturously contemplated the approaching hour of freedom and liberty.

The order was, that we should quit the camp without delay. We were quite willing to obey this behest, had not two of the chiefs, who were friendly disposed towards us, unsolicited sent a message to their master that we were loth to leave without a parting interview. Certainly we had no desire to encounter once more the ash-coloured countenance and vengeance-flashing eye of Theodore. The chiefs knew that perfectly well, and to forestall that sad catastrophe, which they anticipated the commander-in-chief of the British forces would visit with a retributive vengeance, they took every precaution to avert it. Two or three messages flew forwards and backwards from the king to his white captives, and at last the order came that his Majesty would receive Mr. Rassam, and no one else.

Our friend, in full diplomatic uniform,* and surrounded by a whole concourse of chiefs and royal domestics, hurried on to Fahla, whilst the other seven captives and Mrs. Rosenthal, who was a semi-prisoner, and always associated with us, which was not the case with the rest, were driven along a path that lay at the foot of serrated cliffs and shivered rocks that were literally crowded with spectators. King Theodore, we were told, was not two hundred yards from the spot where we stood. This startled us. Go on—stop—to the right, to the left, were the contradictory commands that hissed in whispering notes along the line formed by the captives and their guards.

Hemmed in by dizzy precipices and lofty rocks, the frowning countenance of the king in front, and the anxious and expectant gaze of numerous

* The members of the mission, unlike the old prisoners, were not stripped of their property.

guards in the rear, we resolved not to risk the peril of an unguarded step till we positively knew what course to pursue. Pale and trembling we awaited the issue of the next few minutes. The clatter of shields and the glimmer of spears made me turn to the right, and to my amazement I beheld Theodore threading his way between huge blocks towards the path where we were standing. Instantly we all fell prostrate on the ground and saluted him. He looked flushed, distracted, and wild. When close to me, and I was the fifth in the rear, his fiery gaze lighted for a moment on me, and then in a smooth soft tone, he said: "How are you? Good-bye." It was the sweetest Amharic to which I had ever listened—the most rapturous sentence that ever greeted my ears. It was said that at the very moment when he dismissed Mr. Rassam, his hand grasped a gun, evidently with the design of discharging it at his white captives. Had he done so, the group of musketeers by whom he was surrounded would have followed his example. Impelled by an invisible power, the weapon with the rapidity of the lightning's flash, dropped out of his hold, and Divine mercy, not Theodore's clemency, saved us from a violent death.

Slowly and solemnly we marched on our way. There was no haste or hurry which might have aroused the tyrant's wrath, and brought the executioner upon us, but the measured tramp of men who reluctantly leave a spot where they would willingly linger. Once, however, beyond the hated camp, we accelerated our steps, and did not halt till we were within sight of our liberators' closely ranged conical tents. Evening had already set in, and dark shades shrouded every object from our view. On, on we rapidly strode. Suddenly we heard a challenge. They were Indian pickets. They salaamed us in tones of evident pleasure. We advanced. The hum of voices became more distinct. There was a shout, a cheer, and a hurrah. A clear melodious voice resounded far above the hum and murmur of the wide-stretching lines, it was from its accents the voice of an officer, and the message it conveyed was affecting, solemn, and significant. "God has heard his people's prayer, and disposed King Theodore to let his prisoners go."

It was, indeed, a wonderful deliverance. King Theodore and his few faithful chiefs had no intention to grant us freedom and liberty. They had resolved to immolate us on that very path, which they foresaw our liberators would, ere many hours had elapsed, traverse. One word, and one only would have stretched us lifeless on the hard and rocky ground. God, however, was with us, and He alone conducted us safely through the midst of the murderous band, who were quite prepared to imbrue their hands in the white man's blood. Twice his chiefs, and particularly Ras Engeda, urged him, as we were quitting the camp, that he should wrench off our hands and feet, and thus demonstrate that he feared no enemy and dreaded no danger. "No; I have already killed people enough, let the white men go and be free."

Having yielded to an irresistible power, and given up his most valued hostages, he unhesitatingly complied with Lord Napier's firm and unbending demand, and on the following day, Easter Sunday, surrendered his European workmen and their families. This last act of submission may, perhaps, have been prompted by a faint hope that the commander-in-chief would now withdraw his troops and leave Magdala in possession of a gang of desperadoes, to carry on their atrocious and murderous trade. He forgot the condition imposed on him, and had to learn that a British general is as true to his word as he is faithful to his sword.

I was during the whole of that day in a state of delicious ecstacy and dreamy raptures. Unrestrained freedom appeared to me unnatural. I felt as if I could not divest myself of the idea that I was no longer guarded, that I needed not to conceal every scrap of paper, or burn the letters with which dear friends and kindred in anticipation greeted my safe arrival in the British camp. It was, indeed, a resurrection festival—a foretaste of that glorious resurrection, when the grave will be deprived of its precious treasures, death of its ghastly trophies, and the lap of decay and mortality become the abode of life and everlasting beauty.

In the afternoon, at the request of the senior chaplain, the Rev. E. S. Goodhart, I preached twice in the camp on the solemn subject suggested by the stupendous events of that grand festival of the Church. The roll of the drum, the clash of arms, the long line of troops, and above all, the vague consciousness that I was free, and stood among friends who had encountered innumerable hardships, toils, and privations, to rescue me and my companions out of the fangs of a remorseless tyrant, made my heart gush forth with emotions of the deepest gratitude towards God and man.

Early next morning all the troops marched up to Magdala. King Theodore, to forestall his capture, tried to decamp. His people feigned as if they intended to follow him. There was the usual bustle and clamour of voices, the saddling of mules, and striking of tents; but after waiting for an hour—an hour in which was crowded and compressed a terrible future—he perceived that he was disobeyed, abandoned, and forsaken by the men in whom his last hopes and expectations were centred. In a trice his charger's head was turned towards the mutinous host.

His effort to stimulate their courage and to animate their devotion was in vain. His voice had lost its charm, and his words fell on deaf ears. Indignant, furious, and almost mad, he clutched his pistol and stretched the nearest two dead on the spot where they stood. This outburst of rage did not frighten into submission the rebellious bands, and the dreaded leader of victorious legions, with his few devoted and faithful chiefs, was forced to seek a refuge and shelter from a foe he had so proudly defied, behind the ramparts of a rocky fortress. Desperation imparted vigour to his arm, and valour to his heart. His career of blood was, however, fated to close. He had enthralled myriads and myriads of helpless beings; he had rioted again and again in the throes and agonies of the weak and defenceless; he had literally shed streams of human blood, and now when every prospect looked dark and dismal, that very pistol which had been so familiar with death, became the instrument with which he sealed his own doom.

On the following morning, I rode with Mr. Goodhart and Captain Nicholson up to Magdala. Our path wound along the precipice, where lay in putrefying heaps the slaughtered corpses of the great king's prisoners. The sight made me shudder, and, almost loudly, I ejaculated: "Here my mortal career would have terminated, had not an invisible power interposed in behalf of a helpless captive and the sharers of his misery." On the Amba itself all was activity and animation. There was now no longer heard the clank of galling chains, or witnessed the sad glance of despair. Every one looked happy and content. There were still some prisoners with portions of their fetters dangling on their legs. They had, however, no shadow on their brow; on the contrary, their hearts were overflowing with an excess of gratitude that stifled their voices, and only in broken accents they could breathe forth their true, genuine, and hearty blessings on their deliverer (Lord Napier). It was quite an exciting scene. The whole fortress swarmed with crowds of the curious and busy. Some collected Theodore's treasures, others despatched them down to the camp, and not a few, like myself, idly sauntered about, to have a full view of a spot that will for generations to come live in the history of British enterprise, energy, and valour. The king had not yet been buried. He was laid out on a stretcher, in a hut which for many months formed the dungeon of one of his white captives. To behold that man, whose nod or word had often caused myriads and myriads to tremble, now rigid, gory, and dumb, awoke in me many solemn reflections. I now no longer remembered the tyrant who had transformed fertile provinces into tangled wildernesses, and happy homes into charred ruins. I no longer remembered the sufferings he had inflicted on me for four years and a half. I no longer remembered the throes and agonies of a nation, in which he found his delight to revel. No; my views wandered beyond the limits of time, and the visions that rose before my mind made me rush out of the familiar hut.

The expedition, undertaken in the cause of humanity, and followed by the prayers of thousands, had achieved a most noble, glorious, and bloodless triumph. Magdala, however, still stood out in bold relief from the surrounding scenery, a proud monument of Theodore's conquest and power. Unexpectedly, on the 17th April, a mass of dense smoke rose in circling columns from the centre of the fortress. In a few minutes it became more bright and luminous. The last stronghold of Theodore was on fire. It was a glorious sight—a sight which thrilled with joy the heart of the Amhara and Galla, the liberated captive and the victorious soldier.

On the following Sunday there was a thanksgiving service. The preacher selected for his text the words of the Apostle, "Thanks be unto God, which giveth us the victory." All felt the truth of this significant sentence—all were struck with its solemn import. It was indeed a victory—a victory achieved by prayer, and redounding to the glory of Him who has said, "Thou shalt call, and I will answer."

www.ingramcontent.com/pod-product-compliance
Lightning Source LLC
Chambersburg PA
CBHW022106290426
44112CB00008B/567